Praise for *Drivin*

"Whether you were raised on a farm or in the city, you'll be amazed, entertained, and sometimes shocked by the extraordinary life of this tenacious doctor and single mother who works around the clock through injury, illness, and her own pregnancy to care for the animals she's called to heal."

—DEBORAH ANN LUCAS,
author of *Dance While the Fire Burns*

"Melinda's life story is inspiring. As pet owners, we enjoyed learning fascinating details about a multitude of farm animals, and we were shocked to read about the challenging animal cruelty cases she deals with. Both of us were endeared to the hardworking and smart border collies (Meg, Dot, Cap, Jessie, and Katch) that were reliable companions and copilots throughout Melinda's life and on her adventures along country roads."

—MAUREEN AND CHRISTOPHER HARRINGTON,
authors of *Ivy the Very Determined Dog*

"*Driving Home Naked* is a study in resourcefulness and sheer grit. Anyone aiming to live their best life will tear through Dr. McCall's hilarious and often poignant narrative and find much to admire, and even emulate."

—KIM SAVAGE, author of *In Her Skin*

"Reading *Driving Home Naked* filled me with admiration for the author's dedication, huge heart, and life-affirming humor as she recounted her career as a large animal veterinarian in rural Virginia. Tales of hard work, skill, and passion for animals give us a fascinating insight into this challenging world of caring for farm animals—while showing Melinda's endless energy and her compassion and generosity toward their owners and her colleagues, family, and friends. This book is both eye-opening and heartwarming and an utter delight to read."

—LIZ KINCHEN,
author of *Light in Bandaged Places*

"You will enjoy this passionate memoir, which sets out a strong self-belief, coupled with perseverance, as Melinda shows up and follows her purpose. Her adventures as a veterinarian working in rural communities, joined by her loyal dogs, will inspire you to hold your head high and grab onto your dreams to see them come to life. A woman after my own heart, and a must-read."

—MEG NOCERO, ESQ.,
author of *The Magical Guide to Bliss, Sparkle & Shine*, and
Butterfly Awakens: A Memoir of Transformation through Grief

Driving Home Naked

and other misadventures of a country veterinarian

DRIVING HOME NAKED

and other misadventures of a country veterinarian

MELINDA G. McCALL, D.V.M.

SHE WRITES PRESS

Published 2023

Printed in the United States of America

Print ISBN: 978-1-64742-517-3
E-ISBN: 978-1-64742-518-0
Library of Congress Control Number: 2023905142

For information, address:
She Writes Press
1569 Solano Ave #546
Berkeley, CA 94707

Interior design and typeset by Katherine Lloyd, The DESK

She Writes Press is a division of SparkPoint Studio, LLC.

To all the hardworking vet moms and women in agriculture.

This is not just my story; this is our story. Hold your heads high while you slog through the mud to feed those babies, human and animal, and be proud of the important work you all do. And even on the hardest days, be grateful.

Thanks for the inspiration.

"If you decide to become a veterinary surgeon you will never grow rich but you will have a life of endless interest and variety."

—James Herriot,
All Creatures Great and Small

CONTENTS

Part 3: *Wearing Many Hats*
2012–2021

Part 1
Dressing the Part
1990–2007

A STICKY SITUATION

*I*f I had a dollar for every time I heard the words "Are you sure you want to be a large animal vet?" I could have already paid off my student loans. Most of the concerned citizens who asked this question, including my own father, didn't believe large animal veterinary medicine was "women's work." Others would say, "It's just a really hard way to make a living." But I knew in my heart that it was my calling.

As a young woman growing up on a dairy farm in the foothills of the Appalachian Mountains over forty years ago, I was a minority. Most of the workers on the dairy were men, as were the veterinarians that serviced the dairy. During my childhood, I tried not to ask too many questions. Everyone was in too much of a hurry to explain anything to me. It seemed to embarrass the men if they had to try to explain birthing issues. Most of all, I never wanted the questions to sound dumb. I'd rather seek out the answer on my own from a book.

My mom once asked me before Dad got home, "When you say you're 'worming' the cows, are you giving them worms or trying to kill them?"

"I'm not 100 percent sure, Mom, but what I do know is the wormer is really expensive. If me or Ann spill it, we get our butts beat."

Soon enough, I figured out it was to remove the worms. But my list of questions only continued to grow. I also wanted to know where the old, crippled cows went that left the farm. The sketchy cattle hauler told me they were being served as burgers at my school's cafeteria, but he had such a poker face I could never tell if he was lying.

Growing up in southwest Virginia, I never saw any female doctors, so asking a woman was out of the question. Mom was a nurse, but, evidenced by the question about deworming, she was not well versed in animal anatomy and physiology. I was going to have to learn by watching and reading.

My dad was the herdsman on the dairy, and throughout my childhood, we lived in a small white tenant house overlooking a two-hundred-acre cornfield along the middle fork of the Holston River. The sea of green cornstalks nearly touched the bank of the small creek that branched off the river and flowed in front of our house. As children, we spent many summer days barefoot in the clear water of the creek, catching crawdads. I would occasionally catch one that had only one pincer and try to rehabilitate it on the back porch, but I was never once successful. One sweltering summer afternoon in 1991, when I was twelve, I heard a *tap, tap, tap* on the screen door of the porch. I peeked out and saw Dr. John, a broad-shouldered young veterinarian, in his manure-soaked green overalls. His nose was swollen and bruised, with fresh red blood trickling down both sides.

"How are ya, young lady?" Dr. John asked as he blotted the blood underneath his nose with his dirty finger. "Your dad told me you might have a Band-Aid to spare."

"Looks like I'm doing better than you. What happened to you, Doc?" I asked as I walked into the kitchen to get supplies to fix him up.

"A big ol' mean cow kicked a gate into my face. I hope she didn't break my nose." He wiped away a trickle of blood coming from his nostrils. "This is a dirty, dangerous job. You aren't still thinking of becoming a vet, are you?" he said through the open kitchen window.

I pushed the screen open and brought a wet rag, a Band-Aid,

and a large glass of fresh-brewed sweet iced tea onto the porch. "Yes, I still want to be a vet. Would I be able to ride along with you some-time . . . please?" I started cleaning up the deep gash over the bridge of his nose as he winced. "Here, drink some tea before you pass out."

Dr. John swigged tea. "I reckon you can if your parents say it's OK. But I'm telling you, I rarely get home before dark, and there's a good chance of a tiny thing like you getting hurt. You're a smart gal. There are easier ways to make a living."

I took that as a yes. I smiled and quietly clapped my hands, barely able to hide my excitement.

Dr. John looked defeated as he applied the Band-Aid across the bridge of his nose and slurped his last gulp of tea. "Thanks for the help, Melinda," he said as he headed out to his old vet truck.

"I hope the rest of your day gets better. I'll be calling you about the ride-along!" I could hardly wait for Mom to get home so I could tell her.

Sitting at the supper table that night, I made the big announce-ment to my family. "Great news! I'm going to be doing some ride-alongs with Dr. John this summer."

"Really? Hmmm . . ." Dad replied with one eyebrow raised.

"That's fantastic, honey." Mom shot Dad a look as she took a bite of her freshly harvested garden green beans. "I guess Dr. John isn't going to get your dad's hundred bucks."

"Dad, are you bribing him or something?" I rolled my eyes in disgust.

Ann jumped into the conversation. "Are you bribing anybody to talk me out of anything, Dad? Because I think I'd like to be an artist." Being only nine years old, she didn't have a firm plan for her future, but she did have a flair for the flamboyant.

Dad did his best to stay afloat in the estrogen pool. "I will put up another $100 for anybody who can talk you out of becoming an artist. Have you ever heard the term 'starving artist,' Ann?"

I believe my dad discouraged me out of love; after all, the

only large animal veterinarians he'd ever seen were overworked, divorced, caffeine-addicted men who cursed too much and had multiple scars from injuries and surgeries. The older I got, the more I understood his reasoning for trying to crush my dream into the greasy spot roadkill makes when it's hit by a Mack truck.

After years of working on the dairy farm with my father, he could tell that I was bullheaded enough to pursue my passion and become a vet. In some ways, it was his fault. Before I was old enough to walk, he carried me to the barn every night to check cows. Once I could follow him, I became his shadow. I hiked up the steep hill day after day to get to the barn. I loved roaming around the barn with those docile, large-framed black and white beauties, breathing the fresh barn air with a hint of cow manure. Sometimes dad would "accidentally forget" to take me with him (as a way of discouraging me, I'm sure), but I'd run up the hill and beat him to the barn. There was no talking me out of it, so he started giving me harder and harder jobs to do. I started out feeding the baby calves, then graduated to giving shots, then artificially inseminating the cows and delivering calves. I was always begging for more responsibility.

That same summer when I was twelve, we had a group of Holstein calves to process. Like most of the facilities on the dairy, our cattle chute was lacking—rickety boards attached to wobbly posts with a rusty headgate at the end to catch the cattle's head. With the help of Meg, our trusty border collie, I struggled to push calf after calf up the alley to trap them in the head catch. Meg would go around the calves and help us get them in the pen, and then it was up to me to push them.

When we got to the male calves, my dad told me it was about time I learned how to castrate. I was thrilled that he finally gave me an important job that required a lot of trust, a job that real-life cattle veterinarians do. The bulls were large enough that if I made any mistakes, they could die from blood loss or infection.

My dad's expression was stern; his cheekbones looked even more pronounced as he said, "I will teach you like they teach veterinary students. I'll show you how to do one, let you do one, then make you teach someone how to do one."

We were both hot, tired, and parched. We were covered in blood from dehorning the heifer calves and had run out of water to drink. The first bull calf stepped up in the chute, and I jacked up his tail for my dad to cut him.

"First, you pull the scrotal sack down and cut it off," Dad explained. "Then you pull the testicle down while stripping the cord, and you need to make sure that the cord pulls down really, really far before it separates." Dad pulled the spermatic cord out so far I was beginning to wonder if the calf was going to part with it. "And for goodness' sake, you better have clean hands for this job and put lots of betadine and fly spray on the sack. That's all you can do to prevent infection." He grimaced as he bent over to apply the fly spray. I could tell his back was hurting.

I nodded my head and wiped the sweat from my brow. "Yes, sir. I think I got it. Cut, pull, strip." I knew if I screwed up this job, I'd face either the wrath or the ridicule of my father.

"You know this bull could kick you and break your leg, right? And if you don't hang on tight to that knife, it's gonna end up in your eye or slice your finger clean off your hand." Clearly, Dad was trying to scare me away. I listened carefully.

As I stepped up to the bull, I followed my dad's instructions step-by-step until, at last, I got the robust pair of testicles out without killing the calf or myself. I was so excited that I didn't pay much attention to my aim when I threw the first testicle over the chute. That calf nut headed straight toward my father's cheek—and *stuck!* And man, oh man, the look on his face. I could see the vessels dilating in his temples, and his entire head turned bright red.

I did what any smart girl would have done. I ran! I climbed out of the alley and ran as fast as possible in the opposite direction.

After I'd gotten a safe distance away, I glanced back over my shoulder to see if he had gotten it off.

"What the hell is wrong with you? You better pay attention, young lady," he shouted as he peeled the slimy, sticky organ from his face. He threw it to the ground, and Meg scarfed it up, licking her lips in search of more. At least somebody was appreciative of my work.

In a few minutes, and from a safe distance, I called, "Sorry, Dad. I really didn't do it on purpose!" Deep down, I was still chuckling.

"Melinda, you better get your ass back over here and finish with this calf before you piss me all the way off!" Dad yelled.

After we finished with all the calves, Dad, Meg, and I jumped in the old blue farm truck, and I drove us home. The rule in the country is: if you can reach the pedals, you're old enough to drive. Covered in sweat and blood, I ran to the bedroom to show my mother the fruits of my labor: a big bucket overflowing with bloody bull testicles.

Momma stared at the dirty bucket. "You know I'm proud of you, and I love you, honey, but you better get those nasty bulls' balls out of my bedroom this minute!" Mom was always very supportive, but her nursing stopped with humans. I carted the bucket out to the porch so the dogs could have a scrumptious snack later.

The older I got, the thirstier I became for knowledge. One cold January morning when I was a freshman in high school, one of the cows I was treating in the sick pen had passed away overnight. I wanted to know her cause of death. She was a big Holstein that had calved recently and just continued to go downhill each day. I was sure that by learning why she died, I would be able to change my treatment protocol to help treat the next sick cow more successfully.

It was so cold that I could see the vapors coming from my mouth with every breath and I would intermittently cough as the cold air hit my asthmatic lungs. I had so many layers under my insulated coveralls that I could barely squat beside the frigid corpse. I placed two long plastic OB sleeves over my heavy-duty gloves and Carhart jacket.

I pushed with all my might to work the sharp end of the long butcher knife through the tough cowhide over the cow's abdomen. I backed up and got a run-and-go, which I was told never to do with a knife. The blade slammed against the frozen hide but wouldn't penetrate it, forcing me backward. Out of the corner of my eye, I saw my dad driving by in the old beat-up farm truck. He leaned out the window and shouted, "What on earth are you doing?"

"Well, I'm trying to do a necropsy on this cow, but I'm struggling."

"That cow is frozen solid. Why don't you leave her alone before you cut your arm off? That little knife is never going to work." Dad shook his head and began to roll up his window.

I approached his truck and pleaded, "Do you have a saw I could borrow then?"

"You have to be the most stubborn child on the planet. Yes, hop in, and we'll find a saw." He rolled his big brown eyes so far back in his head that I thought they might get stuck.

Dad dropped me off beside the cowsicle with a medium-sized hack saw. It was very difficult to force the dull edges of the saw through the frozen hide, but it did work better than the knife. By the time I jerked the serrated blade through the liver-colored muscle fibers and shiny white tendons of the bloodless forelimb and the rear limb, I had broken a sweat inside my insulated wardrobe. If anyone was watching, they'd think I was a budding serial killer, but with every fiber of my being, I knew that I wanted to be a large animal veterinarian. And I was getting a good lesson in just how many fibers were in a body. A few minutes later, Dad drove back around to pick me up. "Well, what's the diagnosis?" he asked with a smirk.

"Hypothermia," I said decisively. We both chuckled as we headed home to see if Mom had a warm breakfast for us. I will go to my grave not knowing why that cow died, but I will never regret trying to figure it out.

When I think back to how I started chasing my dream, I remember an elementary school teacher trying to help us figure out what we wanted to be when we grew up.

"Children, what is the first thing you think of when you open your eyes in the morning? Take a minute to think and write it down."

For me, it was easy. My top priority every day was going up to the barn to check the cows that were expecting babies. I was excited by just the thought of getting to witness a live birth, or even better, getting to hold onto those little wet feet protruding from the cow's vulva and assisting her birth. When you find your passion, you love it on the hot days and the cold days, the hard days and the easy days, and the days when you're discouraged and the days you're supported.

I could tell from the start that it wouldn't be easy. Still, I knew my determined, courageous attitude and inordinate amount of "knot-headedness" would make me just the right person for this career. I was more than just a girl looking for a job; I was an educated young lady seeking a rewarding lifelong adventure.

ACCEPTED

*M*y fingers fumbled as I dialed the last number on my Queens College campus mailbox. This was the moment I had been waiting on for months—the day I would receive the letter that would determine the course of the rest of my life. I thought back to my anxiety the day of my veterinary school interview, dressed in my sharp purple pants suit, sitting at that long boardroom table full of intimidating veterinarians. I was shaking on the inside while trying to appear poised and confident on the outside. I clutched the silver bull pendant on my necklace that my friend Sally gave me, so I'd have the balls I needed to get through that interview.

As students and faculty members brushed past me in the narrow hallway, I snatched a lone letter out of the box. The left corner read VIRGINIA-MARYLAND REGIONAL COLLEGE OF VETERINARY MEDICINE (Virginia Tech). I hadn't been this nauseated since I helped my dad deliver a set of dead, rotten lambs from an old ewe when I had the stomach flu last year.

I tore into the letter so fast that the paper cut my finger, and my blood soaked through the paper. This certainly wasn't the first blood I had shed chasing this dream. The first word was "CONGRATULATIONS!" I stood in the hall in complete shock.

"Honey, are you OK?" A small-framed, polite lady from the academic affairs office approached me in the crowded corridor and was concerned.

"Yes, ma'am. I'm actually better than OK. I'm fantastic." I

opened the letter back up. "I just found out that I have been accepted to veterinary school in Blacksburg, Virginia."

"Congratulations. That's wonderful news, dear." As I moved toward the door, the lady called out to me, "My niece Megan started there last year, and she loves it. In fact, I'm pretty sure she's looking for a roommate. Would you like her contact information?"

"Wow. That would be great. It would be nice just to know someone there. Thank you so much."

Within the first five minutes of discovering I had been accepted to veterinary school, I had a potential roommate and friend. I couldn't contain my excitement—I needed to share this news with my advisor, Dr. Martin. She and I had become very close during my time at Queens. She never had human children of her own, but she thought of me like a daughter.

When I started college, I didn't think this would be the case. I first stepped into the second-floor hallway of the science building as a lanky, lost freshman. I nosed around the long, white corridor that reeked of formaldehyde searching for Dr. Martin's office and stumbled into a hidden office, where I saw a woman sitting at her desk.

"Are you Dr. Martin? I'm Melinda, the new work study for the biology department."

"Nice to meet you, Melinda. I'm Dr. Jann, a botany professor. Dr. Martin is located a bit farther down the hallway, but I'm going to warn you. She's not in good humor today, not at all. You may go see her. Just, for God's sake . . . don't bring up the dog."

I entered the small office down the hall to find a middle-aged lady with short brown hair slumped over her desk, her fingers pressed into her temples. She had a stone-cold expression and puffy, dark circles under her eyes. I gazed around the office and noticed a beautiful portrait of a striking black and white dog.

"Hi, Dr. Martin. I'm Melinda, and I have been assigned to your department as a work study. That is a gorgeous dog on the wall. Is she a border collie?"

Her face contorted, and the tears flowed like a faucet. Oh hell, I wasn't supposed to mention the dog.

"Yes, she was my beloved border collie, Misty. I had to take her to the vet yesterday to have her put to sleep because the cancer had eaten her up," Dr. Martin said, her voice trembling. "Life is never going to be the same now. If you don't mind, can we postpone our meeting?"

"I'm so, so sorry to hear about Misty. You just let me know when you're ready to get together." I nervously avoided eye contact with her and the picture of the dog as I creeped toward the door.

The first day of being a real grown-up at age seventeen, and I'd already blown it.

But once Dr. Martin had some time to process her grief, we got along like peas in a pod. We realized that we were both border collie–loving science nerds, and she loved the fact that I wanted to become a veterinarian.

I ran across the quad toward the science building, dashed up the stairs, and burst through Dr. Martin's office door. Excited and out of breath, I shouted, "You'll never believe it. I got accepted to vet school."

This time, happy tears streamed down Dr. Martin's cheeks. I jumped across the desk, and she embraced me.

"I'm so proud of you, my dear. You'll be a great veterinarian; I have never doubted that." It was hard for me to believe that she never doubted it because she was an incredibly tough grader. She held my feet to the fire and loved me while she did it.

WASTIN' TIME

"**M**elinda, you and Ginny will report to school at 3:50 a.m. tomorrow for your trip to prison," Dr. John announced with a grin. I knew the first externship of our fourth year would take us on the prison farm circuit for three days, but I didn't expect him to be so tickled. Dr. John had recently joined the Virginia-Maryland College of Veterinary Medicine faculty, and we often joked about the ploy that backfired.

"By sending you to the prison, I might still have a chance at getting your dad's money," he said. Dr. John might not have gotten my dad's $100 bill, but the vet school was now getting stacks of mine in the form of tuition, which paid his salary. Ironically, the veterinary experience I gained riding along with him and other members of his practice helped me get into vet school.

Still half asleep, Ginny and I climbed into the back seat of the Production Management Medicine vet truck in pitch-black darkness. It was the first day of a very long year, which would require us to change externships every three weeks for seventeen rotations. Ginny and I, both twenty-four years old, had lost some of the enthusiasm we had as first-year students in veterinary school. Back then, the smell of formaldehyde radiating through our pores at the gym was regarded by undergraduate students as a mark of brilliance. Now we'd become immune to the pungent odor and were hoping for fresh air out doing fieldwork. We had suffered through years of sitting for hours on end at a desk, and we had the atrophied gluteal muscles to prove it. It was exciting to be getting the opportunity to apply our knowledge and to get to work on living animals, even if it was technically behind bars.

I was a bit worried about this prison trip for two reasons. First, my professor, Dr. Dee, had a reputation for not making pee stops on long journeys. Some thought it was to torture the female vet students, since he didn't always think this was "women's work." Second, I had never been to a prison. Virginia has several prisons that use their inmates to operate prison farms. Some milk dairy cows, some raise beef, and some have big gardens. This brilliant system allows the inmates to develop job skills while earning a wage and also producing food for the prison. Since the veterinary school is part of the state network, the vets from the school do the necessary veterinary work while training students and, in some cases, conducting research.

Ginny fluffed up her pillow against the window, and I sat in a daze, still half asleep.

"Well, girls, this morning on our drive, we will be discussing the Animal Medicinal Drug Use Clarification Act of 1994," Dr. Dee began lecturing while scratching the bald spot on the top of his head. After an extended period of silence, he turned his head to see if we were still awake. The truck tire caught the edge of the road, and he jerked the steering wheel. The loud noise of the rumble strips startled us so badly that we leaped to attention. I reached to the back of my whiplashed neck to make sure it was still attached to my body.

"And how long does it take to get to this prison, pray tell?" I inquired, wincing.

"A little over three hours, so we'll have plenty of time to discuss it thoroughly," he replied. Ginny and I just shook our heads; it was clearly going to be a very long year.

After what seemed like an eternity, we cleared the barbed-wire security gate at the first prison. Dr. Dee explained to us that there were two main rules we needed to follow while working at the prison farms. Rule #1: Do not tell the inmates any personal information about yourself. Rule #2: Do not ask the inmates their names or what they are in for. The rules seemed straightforward. The warden, a farm manager, and a team of male inmates in tattoos and orange coveralls met us out by the cattle chute to get their briefing from Dr. Dee.

"Today, folks, we're going to process this group of calves. We will need an inmate to catch their heads in the headgate. Ginny, you apply the pour-on dewormer. Melinda, you give the vaccinations. I will record numbers and weights."

We all manned our assigned posts and got to work. Dr. Dee demanded efficiency, so I had the idea that maybe one of the inmates could speed me up by helping me change needles on the syringes. He cracked a half-smile as he said, "Ma'am, we're not allowed sharps."

"Of course not, silly me. I certainly don't want you to get in trouble." I looked over nervously to make sure Dr. Dee hadn't witnessed me violating any rules.

Dust filtered through the smoke-filled air, and sweat started to soak through our clothes. One of the inmates, while struggling to push the stubborn calf up the alley, became increasingly disgruntled. "This sucks! We come out here and bust our asses only to get forty-five cents an hour. A hard day's work will barely buy us a pack of cigarettes."

Ginny and I helped the frustrated inmate get the last calf into the chute and we all cheered. Everyone was equally ready to be done with this grueling task. Dr. Dee instructed us to quickly pack up and load up so we could get to the women's prison.

As we drove along, I figured I'd try to steer the conversation to avoid a fourth hour of discussing half-lives of antibiotics used in production animals.

"So, Doc, I'm kind of interested to see what the women's prison is like. Don't you think like 98 percent of the women are serving time because of some bad decision related to a man?" Dr. Dee raised one bushy eyebrow and glared at me. Ginny snickered as we pulled through the first security gate.

The corrections officer told us the inmates were all in the cafeteria having lunch. Dr. Dee plowed through the cafeteria door at his usual one hundred miles per hour with Ginny and me in tow. He began to scope out the room to locate our cattle working crew. All our eyes were immediately drawn to the commanding presence of an individual standing in the front of the room. There she stood, 6'5", shoulders nearly as wide as a doorframe and a shrewd expression on her face. Dr. Dee whispered to us, "They call her Honey Badger. She's been here for a long time."

"What's up, Doc? Y'all have a seat and have some lunch with us," Honey Badger shouted across the room, waving us over.

Dr. Dee attempted to walk briskly past the table. "Honey B, we'd love to, but we're running way behind, and we really have to—"

"I said sit down." Her frosty glare meant business. All three of our asses hit those seats like somebody pulled a hydraulic lever.

Honey Badger sent her minions over to serve us our turkey dinners. I looked at the dried-up piece of turkey and wondered how I was going to manage to choke it down. When I noticed Honey Badger glaring at me from across the room, I knew I could find a way. I remember hearing the old-timers from home talk about how the prisoners must have it made with three hot meals and a bed to sleep in. Rest assured; these ladies did not have it made.

I slowly chewed the shriveled piece of meat, and it felt as though it was getting bigger and bigger in my mouth. It was so dry I was afraid I might choke trying to swallow. The thought of Honey Badger performing the Heimlich maneuver was too much to handle.

One of the inmates sitting across from me spotted the concern on my face. "Slip the rest into your pocket and you can ditch it when we get to the cattle pen," she whispered. "You don't want to upset Honey Badger." I smiled and carefully smuggled the remaining dirt bird body parts into the pocket of my coveralls.

Once we all "finished" with our lunches, we headed out to the cattle pens to process calves. The inmates were dressed in pale blue loose-fitting shirts with pale blue pants. Some wore earrings, and each woman had her hair styled differently. Some of the older inmates still had long, straight hair and bangs, while several of the younger inmates had shorter, easier-to-maintain hairdos. I looked around at the women and couldn't help but wonder what their dreams started out as. What jobs did they have before they ended up here? Did they have families? And who was raising their children while they were locked up? I had so many questions that I was never going to get the answers to because it was against Rule #2.

Dr. Dee gathered us up to give us our marching orders. "Honey B, you're on the headgate as usual. Ginny, you're going to be vaccinating. Melinda, you're gonna castrate the bulls. And the rest of you lovely ladies just keep the calves coming up the chute. It's getting hot, and we need to work quickly."

Calf after calf came through the chute. Only one so far had slowed us down—the orphaned calf the ladies made into a pet. They'd used the money they earned working to buy her snacks so they could lure her up the alley. They gently and compassionately assisted the calf step-by-step with the peanut butter crackers. It was easy to tell many of them were mothers. The infinite patience they demonstrated with their pet's stubborn behavior and the gentle touch of their roughened hands to encourage her to move spoke volumes about their character.

It was getting warmer with every passing minute, and my back and arms were getting tired of being bent down under those calves, pulling and stripping testicles. After a while, Dr. Dee announced loudly, "Ladies, Melinda here thinks most of you all got in here because of a man."

I was mortified. If he didn't like me, why didn't he just fail me or shoot me or something?

Honey Badger shouted, "I sure as hell didn't get in here because of no damn man. I beat some girl's ass to a bloody pulp."

Dr. Dee tried to rein her in: "Language, please, Honey B . . ."

A small-framed inmate with short dark hair and about twenty piercings up and down each ear chimed in, "I didn't get in here because of a man, but that's a long story for another time."

Dr. Dee looked over at me. "See there, Melinda, you're wrong." I clearly remembered Dr. Dee telling us in a lecture that we could never, ever trust an experiment with an n of 2 because it was not statistically significant. I chose to bite my tongue as he broke his own rule.

By the third grueling hour of manual labor, I felt like we were all being punished for something. I thought back to my first year of veterinary school, when Dr. Tom came to a Mentor Day. He had been a large animal veterinarian for quite a while. One of my class-mates asked him if women could really do this job. She said, "All we ever see are men doing it."

Dr. Tom replied, "Of course they can. There aren't very many women in the country doing this job at this point, but they all have one thing in common, and that's grit."

We were down to the last few calves left to process. When I reached under one bull calf, I realized something was different. I felt only one pronounced testicle and maybe just the start of another one. I asked Dr. Dee to cop a feel.

"Well, Melinda, that calf is a unilateral cryptorchid. I think he's only partial, though. You oughta be able to get him—you're a farm girl."

I carefully reached under and split his scrotum with the knife. The first testicle popped right out, stripped easily, and pulled loose. I squatted down behind this calf for so long my quadriceps began to burn and tremble. I was determined to prove to Dr. Dee that I was fit for this career. I reached farther and farther up toward the calf's groin, trying to squeeze out the small, slippery nut while praying he wouldn't kick my teeth out. Sweat ran into my eyes as I searched, surrounded by a sea of blue shirts expectantly watching.

Honey Badger let out a loud sigh. "Dr. Dee, wouldn't it just be faster if you did this yourself? I'm gonna die of old age waiting on this rookie. Does she even know what she's doing?" She made several more disparaging remarks while the other inmates stared in anticipation.

The pressure was on. The whole operation had come to a halt waiting on me. Just as I latched on to the problematic organ, Honey Badger asked, "Are you about done? Because you are wasting my damn time!"

I was so focused on pulling that testicle out that without thinking I blurted, "Well, that's fascinating, Honey Badger, 'cause all you got is time." Right then, the slimy, undersized testicle popped out. I dropped the testicle behind the calf and ran out the door leading to the opposite side of the chute. I felt like I was the prisoner as I clutched the metal bars on the side of the chute for protection.

Honey Badger glared at me. The inmate who'd helped me dispose of the turkey had also explained that Honey Badger was getting out soon if she could remain on good behavior. I prayed that Honey Badger was considering that. After the longest thirty seconds of my life, she turned and walked away. She must have realized that crushing a measly vet student to a bloody pulp wasn't worth another twenty years. Honey Badger taught me something important that day. We all have goals, whether the goal is getting out of prison or graduating from veterinary school. We must be willing to do what it takes, no matter how difficult it is, to keep working toward the goal.

PORCH LIGHT RESCUE

*F*or years, I wondered why they used Virginia Tech degrees on the walls in movies. As I stood gazing at the wall above my desk, I suddenly understood. That large pearly white veterinary degree surrounded by its dark cherry frame and deep maroon matting with gold accents shone like a diamond—and cost more than one too.

I had just accepted a position as an associate veterinarian at a practice in the central part of Virginia. Dr. Kate, who had been a solo practitioner for nearly fifteen years, was desperate enough for some help that she hired me even though I was a new graduate. I had completed an internship with her two years earlier. Dr. Kate was an intimidating woman, standing six feet tall with a razor-sharp mind and a don't-screw-with-me attitude. I was twenty-five years old and eager to get out there and help animals, and I most certainly didn't want to do anything to disappoint my new boss.

Tap, tap, tap. I hammered the last nail into the wall to hang my colorful Irish tea towel with intricate Celtic patterns. Just as I reached down to grab the picture, the phone rang, interrupting my fleeting moment of domestic bliss in my one-bedroom apartment. My little apartment was nestled at the top of a beautiful historic home called the Cuckoo House. Multicolored flower gardens surrounded the home, which also had a small pond and walking trails that led back to an old family cemetery where the family dog was also buried. The small brick patio outside my apartment was perfect for sipping margaritas and sunbathing. And there was a groundhog that was smart enough to know that my swimsuit didn't have enough room for the pistol.

"This is Dr. Melinda. Can I help you?" I said into the cordless phone.

"Doc, I hate to bother you so late in the evening, but I'm afraid I'm gonna need your help with a down cow. She calved yesterday and can't stand tonight. We need her to get up so she can feed this baby."

"No problem, sir. I'll be on my way momentarily. Please leave the porch light on for me since I'm new in town." This would be my first real emergency call as an actual bona fide veterinarian. My hand shook as I hung up the phone. I had the piece of paper that said I graduated from veterinary school, but should I really be responsible for an animal's life?

Down cows aren't always an emergency, but if they lie on their side for too long, they could potentially bloat and die. I laid my picture-hanging supplies on the small hand-me-down love seat in my apartment and jotted down the directions to George's house on the back of a receipt. I blew out my vanilla candle, pulled on a pair of boots, and rushed out the door.

I wasn't looking forward to navigating with paper maps in the dark, so I was hoping I'd be able to see George's porch light. In the mountains of southwest Virginia where I grew up, the porch light was used as a form of communication if you were expecting somebody.

Cornstalk after cornstalk lined the winding country road as the sun tucked itself into the Blue Ridge Mountains. I couldn't just look for cows—most everybody in the community had cows. Then I spotted a small white house near the road with the porch light on. When I hopped out of my dusty green pickup truck with the shiny white vet box on the back, two desiccated french fries fell onto the ground. I zipped up my crisp clean green overalls with the bright yellow caduceus on the left chest. A middle-aged lady with a worried and expectant look was on the porch, waving me into the house.

"She's in here." She grabbed my hand and pulled me inside. It was clear that there was no time for introductions. I braced myself for a cow in the living room.

When we stepped through the doorway, there was only a feeble-looking elderly woman slumped over in her recliner. "Ma'am . . . that's an old lady . . ."

"What were you expecting?" she asked with a confused look.

"A cow."

She looked even more puzzled. "Wait, what? You're not from the rescue squad?"

After we established that I was a veterinarian looking for George's down cow, we had a short laugh. I apologized to the elderly lady and told her I hoped she'd get some relief soon. Her daughter pointed me to George's house.

"Any chance you could swing back in after you finish with the cow if the rescue squad hasn't made it here yet?" she asked, clearly desperate.

I finally found Mountain View Farm and my actual patient, the old cow stretched out on her side. I knelt beside the cow and pierced her large jugular vein with the needle. I listened to the slow glug, glug of the calcium entering the thin IV line from the bottle. George's bright white hair glistened in the moonlight as he held the bottle and looked down at me with his small round glasses. When I told him the story of meeting his neighbors, he laughed. "So, are ya going back over there when you finish?" The cow started to come to life, her muscles responding to the calcium. She leaned her head up as if she were listening to us.

"George, the only thing I could do for the old lady would be to walk in there with one of the long obstetrical sleeves on my arm and see if it shocked her heart back into rhythm." He laughed and shook his head.

Pulling out of the long farm drive, I looked back over to the little white house with the porch light on. To my relief, an ambulance and two strapping young men from the rescue squad were wheeling the elderly lady out on a gurney. While driving home, I said a little prayer for both the little old lady and the cow, and I wondered if every day was going to be like this one. I was relieved that I had at least one marketable veterinary skill.

A WEAK MOMENT

*D*r. Kate and her boys waved to me in the rearview mirror of the Yukon as they headed north to Maine in search of cooler weather, rest, and relaxation. It was the first time she'd had a vet from her own practice she could leave behind to cover the calls. I was at the office applying a fresh coat of paint to the walls and hoping for no drama while Dr. Kate was away. I was barely two months out of school and wanted nothing more than to take good care of the practice. Our work is physically demanding, and being able to take breaks is important for all vets. When you work for people who are making a living farming, you don't get many vacations, and neither do they.

The next day, I got my first emergency call from a middle-aged husband and wife team of farmers whose cow was having a difficult labor. It was getting late in the day, so I loaded my obedient border collie, Jessie, into the truck, and off we went. I wasn't too nervous about the call; I had grown up pulling calves on the dairy. In fact, delivering babies was what inspired me to choose this career. I find nothing more gratifying than clearing the afterbirth off the newborn baby's head as it draws its first breath.

When I arrived, my anxious patient was waiting in the headgate. I pulled on my plastic sleeves and reached into the cow's vagina. I immediately realized from the severely narrowed cervix that she had a uterine torsion . . . a bad one! Cathy and Stan could tell by my scrunched-up face that there was a problem. The cow's womb was turned counterclockwise at least 180 degrees, which made her cervix completely closed with no way for the baby to get out.

"With a team effort, I believe we can get her untangled," I said, struggling to sound positive.

"OK, dear, you just tell us what you need us to do. Just remember we're not spring chickens anymore," Cathy said. I sedated the cow and laid her on the ground. Now was the part where we needed more muscle. We had to roll the gigantic mama cow in the direction of her twisted uterus. All three of us grabbed a leg and heaved her over, once, then twice. When I reached back in, the torsion was still present—somewhat less than before, but it was clear that no calf was going to pass through that blocked tunnel. I reached into the cow's vagina, and we tried one more time to roll her as I held the calf's feet steady from behind. I was barely able to see that black cow's huge back legs pass by my face because of the sweat running into my eyes. By this time, we had all sweated through our clothes and were exhausted. I explained to them the only other option to get the calf out was to do a Caesarian section.

I was not looking forward to doing a C-section on a down cow with night approaching and no trained assistant, but that was looking like our only option. As I prepped the cow for her surgery, I asked Stan to hold the flashlight and Cathy to be the person who held the copious amounts of guts in the hole while I worked to get the baby out.

After about an hour of intensive surgery, it was getting harder and harder to see what I was doing. I looked over at Stan to see if the flashlight battery was going out. Stan's slender body was sliding down the fence like he was melting.

I ripped off my bloody plastic sleeves, now full of water from sweating, and approached Stan to feel for a pulse. There was a pulse and he was breathing. Maybe it was the sight of so much blood that had made him faint? Maybe he locked his knees, like veterinary students often do?

"Don't worry about him; he had a colonoscopy earlier today," Cathy said. "I told him he should have eaten and drank more before he came out here in this heat. He'll be fine. He should have listened to me." I propped him up against the fence with the flashlight carefully positioned under his chin; it looked like a scene from *Weekend at Bernie's.*

I gloved back up to resume my work, and an inquisitive neighbor named Linda came by just in time to lend a helping hand. While I was wrapping up the surgery with the last layer of sutures, Jessie was getting impatient in the truck and started honking the horn. The honking horn seemed to rouse Stan, who slowly began to rise. Cathy, Linda, and I propped the cow up and made her comfortable. The cow looked as dazed and confused as Stan. I dragged her deceased baby out of the pen. The calf's blood supply had been compromised far too long for it to have any chance at survival.

As they helped Stan to the truck, I cleaned up my gear and headed out. Dr. Kate had only been gone for two days, and I was ready for a vacation.

MIMI THE SHEEP
GOES TO DC

"**O**ld buddy, old pal . . . do you want to hear a sad story that I think you could help turn into a happy story?" my friend Laura asked in a desperate tone. Laura had recently opened a charter school right smack in the middle of Washington, DC. This school was unique in that the administrators paired underprivileged children who had a willingness and aptitude to learn with enthusiastic, passionate teachers.

"You know I'd pretty much do anything for you. Try me," I replied. Laura and I had been friends since our childhoods in southwest Virginia. Now we were two young professionals in our mid-twenties excited about changing the world. I was well into my second year as a practicing veterinarian and was eager to share my knowledge with anybody who would listen. I rarely said no to anything or anybody.

"My kindergarten class is going on a field trip to a pumpkin patch, but the pre-K class isn't able to go due to car seat regulations. I realize this is a tall order, but is there any possible way you could bring eighty-five pumpkins and a few animals for the kids to pet?"

The next day, I rang up my client and friend Heidi for help. Heidi, like Laura, is kindhearted and dedicated to educating children, especially about farm animals, and she just can't seem to say no to anyone. She is the quintessential little Italian mother to everyone she meets. I had worked on Heidi's small farm for a few years now. She, her husband, and their four children raised goats, sheep, and chickens to provide meat and milk for their family. I enjoyed helping the dairy goats deliver their babies. Sometimes a doe would have enough babies that I could hand each child a tiny baby goat to dry off.

"Heidi, how would you like to go with me to visit our nation's capital? And, oh yeah, we need to take pumpkins and farm animals. Are you in?" I pleaded.

Heidi was instantly on board.

Before the crack of dawn that Monday morning, we loaded eighty-five pumpkins donated by Whole Foods, Mimi the pet sheep, and two relatively well-behaved goats into the long bed of the old white GMC pickup truck that had been retired from veterinary service. We cranked the tension down on the last ratchet strap that held the crates in place and dusted off the bits of hay from our clothes.

"We can't be looking like rednecks going to the big city," I said. Heidi proceeded to spew coffee out of her nose. Formerly from upstate New York, Heidi realized how out of place farmers look in urban areas.

Heidi and I buckled up and headed north on the unmarked winding country roads that soon turned into the jam-packed I-395, the inner loop of the Capital Beltway. How could all four lanes of traffic headed in the same direction be sitting still? To pass the time, we were jamming to "Goodbye Earl" at the top of our best Dixie Chicks voices when the truck started making a little noise of its own. The loud dinging alerted us to the blinking alternator light. I called my favorite mechanic.

"Les . . . man, I'm in a bind on 395. How many more times will this truck start if the alternator light is on?"

"Get to the school and do what you gotta do," he said. "The truck will start one more time, so get yourself to a mechanic right after you leave there."

Heidi and I arrived at the school and were greeted with hugs and smiles from Laura and her staff, all wearing bright orange T-shirts with the motto "Work Hard. Be Nice." We entered the yard surrounded by walls painted with beautiful rainbows and murals.

"The play space must be enclosed to protect the children from the violence and turmoil that rages outside these walls," Laura explained. "It's nothing like where we grew up, Melinda."

We all worked together to arrange the pumpkins and bring in the animals before eighty-five smiling, excited children bounded through the doors, many with their plush cheeks painted with bright rainbows. The children didn't know what to think about Mimi at first; many had never seen a live animal of any sort. Some kids were curious about her, some were a little too eager to love her, and some were scared to death of her. Heidi would take the children's hands and help them feel Mimi's shiny, crimped white locks. One shy wisp of a boy whispered, "Awww, Mimi, you are soooo soft like a pillow," as he laid his head across the fleece covering her wide back.

After the initial excitement had worn off, we sat the children down in a circle and read them some books and talked with them about where agricultural products originate. "Children, do you know where your food comes from?" I gazed across the sea of children, and hands sprung up into the air.

I called on a girl in the front row with a head full of braids, each with a brightly colored bead. She shouted, "The grocery store!"

"How many of you think she's right?" Nearly every hand reached toward the sky. Heidi and I looked at each other with equally big eyes.

"Miss Heidi is going to hold up the picture of an animal, and you all try to help us figure out what comes from the animal," I said as Heidi flipped through one of our books to find a picture of a cow.

"This cow gives us milk and meat. And Mimi here, what does she give us?" I reached down to part Mimi's locks, hoping to give the kids a hint. Heidi encouraged a child from the front row to touch a ball of yarn. "Sheep give us wool to make clothes, and meat too. And what about these crazy goats? What do they give us besides a hard time?" Heidi gently tapped one of the goats on the nose when she noticed it munching on the shoestring of a little girl in the front row.

After a few seconds of silence, Heidi piped up and said, "Goats are actually the best! They give us milk and meat, and some goats give us fiber to make clothing, like mohair and cashmere."

Heidi and I could see we had gotten the little wheels in their minds turning. Everyone, kids and teachers alike, was amazed to learn that only 1 percent of our population is directly involved in animal agriculture and 1 percent raises crops. Literally 2 percent of the population produces the food, while 100 percent of the population eats it.

All too quickly, our time with the kids was over. They kissed Mimi and the silly goats goodbye, gave us hugs, and marched out clutching their little orange pumpkins. We loaded up the livestock and said our goodbyes, praying the truck would start just one more time.

Moments before we exited the building, we heard gunshots. When the coast was clear, the armed school security guard motioned for us to exit and we made a beeline for the truck. I slammed the driver's-side door shut just as the police rushed onto the scene. Across the street, a man lay bleeding on the sidewalk.

"Holy crap! Is that dude dead?" Heidi blurted out. "I don't think I've ever seen a dead person before."

When the engine turned over, we were thrilled. Our hearts raced as we sped off to flee the murder scene and look for the closest mechanic.

Suddenly, we turned a corner and saw the majestic Capitol building at the end of a long street. On this street, it was not hard to appreciate the diversity in our culture. People everywhere: rich and poor, brown and white, English-speaking and non-English-speaking, dressed in every kind of clothing imaginable. As we approached the stoplight in front of a mosque with the increasingly vocal goats, two men yelled through my open window. They offered us cash for the goats, hoping to provide a meal for an upcoming religious feast. Heidi politely declined, shaking her head no while trying to hide the panicked look on her face. We spotted a small gas station and pulled in.

We were greeted by a mechanic named Heinrich. He was an older, gruff German man with a snow-white buzz cut and robust stature. He agreed to put a new alternator on the truck.

"Buddy, we'll pay you extra if you promise to keep the sheep and goats safe while we walk down the street for a quick lunch. They are kind of in high demand around here," I said and handed him the truck keys. Heinrich made it clear that he had no patience for thieves and vowed to protect the livestock at all costs, complete with a dissertation about his German heritage.

After Heidi and I visited the local pub for lunch and a well-deserved cold beer, we settled up with Heinrich, who smiled and handed us the truck keys. We jumped in with our rambunctious, small ruminant buddies, declined three more offers to sell, and headed home to our peaceful, self-sufficient lives back in the country.

TRACTOR BUCKET SHARPSHOOTING

I pulled my legs out of the filthy coveralls and tossed them into the laundry. Dr. Kate and I compared stains after a busy day's work.

"Oh hell, you better ditch the shirt too. The dried blood in your armpits is going to get uncomfortable after a while." Dr. Kate tossed me one of her clean T-shirts.

When I turned toward her to grab the shirt, she shook her head and squinted. "That *was* a nice bra. What did I tell you about wearing those to work, Melinda Gayle?"

"I know, I know. Young, single women do tend to have a disproportionate number of nice bras, you know." I tried to change the subject. "What's the story with those ripped coveralls? Cougar attack?"

"I couldn't get my truck all the way to that down cow the other night. By the time I'd crawled through the barbed wire fence six times, the coveralls were shredded, and my skin wasn't much better. When I walked through the door, James didn't know what to think! He got a tube of antibiotic ointment and took his turn at doctoring after I showered." Dr. Kate blushed with a devilish grin on her face. "It turned a bad night into a really good one."

We'd been working together for nearly a year now and enjoyed the camaraderie at the end of a long day. Dr. Kate said, "MG, I think we deserve homemade margaritas! Do you concur?"

"C'mon, Kate, have you ever known me to turn down a margarita?"

We decided it would go faster if one of us squeezed the limes while the other made the syrup. I nearly always had to squeeze the limes because I wasn't much of a cook. Growing up on the farm, I did the manual labor outside and always missed out on helping cook supper. Just as the tart juice of the first lime hit the bottom of the container, the phone rang.

It was one of our older farmers, Clint, calling with a cow in labor out in the pasture. The cow and the farmer were both upset; there was no way he would be able to get her to a pen. Dr. Kate and I decided to tag-team it. We stuck our margaritas in the freezer, hoping to get back to them before dark.

We grabbed clean coveralls and jumped into her dusty silver GMC pickup with the white vet box insert filling the bed. Speeding down the winding back roads through the flat county terrain, we passed pine forest after pine forest, interrupted only occasionally by a fenced pasture with a small herd of beef cows or a few horses.

When we arrived at the farm, Clint was there in his tattered denim overalls and John Deere cap with little bits of hay nestled in his dark mustache. He'd watched the cow for most of the morning and tried all afternoon to get her confined where she could be helped, and there'd been no birthing progress. Dr. Kate made eye contact with Clint and said loudly to compensate for his deafness, "We need to tranquilize her with a blow dart. Show us to her most recent vicinity." We loaded a dart with sedative, pressurized its rear chamber, and assembled the five-foot blowpipe.

Easing up as close as we could, Dr. Kate fired a shot at the cow from the truck window. At the last minute, the cow made a hard right and dodged the dart. Dr. Kate gritted her teeth. "Damn it!" She spotted the bright red and yellow flight of the spent dart in the clump of grass, reloaded with a fresh needle, and eased close once more. She took a deep breath, then shot the loaded dart directly into the cow's backside.

"Good job! See, you haven't lost your touch," I whispered to Dr. Kate. We waited the ten minutes for the sedative to work, hoping the cow's adrenaline was not high enough to block the effect. Fifteen minutes later, she was still unapproachable and acting like a lunatic, running in the opposite direction while bellowing. All of us were losing our patience.

"Mind if I give it a try?" I asked as Clint pulled up to us in his tractor.

"Knock yourself out," Dr. Kate said.

I loaded the dart with another dose of sedative and jumped up into the tractor bucket. I crouched down in the bucket as Clint lifted me nearly ten feet in the air so he could see to drive. "Clint, buddy, get me as close as you can to that cow," I shouted, hoping Clint could hear me.

For Clint, this was probably terribly exciting, like a high-speed chase (at low speed). For Dr. Kate, this must have been terrifying; her young employee, covered under her workman's compensation, was now in a six-foot-wide tractor bucket dangling a dart full of sedative with an eighty-year-old chauffeur. And for me, well, I was living the dream. I always thought it would be super fun to dart something from a tractor bucket, and now I was on a mission with a chance to be the hero. With the wind blowing through my hair, I was trying to scope out my target, all the while trying not to fall out of the bucket each time we hit a groundhog hole.

As the cow joined her herd mates to run from the tractor, I hollered, "We need the one with the blow dart and the feet sticking out of her ass." Clint hung a right, and we were back on track. I spotted her and took a deep breath to fire the dart. The dart sunk deep into the muscle on the cow's rump. A direct hit!

"Halle-freakin'-lujah," Dr. Kate cheered as she readjusted her worn-out ball cap.

I instructed Clint, "Back off her now and let her have some space." Ten minutes later, the old gal finally conceded and lay down.

Dr. Kate put a halter on the cow and tied her to Clint's tractor. "MG, I never want to see you tie a cow to a vet truck, especially not a truck I own."

I nodded my head, pretending like I never tied a cow to a truck before.

We gloved up, and Dr. Kate cleaned the cow's vulva with warm, soapy water. She placed the obstetrical chains on the calf's front feet and lubricated the vaginal vault while I assembled the calf jack. This double-ratcheted instrument is worth its weight in gold, as it allows us to safely apply traction on oversize calves without wrenching our backs or harming the babies. Dr. Kate hooked the chains to the hooks in the jack, and I began to crank. With every crank of the jack, there was visible progress. One foot would come out farther, then the other, until we could see the calf's large, swollen tongue begin to appear.

"With a tongue that swollen, I'd say that thing is dead as a hammer," I said, continuing to crank the jack.

We all thought the calf would be dead. Clint had been trying to catch the cow for several hours, and on top of that, we sedated her (and she shares a blood supply with the calf).

Right then, the calf's fat tongue moved. Just a little, but it was a sign of life that lent urgency to our actions. Dr. Kate turned to me and said, "Look at that. Let's get this thing out of there."

Once the shoulders were clear, I raised the angle of the jack to reduce the pressure on the calf. Dr. Kate quickly reached in with a handful of J-Lube (or as the farmers call it, "instant snot") to apply to each of the calf's hips. Now keeping the jack in line with the cow's spine, I renewed pressure as Dr. Kate rotated the calf's body a quarter turn so its wide hips could clear Mama's constricting pelvis. With that, he came out in a rush.

Clint was thrilled to see that the calf was alive. "Man, it's a whopper! No wonder the mama cow couldn't deliver it. I'm sure glad I called y'all for help."

Once the calf was out, I started drying his long, wet body with towels, while Dr. Kate checked the cow internally. I reckon he must have weighed nearly ninety pounds. I especially concentrated on getting his nostrils clean and open. Clint passed me a rigid, pointy stick of hay from his tractor bucket, and I shoved it in the calf's nose, as my dad had taught me on the dairy. It seemed evil to poke a baby in such sensitive tissue with something so hard, but by God, it sparked a reaction and made the calf gasp for a breath every time. Right then, the calf shook his head, flapping his long slimy ears, and drew a big breath. He was a fighter for sure.

"MG, mix him up some powdered colostrum. You'll probably have to dig around in the mess to find the feeding tube. I will get her some pain meds and antibiotics." Dr. Kate slipped on her reading glasses so she could read the bottles of medicine.

"I'm a bit worried about reversing that sedative. Any chance she might get up and try to kill us?" I asked while pulling the reversal up into the syringe.

Dr. Kate and Clint seemed apprehensive as well, but in the end, we felt it would be in the best interest of the calf to levitate his mother. As I pushed the reversal drug slowly into the cow's tail vein, she gradually sat up cow-fashioned, on her chest with her feet under her, and slowly rose to her wobbly feet, glaring at us while drool poured out of her mouth.

Lately, it felt like nearly every birth I assisted was for a dead baby. Delivering live babies was the spark that made me choose this career, but ever since I'd started work, it seemed like I got all the difficult cases, usually involving death.

We decided the cow needed some alone time to get her bearings and bond with her oversized bundle of joy. Glancing in the rearview mirror of the truck, I saw her totter over to her baby and start licking him behind his ears.

YOU ARE MY SUNSHINE

*D*o the epidural first, clean the prolapsed vaginal tissue, replace it, and use the long needle to place a purse-string stitch to hold it in. I repeated the instructions Dr. Kate had given me to perform the vaginal prolapse repair over and over as I drove to my next patient. I was on the lookout for the unfortunate cow with her lady parts flapping in the breeze. I had been practicing for two years now, but I hadn't repaired many prolapses, so I was lucky to have someone more experienced to coach me.

I parked my dirty green pickup at the site and walked into the barn. When I looked around the door, a part of me thought the barn looked vaguely familiar.

Of course it did—it looked exactly like the one Jesus was born in. There was a big Hereford cow staring right at me and no sign of any kind of chute or head stanchion. An elderly lady walked in and introduced herself. "Don't worry, I have some help on the way. He should be here any minute."

"Ma'am, how do you normally restrain cows in this barn? I don't see any sign of a headgate." I scanned the barn for anything, even a rusty gate, to push the cow behind.

"We usually just put a rope on the cow's neck and push a gate around on them."

I grudgingly tossed a lariat rope over the cow's head and cinched her up to a post, praying she wouldn't pull the whole barn down on us. I started to look at the cow closely but realized quickly that the body part sticking out was *not* her vagina. It was her rectum. And it had not simply been out for a day—it was likely out more than a week. It was long, swollen, dark, and nasty, the grossest oversized Tootsie Roll you could imagine!

While we waited for the helper to arrive, I called Dr. Kate on the CB radio to get some modified guidance on how to handle the cow's half-rotted rectal prolapse. I knew what came out must go back in, but how, when the tissue was so filthy and friable? Dr. Kate started on a diatribe as if she were reading from a surgical technique manual.

"First, give the cow an epidural. Then place a teat inflation in the prolapse and pin it with cross-pin fixation before you start removing the necrotic tissue using two circumferential incisions. Then make a longitudinal incision to connect the other ones before you start blunt dissection down to the healthy submucosal plane. And good luck tying ligatures around all those blood vessels that shoot blood at your face while you're working. Finally, align the mucosa with four simple interrupted sutures around the circumference of the prolapse. Got it, chica?"

What?

Here I was, standing in the field by a barn, with no pen or paper, trying to visualize this procedure in my head. I took a stab: "Cut off the bad stuff until I get to the good stuff, try to control the bleeding, and sew the good stuff to the good stuff? Got it."

I repacked my plastic carrier with medical supplies and went back to the barn with the helper. He was a scruffy, middle-aged guy who seemed strangely happy to be part of this ordeal. Pushing the gate around on the cow so I could give her the epidural, he began to tell a joke and burst into laughter before he reached the punch line. His breath smelled like he'd downed a fifth of Jack for breakfast. He was as drunk as a monkey. It was at this moment I decided to just sedate the cow.

One of my veterinary school interview questions had been

"How would you handle the situation if your help showed up drunk?" Either that professor was psychic, or this was a common occurrence.

I started filleting the rotten tissue off the feces-covered rectum while trying to remember Dr. Kate's explicit instructions and tuning out the singing from the drunk "helper." It was easy to tell when I reached the healthy tissue because the blood started flowing like crazy. It was like being shot in the face by the little dish rinser in the sink, except with blood. The elderly lady, who was standing up against the barn wall, grew increasingly pale and buckled at the knees. I ripped off my bloody plastic sleeves and ran to catch her as she began to faint. I supported her large frame as she melted in my arms. I laid her carefully on the ground and wiped her head with a cool rag to rouse her. Me and my intoxicated sidekick hoisted her up and put her on the front seat of my truck. I carted her up to her house and guided her into her recliner, where I left her with a large cup of ice water.

When I got back down to the barn, my patient was still lying peacefully without a care in the world, other than the small pool of blood she'd lost behind her. Once again, I started trying to remember Dr. Kate's dissertation on rectal repair, which was not coming back to me very easily. I tied off the large vessels one by one until I ran out of sutures. Then I pushed the tissue back in and placed a purse-string suture to secure the tissue on the inside of the cow. Scruffy was clapping, cheering, and telling the cow how pretty she looked. I was starting to wonder why drinking breakfast was so frowned upon in our society. If we could all start out every day as happy as this guy, the world would be a better place.

After I finished with the cow patient, I thanked Scruffy and went to check on the human patient, who was relaxing in her chair. I reiterated several times that repairing the cow's rectum was strictly a salvage procedure and that she needed to be sold soon.

"I understand, dear. Thanks for everything today. Sorry I wasn't much help," she replied.

When I arrived home I needed to tell somebody about my crazy experience, so I dialed up Ann. "Hey, sis. What are you up to today? You won't believe the call I just went on."

"Girl, I'm having one of those days, but it sounds like yours is worse. If it involves blood or guts, you know I don't want to hear it. That crap makes me queasy and then I feel sick while I'm decorating my wedding cakes," Ann said as she fired up her industrial-sized KitchenAid mixer.

"The whole story is blood and guts, oh yeah, and a drunk guy, so I guess I will just holler at you later. I hope your day gets better." I hung up shaking my head, wondering how my sister and I could be so different.

Exactly one year later, I received a call for a cow with a vaginal prolapse. Initially, the address didn't register as familiar. When I pulled up to the barnyard, I recognized it immediately. Why, of course, it was the barn Jesus was born in, and it was still standing. When I walked through the door, it was the same cow, with the same prolapsed rectum. I started shaking my head when I heard an all-too-familiar voice. There he was, my little half-lit scruffy buddy. He looked over at me, grinning from ear to ear, and said, "Every time I see you it's like sunshine!"

A POT OF JASMINE
AT THE END OF THE RAINBOW

One afternoon in the late fall, Dr. Kate was called to see a newborn alpaca at a local alpaca farm just outside of Richmond. The owners specifically requested her because these alpacas were very expensive and they sought her level of experience.

Dr. Kate was known in the agricultural community for telling it like it is. She was extremely intelligent, but not always the most empathetic person. One day at the vet clinic, she answered the phone in her brusque tone: "Do you want the nice one or the mean one?" She didn't even try to pretend that burnout wasn't dragging her down. I was flattered to be known as "the nice one."

Dr. Kate diagnosed the cria, baby alpaca, with a congenital condition called choanal atresia, a genetic abnormality in which the nasal passages are too narrow to sustain life. The owner was away at a national alpaca show, and alpacas were still a relatively novel species in the United States, so the owner suggested it go to the veterinary hospital at Ohio State University to see an alpaca expert.

Since the cria was having difficulty breathing, the owner wanted a veterinarian to accompany it and offered to pay one to do so. Dr. Kate offered me up like a sacrificial lamb.

"Dr. Melinda can drive your van up to Ohio with the cria.

She'll have to take the mother alpaca too. I'll send my son Brian to help keep her awake."

I had worked all day and had already been up for twelve hours, so I was really looking forward to an eight-hour journey north with a twelve-year-old.

The client thought this was a great idea, and her husband helped us load the animals. He gave us the keys to the dark blue older-model minivan, warning us, "The van has fuel, but the gas gauge can be a little funny. You all be careful and have a safe trip."

On the second hour of our journey, I turned to head south on Interstate 81. The setting sun created layers of pink and orange hues in the sky as it tucked itself into the mountains over the green pastures speckled with grazing black cows. This job seemed too easy to be true. By the time we switched interstates again, only two and a half hours into our eight-hour voyage, young Brian was fast asleep. Darkness closed in on us, and I was getting quite tired myself. Cresting one of the steep West Virginia hills, the minivan began to sputter as if it were running out of gas. This couldn't be—the gauge was at three-quarters of a tank! I guided the rapidly slowing vehicle onto an exit ramp, wondering what I was going to do with an empty tank, a sleeping boy, and two alpacas in the middle of the night in West Virginia.

Shortly, a car pulled over, and a gentleman shouted out of his window in his thick West Virginia accent, "Y'all need a ride to a Walmart to get some gas?"

"Yes, sir. Thank you." I roused sleeping Brian and helped him into the stranger's car.

I glanced into the back of the van. The mother alpaca was comfortably seated in a cush position, upright with her feet tucked under her, by her tiny cria. I instructed, "Y'all behave while we are gone."

While chatting with our driver about his all-day fraternity

alumni golf tournament, I noticed how poorly he was driving. It dawned on me that we were riding with a drunk driver. As we got back to the van, the heavens opened, pouring rain. It was a toad-strangler for sure. Brian jumped back in the van to check on the alpacas, and I stood in the driving rain, attempting to pour five gallons of gasoline into a hole the diameter of a quarter in the pitch-black night while our intoxicated taxi driver sped away. Yes, chivalry is dead in West Virginia. I called the police to warn them that there was a drunk driver on the road, and they told me there were checkpoints everywhere that night because the governor was cracking down on drunk driving.

Once we were all back in the van with the broken gas gauge, we continued north, attempting to find a gas station and food for starving Brian. Two exits passed before we spotted the glorious neon lights of a gas station with gas and food. When I pulled off, blue lights and state troopers were everywhere. Sure enough, it was one of the governor's checkpoints. An officer shone a bright light through the window into my eyes and said, "Ma'am, I'm going to need you to blow into the breathalyzer and perform a field sobriety test."

The breathalyzer was a real struggle. I tried repeatedly to blow air into the machine for the required seven seconds, but by the fifth second, I'd start gasping for air while my lips turned blue. My childhood asthma and resulting bouts of pneumonia had really damaged my lungs. When this happens to calves, we call them "lungers." Most of my childhood doctors tried to dissuade me from large animal medicine because of the dust in the barns and the hay. They were sure my allergies and asthma would be a constant issue.

I decided to level with the deputy sheriff. "Sir, I'm having a really crappy night. I am craving an adult beverage, but I haven't had time to drink one. We need to get this baby alpaca to the hospital because it breathes worse than me." I'm not sure if he believed me or got tired of hearing me talk, but he let us get back on our way.

Finally, we were able to get some fuel for the van and for ourselves. I chose a Mountain Dew Amp as my upper of choice and made the rest of the journey. It was nearing 5:00 a.m. when we pulled into the veterinary teaching hospital. We unloaded the cria and her mother and headed to a hotel to get some much-needed rest before the alpaca expert came in. But after only about an hour, Brian and I began to hear what sounded like festivities, complete with trumpets and sirens. As we peeped through the curtain, all we could see were rainbows and a crowd of people marching through the streets gathering for the annual gay pride parade through the middle of Columbus. After we determined that our chance of getting any rest was over, we grabbed a quick breakfast and went back to the veterinary hospital.

The expert veterinarian strutted in, dressed in pristine green overalls, to examine our cria. He took one look at the cria and pronounced, "This cria has choanal atresia and it needs to be euthanized. I will call the owner and speak with her." After a quick phone consultation with the owner, he ordered a veterinary resident to euthanize it. Brian and I glanced at each other, then at the lifeless baby alpaca on the concrete floor, her big brown glassy eyes fixed. I'd fully expected this to be the outcome, but in that moment, I was overcome with emotion. I'd been hired to do everything in my power, including a tracheostomy, to keep this baby alive, and now I was standing by her dead body. It was at this moment I decided I wasn't going to be an alpaca EMT as a side hustle anymore.

Now we had to load the angry, grieving mother back into the van without her baby. As the 175-pound, jet-black mama was being led away from her lifeless baby, she squealed and clucked loudly and repeatedly. You could hear the anxious desperation in her cries. Every time the veterinary student would try to pull her toward the vehicle, she'd jerk her head around to look at her baby and spit green, putrid cud in our faces. Brian's pupils dilated as he realized we'd ridden in a van for eight hours with an animal that was capable of spitting as a defense mechanism.

Our journey home was off to a rocky start. We were both exhausted. The van reeked of gasoline from the wet jug and putrid alpaca spit. The mother alpaca was raising Cain in the back of the van, making deafening noises and trying to stand up. The smell of gas was so bad it was starting to give us both a headache. Brian piped up, "Why don't we pull off and get an air freshener?"

We pulled into a rinky-dink gas station and grabbed a clip-on air freshener, complete with a little glass vial of a bright pink, scented liquid labeled Jasmine Mist. I was excited that the station also had fountain drinks, even though they were out of lids. I placed my Coke in the cup holder, and Brian clipped our air freshener to the vent. It seemed things were looking up for us. At least it was starting to smell slightly better, and we had caffeine and ibuprofen.

After a half hour or so, I looked over to Brian and asked, "Has the air freshener spilled?" He argued incessantly with me (because Brian always argues) that it had not.

All I could smell was Jasmine Mist, everywhere. I literally felt like the lady on the commercial where the flowers are streaming into her nostrils. I finally yelled, "Brian, find the freaking spill!"

He found it all right. The small glass vial of Jasmine Mist had fallen directly into my uncovered Coke. I had just consumed two ounces of air freshener.

The bright side was that the van did not smell like gas anymore. The downside, as Brian discovered from the box, was that we needed to call Poison Control.

At Poison Control, a polite young man answered. I explained my predicament, and he said apologetically, "I'm sorry, ma'am, but I have no idea what's going to happen to you. I'm just a veterinary student working at Poison Control for extra money to help with my student loans."

"OK, let's pretend I'm a dog, then."

"I suppose if you were a dog, you'd vomit uncontrollably, but I doubt you'll pass out. It's probably fine to keep driving. Good luck to ya."

The vet student's prophecy was fulfilled in the hours to come. I started with abdominal cramps, including excruciating menstrual cramps (because they always come at a great time), and became severely nauseated. Doubled over at the waist and belching jasmine, I struggled to hold the van on the road.

The final few hours of the journey were the hardest. The mama alpaca finally settled down, just in time to be dropped off at her house, where she'd have to adjust yet again. I handed the van keys back to the alpaca owner's husband. He asked, "How was the trip?"

Exhausted and dehydrated, I said, "Hellfire, man. The gas gauge on your ride is broken. Not 'a little funny,' broken. And that was just one of the many things that made this trip *suck*! And, oh yeah, sorry about your cria, and good luck with her grouchy-ass mother."

I collected the cash and sped away. When I pulled into my driveway, Brian and I both got out, dropped to our knees, and kissed the ground.

A MERCIFUL END

While speeding back to the office, I fantasized about being in a spa, facedown on the table, a plush white towel covering my bum, with candles and incense burning all around the table. A strong, handsome masseur skillfully working the warm oil in between the rigid muscles of my shoulders, slowly releasing the tension from my overworked body. I had hit a wall of mental and physical exhaustion and was in dire need of a break.

It had been a long, hard spring my second year at the vet service. Even though I was only in my late twenties, my body had to acclimate to the repetitive physical nature of this type of work. Thousands of cows and their calves had come through the cattle chutes to get vaccinations, deworming, and pregnancy checks. When I pulled into the office, Dr. Kate was sitting in her comfy chair on the porch with a glass of chilled Pinot Grigio in hand. That shady, peaceful screened porch was our favorite hiding place. It wasn't even really hidden—it just seemed like testosterone inhibited the ability to look very hard for us.

"You look like you could use a drink," Dr. Kate said.

I eased into my chair and nodded. "My back is killing me. Could you grab me an ice pack when you bring my wine?"

"Absolutely. I'm going to grab one for my elbow as well. That thing got smashed a few weeks ago with a damn gate and it still hurts. I knew I should have charged them more."

Our peaceful porch retreat was rudely interrupted by the

obnoxious ringtone of my cell phone. I answered in case it was something I needed to deal with before I drank too much wine. On the other end of the line was a very sweet sheep farmer, Nelly. In her heyday, Nelly was a crackerjack sheep farmer. She bred beautiful Shetland sheep to harvest their fleeces, some of the nicest fleeces in the country. Nelly and her husband, Bill, now both in their early sixties, were a team, working side by side day in and day out tending their livestock and working their Australian shepherds.

I first met Nelly when she decided to sell her sheep due to her illness. She was diagnosed with a rare autoimmune disorder that had rendered her incapacitated. Bill was now spending his time caring for her, and the sheep fell through the cracks. Being responsible farmers, they knew it was time to downsize, as they had no children to take over the farm. They sold their flock to a young couple with four children.

When I first answered the phone, I was confused as to why Nelly would be calling a large animal veterinarian when she didn't have her sheep anymore. "How are you all doing? Missing the sheep already?"

"That's the reason for my call, dear," she said with a trembling voice. "My husband has been having some personality changes, and he was recently diagnosed with an inoperable brain tumor."

"Oh no! I'm so sorry to hear that. How bad is it?" I asked, my shoulders tensed as I sat more erect in the chair.

"The doctor said it will grow fast and that his condition is terminal. I'm absolutely devastated at the thought of losing my caretaker and best friend." Nelly sniffed loudly and repeatedly.

After a short pause, I asked, "Is there anything I can do for you? Anything at all?"

She replied, "There is one thing, and I'm sorry to have to ask you to do this. Would you be able to come out to the house and euthanize Tess and Gus, our Australian shepherds?"

"Yes, certainly, I can do that for you. How soon would you need me?" I took a sip of wine and looked over at Dr. Kate.

"I don't know. Maybe next week? They are both fourteen years old now and they are very arthritic, and you grew up with border collies, so I know you understand that these working dogs are only good with us. I can't bear the thought of them being here without us."

Dr. Kate pulled her glasses down a bit and glanced at me with a curious expression. "What's up? Everything OK?"

I explained the situation. "Have you had enough wine to agree to come help me with this?" She willingly agreed. We sipped our wine and contemplated what lay ahead.

Monday afternoon rolled around. I picked up Dr. Kate, and we set out to do the job we were both dreading. Going into sick people's homes was nothing new to me; I fondly remember my sister and I playing dominoes in Mr. Ed's living room while my mom provided nursing care to his wife dying of breast cancer in the next room. In all the years of working alongside my mother, I don't remember a situation with a terminally ill couple, though.

When we arrived at the farm, Nelly and Bill were lying in their respective recliners, each with an obedient dog curled up on a comfy dog bed by their side. The dogs jumped up and barked incessantly as we entered. Dr. Kate and I visited with the couple briefly and discussed how they thought the dogs would be most comfortable. Nelly said, "I'd like to hold my girl Tess in my arms for her sedation. She's not the friendliest." I lifted the dog into the chair with her and braced her head while Dr. Kate injected her with the sedative cocktail. Nelly's sadness was palpable as she stroked her old friend lovingly and gently kissed her on her head.

"It may be best if you all sedate Gus and then place him in Bill's lap, because his coordination is very impaired," Nelly explained. We did just that.

With both dogs lying comfortably in their parents' arms, I made certain they had a gravedigger coming to bury the dogs, and we expressed our sympathy. "I'm so sorry you all are having to make such a difficult decision, but I admire your strength and courage."

Once the dogs began to "see the pink elephants," as my anesthesia professor used to say, Nelly whispered to Bill, "I can only hope our deaths will be this peaceful and kind."

Dr. Kate pinched off each dog's vein to raise it so I could inject them with euthanasia solution. As the pale pink solution traversed the IV line and entered the vein, the dog's bodies relaxed. Both Nelly and Bill wept as I intently listened to each dog to make sure their heart had stopped beating. Both dogs passed very peacefully. I often wrestle with the fact that we are so much kinder to our animals than we are to human beings. I gave Nelly and Bill each a hug and kiss on the forehead, and we left.

When we got to the truck, I glanced over at Dr. Kate, who had tears rolling down both cheeks. That was the first time I had ever seen her cry. I suppose veterinarians develop a hard outer shell to protect their hearts so they can continue to do these emotionally difficult jobs.

HELL ON WHEELS

It is not uncommon for young, eager veterinarians starting out in their careers to agree to most anything: performing surgery on a turkey, neutering a tomcat on the tailgate, or euthanizing a squirrel. Starting on year three at the practice, much to Dr. Kate's dismay, I hadn't quite gotten this out of my system. I invested all that time and energy in learning how to work on so many types of animals and perform so many medical procedures, and by God, I was going to try it all at least once. In this instance, a very nice draft horse client, Wendy, asked if perhaps one day I could castrate a mule for her. She explained that the mule and his sister were a pulling team and he was getting to the age where his testosterone would be a problem.

Wendy was a small-framed woman, but she commanded the respect of her horses, even the 2,500-pound Suffolk punches she used to pull logs out of the forest. She was certainly the type of horse person I enjoyed working with. Her proposition sounded quick and easy. After all, I had castrated several huge workhorses for her before, and it had always gone well. Why should this be any different?

I arrived at Wendy's farm and saw her standing with her small, dark-coated mule on a halter, eagerly awaiting his procedure (presumably because he didn't know what the procedure entailed). She said his name was Hell, and when she saw my puzzled look, explained, "Hell's sister is named Wheels, and they are a pulling team, so together they are Hell on Wheels."

I chuckled as I pulled up the sedative in the syringe, just as I would for a small pony, and pushed the drugs into his vein. He was getting predictably sleepy, so I gave him the shot to make him lie down, then tied his back foot securely around his neck and shoulder with a long rope. I made the first cut over his robust, moist testicle and began stripping the excess tissue away from the spermatic cord to pull it away from his body. My sweaty palms squeezed the long arms of the emasculator, crushing the tissue beneath. Unexpectedly, the mule raised his head with a panicked look in his eye. I crawled back up to his neck and quickly injected more drugs. Hustling back down to the southern end to remove the clamp, I noticed the mule was trying to get up. He was determined to keep his manhood! I narrowly got the emasculator off containing the testicle and loosened the rope to help him avoid breaking his leg. Hell jumped up and began to run like the wind.

Wendy and I looked at each other in amazement. What was I going to do? This job was only half done, and I was pissed! I did what any young, stupid veterinarian would do: I caught him. Boy, was he surprised to see me when I grabbed his halter and tied him to a board fence. I unsuccessfully attempted to give him more sedative, which was a dumb idea because the sedative was no match for the adrenaline pulsing through his veins.

Wendy's daughter Anna, a budding rock star, suggested singing him a song to calm him. Wendy began humming the Alpo dog food jingle, which helped break the tension. I reached under the mule and felt the one remaining testicle, hoping I could get it out before he bolted. The instant he felt my fingers wrap around his large testicle, he took off, dragging the pieces of the broken board fence with him. I'm sure there was smoke coming out of my ears! In that moment, I remembered the words of one of my wise veterinary school professors: "When you get to the point of anger, it's time to walk away from the anesthesia drugs because something bad will happen."

"I think we'd better let some of the drugs wear off before we try again," I said to Wendy. "He's had enough drugs to kill an elephant. We're gonna need two strong men for round two. You bring your husband, and I will bring my boyfriend. Sound like a plan?"

Two days later, I pulled back in with my 6'4" corn-fed farmer boyfriend, William, in tow. In front of us stood Wendy; Hell; and Wendy's tall, strapping cowboy husband, Sheldon. All of the pieces were in place to guarantee success. We took the mule under a huge tree so we'd have a place to secure the ropes.

When the men met, they immediately began making fun of us. "You girls let a little three-hundred-pound jackass get the best of you?" William and Sheldon laughed at our expense. Wendy and I were getting mad. If those boys weren't careful, their only chance at getting a piece of ass was from the one about to lose his balls.

I gave the little ass his first dose of sedative in the vein, twice as much as before. Once he looked sleepy, I gave him the shot of ketamine to drop him to the ground. He lay down peacefully, and we moved in like a NASCAR pit crew, tying ropes to every part of the mule that looked like it would hold a rope. We snugged every rope to the big tree. I made the cut over the testicle and started squeezing the testicle out of the hole, with the clamp right beside me. Hell began to squirm.

"Hold his head down, boys," I yelled as I crushed the clamp down. It stayed on for all of twenty seconds before I had to pull it off.

The obstinate mule jerked his head up and sent both large men flying backward to land flat out in the dirt.

"That son of a gun threw me onto a rock," William shouted to Sheldon, wiping dirt out of his eyes with his shirtsleeve. Hell brayed loudly as if he were telling us all where to go. I pulled the last rope off his leg just in time.

Hell ran off into the sunset, this time as a changed man. He might stay mean for the rest of his life, but he wouldn't have the testosterone to back it up. The guys continued to compare battle scars, while Wendy and I shook our heads.

"There's a reason the women bear the children, you know," Wendy said with a grin.

"What's wrong, boys? Did that little mule just whip y'all? I think you all owe us an apology." I smirked and started to clean up my equipment.

"You gals really weren't joking when you said that little devil was a tough customer," Sheldon replied as he pulled his cowboy hat off to pick the gravel out.

I really wanted to take the last testicle to a taxidermist to make myself a trophy for completing what seemed to be an impossible task. Clearly, the only one more stubborn than a mule is a hardheaded veterinarian trying to prove herself. Wendy and I exchanged a hug.

For years to come, she competed with Hell on Wheels in the cart-pulling event at the Virginia State Fair, where he beat up at least two more cowboys.

OFF WITH HER HEAD

One clear, sunny day in the early summer, I drove across the long two-lane bridge over the cool blue water of Lake Anna. Some people were jetting around in their jet skis while others lay on their floats like toads on rocks, basking in the sun. It was hard not to be jealous of them enjoying their weekend when I was headed to see a down cow for a new client.

When I pulled up to the farm, a dark-haired, middle-aged woman waved me toward the outside of a small barn where a mixed-breed cow sat, looking desperate to stand. The woman, who introduced herself as Julie, gave me a brief history of the cow.

"She's five years old, and she hasn't eaten for two or three days," Julie explained. "My husband and son put feed and water in front of her and she acts like she wants it, but she won't partake."

Julie had some experience working on a dairy in her younger years, so she'd given the cow calcium paste by mouth in case she had a condition called milk fever. "Nothing I'm doing is working," she told me, puzzled. "The cow has been housed in a dry lot and seemed like she was in a raging heat, complete with incessant mooing before she went down. It was weird."

With my gloved hands, I carefully examined the cow from head to tail. Her temperature was low, her stool was hard from dehydration, and her gut sounds were diminished because of her lack of appetite. I treated her symptomatically for all the usual suspects: metabolic problems, a form of cancer called lymphoma, and musculoskeletal injury. I'd been doing this for three years now, and I knew the issues that would take a cow down in central Virginia. One of my veterinary school professors said, "Common things happen commonly." But something was different about this cow. Despite being down, she was far from weak. When I haltered her and pierced her big jugular vein with the needle, she barrel-rolled—twice! How on earth could this cow have enough energy to fight when she hadn't eaten for three solid days?

Trying to impress my new client, I was mostly concentrating on hitting the vein with the needle. When I started thinking about the cow's neurological system being impaired, the nymphomania, and the inability to eat and drink, I realized there was one thing I hadn't considered: rabies!

I carefully approached the cow's head and grabbed her tongue to examine it. Sure enough, she had no muscle tone in her tongue. She wasn't eating and drinking because she couldn't. "Ma'am, unfortunately I am going to have to consider rabies as a possible diagnosis for this cow," I explained.

Julie flew off the handle and started acting like she had rabies herself. She berated me and peppered me with questions about this lethal neurologic disease. "Well, how could she have gotten rabies?" she demanded. "That is ridiculous. Why would you even suggest that?"

I understood her frustration and confusion, but it didn't make my job any easier. "Ma'am, cattle don't foam at the mouth and bite like dogs with rabies. They get what's known as a dumb form of rabies instead of the furious form."

"OK, if you think the cow has rabies, then test her . . ." Julie challenged.

"There's one small problem, ma'am," I said. "The only way to test the cow would be to euthanize her, remove her head, and send it to the state lab for testing. If the cow turns out to be rabid, you and your family will need to get post-exposure shots to help prevent you from becoming infected with the virus."

She maintained a blank expression. I wasn't sure she'd processed one word that came out of my mouth. The more I spoke, the angrier she got. "I'm getting ready to go across the country on a business trip. I don't have time for rabies!"

Let's face it, who *does* have time for rabies?

"Leave the cow alone for the night and think about what I said. If the cow becomes more neurologic or dies overnight, I will need to come back tomorrow to remove her head." I scribbled my cell phone number down on the back of a losing lottery ticket and handed it to her.

Sure enough, at the opening of the next day, Julie rang the office to say the cow was becoming more neurologic. I went back to sedate the cow so I could inject her with the special pink juice. The cow, through no fault of her own, was crazy as a shithouse bat. Getting her sedated enough to euthanize her was a struggle.

Once she finally succumbed to the liquid relief and took her last breath, I placed a second pair of gloves on my sweaty hands. I fetched a gift from my dearly departed grandmother. Most kids' grandmas give them money, or jewelry, or furniture. Not my grandma; she gave me a special hickory-handled knife that we used to cut up the hogs at hog-killing time. It was an awesome knife, and I cherished it. I sharpened the old knife and carefully removed the cow's head at the atlanto-occipital joint, using great care not to splash any possibly infectious blood on myself or the clients. I placed the large, bloody head into a five-gallon bucket with ice I had purchased from the boat dock.

"If the cow tests positive for rabies, the health department in your county will contact you as soon as they get the results," I explained.

Julie paced back and forth, still frustrated and in disbelief. It's hard to imagine being a mother thinking you inadvertently exposed your family to a lethal disease just by trying to raise food to stock the freezer.

I hauled the head through the doors of the local county health department. Man, do you get some weird looks from the chicks who are just waiting in line for their pregnancy test when you come through carting an entire cow head in an ice bucket. I could pretty much tell you which ladies were pregnant by the ones who were retching as if they were going to vomit on the floor. Surprisingly enough, this is considered an acceptable way to transport a potentially rabid body part because the virus dies within thirty seconds once it's out of the animal's body. I delivered the bucket to the unlucky recipient, turned over all the necessary contact information, and went to my next job.

Less than twenty-four hours later, I got a call from the health department.

"Hi, ma'am. I'm calling to let you know that the cow we tested for you was in fact rabies positive."

"Thanks for the information, buddy. Good luck calling my client out in California to break the news to her. I'm gonna warn you . . . she ain't gonna be happy."

That night, I went to the emergency room and waited for eight hours to get my rabies booster shot. They told me I only required a booster shot since I was vaccinated in school and apologized for the hellacious wait.

I didn't hear anything from Julie for a couple of weeks. I prayed for them every night and hoped they were tolerating their post-exposure shots well. I figured no news was probably good news.

Two weeks later, I received a handwritten letter on a plain sheet of notebook paper with a crisp $100 bill in it. It read:

I want to extend my sincerest thanks for your prompt attention and follow-up in the handling of our rabies incident. Thank you for being diligent about getting to the source of the problem as your actions may clearly have saved my life. I was very impressed with your concern for the health and well-being of

*myself and my family. You are a wonderful doctor and it was
very fortunate for us that we found you in our time of need!*

My broad shoulders sank as the tension left them. I felt so
relieved. That letter was exactly the encouragement I needed to
remember that being a veterinarian was about saving the lives of
animals—and, on occasion, people.

WHAT WOULD JOHN WAYNE DO?

"**M**G, any chance you could go out and euthanize a cow?" Dr. Kate asked on the other end of the line. "I pulled a huge calf out of her several days ago, and she has been paralyzed in her rear limbs for three days now."

"Sure thing, it's my weekend on call anyway. I don't have much more to get done here at the apartment."

Dr. Kate continued, "There is one more thing you should know. The owner, Tommy, has some serious mental impairments, but I have discussed all the options with him and he's OK with you coming out to put her down."

I hopped in the vet truck and ran by the office to pick up a few supplies when I was spotted by Dr. Kate's preteen sons, Brian and John. The boys jumped into the truck, and John yelled to his mom, "We're going with Dr. Melinda on an adventure." I chuckled at their eagerness and figured they were just looking for an excuse to get out of the house.

Brian struggled to pull the seat belt over his head of fuzzy blond hair. "Wow, Dr. Melinda, it reeks of cow crap in here. Maybe you should get an air freshener? I hear jasmine ones smell and taste good." I glared at him while John burst into laughter in the back seat.

The boys and I zoomed down the winding country roads, singing along to Josh Turner's "Firecracker."

"Do you have a crush on Josh Turner?" Brian asked as he struggled to push the seat back to give his excessively long legs more room.

John followed along, batting his long eyelashes. "Yeah, you always look dreamy and turn red when this song comes on."

"I don't know what you're talking about, boys. No, I do not have a crush on Josh—OK, maybe a little one," I confessed. "I just think his deep voice is sexy."

I always felt like the boys' big sister who helped them understand complex issues in life. They were just beginning their teenage years, so they had a lot of questions they didn't feel comfortable discussing with their parents.

John asked, "Big sis, any chance we make a pit stop to grab a Mountain Dew and a candy bar for the trip?"

"Sure thing. I'm kinda thirsty myself. Maybe a snack will keep you two occupied while I work?" I pulled into the small convenience store close to the farm.

When we arrived, the owner was sitting beside a huge geriatric Hereford cow with a worn-out look on her face and bed sores on her hocks from being down for several days. The boys sat in the truck jamming to the radio and eating candy while I slipped out to speak to the owner.

"Hi, Tommy. My name is Dr. Melinda, and I'm here to help your cow. I'm going to start by giving the cow some sedative to make her sleepy. Then I will give her a lethal injection of pentobarbital in her jugular vein that will put her to sleep," I explained. He nodded as he stared at me blankly. I hoped he understood what was about to happen.

I went back to the truck to fetch my supplies from my brand-new Porta-Vet box on the back of my GMC pickup. I was in love with the box. It had lights, a refrigerator to keep my drugs and vaccines cold, and a water hose that squirted warm water. All the schoolchildren I did talks for were most impressed by the water hose, but my favorite part of the box was the sliding drawers with numerous sizes and shapes of compartments to store my drugs and equipment. I loved being organized, and I felt like it made me a better doctor.

The old cow got very sleepy from the sedative, and I began to inject the fatal solution into her distended vein. She soon lay over on her side, in lateral recumbency, and began to snore. It was clear the cow was resting very comfortably, but she certainly wasn't deceased. This was a bit disturbing. Every time I had ever seen or injected the pink juice, death had been the result.

Tommy and I chatted while we waited for the cow to pass, and after several minutes, it was clearly not happening. I walked over to the truck to peek at the boys, who appeared to be throwing M&M's at each other, then meandered back to the cow, hoping she had crossed the rainbow bridge. Tommy and I looked at each other and shook our heads in disbelief. I went back to the truck, fetched the whole bottle of night-night potion, and emptied the rest of it into her jugular vein.

Fifteen very long minutes passed with the cow just snoring away, getting the best rest she'd had in her entire life. Now what? I had used every bit of the solution I had in the truck. As I stood there, I could hear one of my wise professors from veterinary school saying, "The only way to mess up a euthanasia is to leave it half done." I have never been a half-ass at anything, and I wasn't about to start now. I was a country girl way before I was a veterinarian, and you know what all good country girls have in the truck? A gun!

I made eye contact with Tommy and began to explain. "I do apologize that the injection did not end this cow's life. It did put her to sleep, but only to sleep, and she is in no way suffering right now. I'm going to have to load my gun and shoot the cow. Is this OK with you?"

He nodded and said, "Do whatever you need to do, ma'am. I trust you."

I checked on the happy, oblivious boys and stealthily slid the .357 from underneath the truck seat. I loaded seven rounds of .38 hollow points into the revolver. I marked the cow's head with lines to dictate the correct placement of my bullet. After all, I am a professional.

"Step back, Tommy. It's going to be very loud, and I may have to shoot her more than once," I warned him.

I pulled the hammer back and fired right into the center of my X on her forehead. The shot was incredibly loud, followed by stark silence. Thank goodness, the ol' cow was finally at peace. After about thirty seconds, I was sure the job was done. Moments later, the cow started up with loud snoring and breathing. I couldn't believe it. I shot her again, this time behind the ear.

Brian and John got out of the truck to see what on earth was going on. Tommy looked surprised to see the kids, so I explained to him that they belonged to Dr. Kate. The boys had never seen their mother use a gun on a vet call, so this was a whole new experience for them. I attempted to brief them on the situation.

Brian interrupted, "Down at my grandparents' house, I saw this cool old Western where John Wayne pulled out a gun and shot the cow in the heart. Maybe you should try that?"

I certainly wasn't above it, and it seemed like a quick, humane death, right? The heart is a key organ, and the cow was left side up.

I commended Brian and looked at Tommy. He said, "I love John Wayne. I think you should give it a shot." I ushered the boys away from the cow and made them cover their ears with their hands.

Boom. Boom. I fired two shots right into the lung directly over the cow's heart. We all came back around her and watched in anticipation.

Both boys jumped about a foot in the air when the cow began to snore even more loudly than before. But this time on the expiratory part of the snore there was air flowing out of the lung space; I could feel it with my hand. Even though all of us were completely freaked out by this seemingly immortal animal and her weird noises, the cow still seemed to be getting the best sleep of her life.

"So, Doc, what's plan C?" John asked.

Exasperated, I asked, "Well, boys, you all got any more bright ideas? Does anyone remember any scenes with Chucky from *Child's Play?*" Nobody seemed to get that but me, so I didn't even try to explain.

I was losing patience with the whole ordeal. Contemplating my next move, I remembered Grandma's old hickory knife. I went back to the truck, dumped the extra bullets out of the revolver and stashed it away, then pulled the knife out of its sheath made from an old teat inflation. I ran the long blade of the knife back and forth, over and over, up and down each side of the file to sharpen it. As I sharpened the knife, I thought of the Road Runner cartoons, in which Wile E. Coyote never gets Road Runner. I was beginning to wonder if this job would require a large boulder being dropped from the sky.

I was determined that plan C was going to work. I explained to the very patient and understanding client what plan C entailed, and he was on board. I approached my unconscious patient and put my fingers in her nostrils, slightly lifting her head, while my other hand pulled the razor-sharp knife across both jugular veins in one fell swoop. The cow didn't even make a noise. I tenderly laid her head back in a resting position, and she started to bleed out. After the cow had lost about two gallons of blood, her tired heart finally beat its last beat. Peace at last for the sweet mama cow. The boys returned to the truck, relieved and amazed, as I cleaned my equipment. I gave the client a big hug and apologized.

"Thanks so much for your patience and understanding, Tommy. Sorry it didn't go as planned, but isn't that typical in farming?" He nodded repeatedly, as if he were still trying to process what had just taken place.

The boys and I returned to the office just in time to get them to their grandmother's house for lunch. Sitting at the old wooden table with their grandparents and father, they enthusiastically told the tale of our adventure as everyone's eyes got bigger and bigger.

"I vividly remember when ol' John Wayne slung that gun from his hip and popped the ol' cow in the heart. Boy, I'm proud of you for remembering that." This was high praise from their grandfather—getting a compliment from that man was harder than getting a swollen-up rotten calf out of a heifer. Brian was so elated he thought it would be great to write up a short story for a school project. Fearing fallout from animal rights activists and certain that important details would not be conveyed correctly, their mother forbade them to repeat the story to anyone ever again.

I FELL TO PIECES

One sweltering summer afternoon, I had just sat down at the picnic table at the country store to take the first bite of my well-deserved turkey sandwich when I got a call on the flip phone from our secretary, Gale. She told me to go to a small dairy farm close by to help a cow that was having difficulty calving. I had been looking forward to eating while not in a moving vehicle, and I was not looking forward to this job. Dairy farmers are proficient when it comes to delivering calves. The only time they call a vet is when it's a disaster, not to mention it was nearly one hundred degrees outside.

When I arrived, Gil met me in the driveway sporting a soaking wet T-shirt with two blood-soaked sleeves. Nearly out of breath, he said, "Thanks for coming, Doc. I have been working the cow for over an hour. She's a huge Holstein and I can't seem to budge the calf."

I do love a challenge, but I didn't have a good feeling about this delivery. I pulled on the yellow, shoulder-length thin plastic sleeves, clamped them to my T-shirt, and entered the stanchion barn to assist the cow. The cow looked back at me with her big brown eyes as if begging for relief. I cleaned her long, mucous-covered vulva with soap and warm water and used copious amounts of obstetrical lube on both arms. As I examined her internally, I could feel a huge set of feet, and I could tell the calf was no longer living. There was no reaction when I pinched its foot, and the cow

67

had been struggling for too long. At this point, this job was about saving the cow's life.

I placed chains on the calf's feet, and I went back to my truck to get my ratcheted calf jack. I attached the handy gadget to the chains on the calf's feet and slowly cranked the jack one click at a time, to no avail. The calf's head was entirely too large to come through the mother's bony pelvis. The cow plopped down in exhaustion.

"That calf is dead as a doornail, and the cow is exhausted," I explained to Gil. "Our best bet is going to be to take it out in pieces. See if you can get us some helpers. Just tell them you have cold beer in the shop. Don't tell them about the sawing, or they might not come."

As I went back to the truck to fetch the fetotome and wire, Gil phoned some friends. Gil was a social guy who hosted a steam and gas show every year, so he had no shortage of friends. By the time I got myself positioned on the ground behind the cow and inserted the fetotome and wire around the calf's head, there were two extra helpers in the barn. The fetotome protects a cow's delicate feminine tissue from getting cut by the wire. It requires one person to hold it in place while another person uses the wire handles to saw through the calf's bones.

One of the guys rolled up his sleeves and grabbed the handles attached to the wire while I continued to hold tension on the instrument.

"Slow and steady wins the race, buddy," I warned him. "It's not a he-man contest. Don't pick up speed until we get this wire seated." Pretty soon, though, my strong, gruff helper pulled on the wire hard and began to saw faster and faster. After a few seconds of sawing, the wire popped, and he fell ass over teacup into the opposite gutter of the barn.

Once he picked himself up and dusted himself off, I encouraged him, "You want to give it another shot? This time try longer and smoother strokes, like a Nordic track." I replaced the wire, and my sore helper started again. As he sawed slowly and deliberately back and forth, he started to sweat through his clothes.

"You're doing great, man. Keep it up. You're almost through," I told him just as if I were his coach. Right then, the sawing got easier, and his wire made it all the way through the head. When I pulled the large dead calf head out of the cow's vagina, you would have thought I had a trophy buck's head. The guys were impressed, not only with the size of the calf but with the fact we got a piece of it out. I placed the wire around one front leg, we got it removed, then with a quick break to switch lumberjacks, we got the other leg removed. Thirty minutes in, we were finally making some tangible progress.

We stopped for a quick water break and moved to the chest cavity of the calf. I explained to the guys, "Brace yourselves. We're about to saw through all these rib bones, so the sawing is jagged and frustrating." I continued to work tirelessly, and we took breaks to switch people sawing between each piece of the chest cavity. Never did ripping something's heart out feel so gratifying! With every piece we brought to the outside of the cow, her chance of survival increased exponentially.

When we got the last piece of the chest cavity delivered, the cow was finally able to urinate. Dark, foul-smelling urine flowed out of the cow's urethra like a river. It quickly filled the gutter behind the cow, and my hair soaked the urine up like a wick. Pretty soon, my long, straight highlighted hair was curly. Gil, while belly laughing, asked me, "Did you ever think you'd spend over twenty years in school only to end up in a puddle of urine and fetal fluid behind a cow?"

"What are you talking about, man? I'm living the dream." I smiled as my mind drifted. Did I really borrow ninety grand to end up in a situation like this? Is this what "living the dream" looks like?

After a quick laugh, me and the guys started back to sawing on the abdominal cavity. Another hour passed as we continued to deliver the calf piece by piece. To entertain ourselves, we started a betting pool on who would get heatstroke first. About that time, Gil's father, Bill, walked into the barn. He looked at us like we were all crazy. Bill was nearing eighty years old; he was a stout man with a chiseled face. As he stood there staring at us, "I Fall to Pieces" came on the barn radio. Bill stated in his assertive tone, "I have one rule: if a Patsy Cline song comes on the radio, you must always stop and dance."

I love Patsy Cline and I love to dance. I stripped off my long, fluid-filled sleeves, and he reached for my waterlogged hand. He helped me up from the concrete floor and tenderly clutched my waist with his right hand and pulled me close. Bill placed my hand in his and began to guide me around the middle of the barn while the music played. This was a side of Bill I had never seen.

When the song ended, it was back to work. Now starting the fourth hour, only the hips of the calf remained—the big, swollen hips. Placing the wire around the hips required an additional instrument to help gain length, and it required me to stretch every muscle fiber in my right shoulder and arm to its physical limit. After two failed attempts, I was about to cry, but I was too dehydrated to generate any tears. Right then, a burly, arrogant man came marching into the barn, strutting like a banty rooster. He'd stopped by the farm to deliver a piece of equipment and had been driving an air-conditioned truck around all afternoon. He couldn't understand why we were all so exhausted and frustrated.

"I'm good at getting calves out," he boasted. "Y'all seem to be struggling, so why don't you let me give it a try?" He ripped off his shirt, spit tobacco juice on the ground, and got behind the cow.

"Whoa, buddy, hold up. If your arms are going to enter this cow, by God, you're going to wash them and lubricate them first." I squirted his big hairy arms with soap and handed him a wet rag.

"Can I borrow that thing that looks like a meat hook to hook into the calf?"

"I'll allow it, but I'm going to double-check it after you get it placed. I have worked way too hard on this patient for you to rip her to shreds." I climbed down behind the cow and reached in to cop a feel.

He attached a chain to the hook and some ropes to a pulley. "OK, boys, pull. I'm going to show you how a professional does it." He stood there with a big smile on his face, anticipating victory.

The tension on the pulley was maxed out as we all stared at the rope. Flying out of the back of the cow came the hook—with one tiny tuft of fur in it. Bill and I laughed loudly and unapologetically. The man wiped the blood off his arms, put his shirt back on, and stormed out.

Dealing with the arrogant helper gave me and the guys just enough stamina to finish removing the last two pieces. As we brought out the last piece, we all cheered, too incredibly exhausted to jump for joy. One of the guys shouted, "Dang, girl, you got some grit."

Those words brought a smile to my dirt-smudged face. I thought of Dr. Tom saying that all the successful women large animal veterinarians had one thing in common, and that was grit.

The guys carried my filthy equipment into the milk room and helped wash it up. Once we got most of the slime off, we celebrated with the best-tasting cold beer I have ever drunk.

A MOST DIFFICULT DECISION

*L*ogging is a big industry in Virginia, which contains sixteen million acres of forestland. Day in and day out, the men perform the dangerous task of harvesting trees and transporting them to timber- and wood-processing facilities. You'd imagine they would grow tired of being in the woods, but during hunting season, these men gather to take their dogs deep into the forest to hunt deer. They enjoy hearing the choir of hounds in pursuit of their prey as they run through the loblolly pines. Many of these hunters put the deer in the freezer to feed their families throughout the year.

One peaceful October day, my client and friend Maureen, the matriarch of the Lynch family, a respected family of loggers, rang my phone in distress. "One of Alan's puppies was bitten on the nose by a raccoon. You know Jimmy—he ran in and grabbed a gun and shot the coon, but it tested positive for rabies."

Maureen and I had met when I was searching for my boyfriend's lost hound puppy. We'd been friends for nearly the entire three years I had been at the practice.

"Oh no! I'm so sorry to hear that. Were the puppies old enough to be vaccinated?"

"No, ma'am. They were just a little too young yet. The pup seems OK. What should we do? I value your opinion as a friend and as a professional."

The biggest problem with this scenario was that Top was too young to have had his rabies vaccine, and he was bitten in his face, very close to his brain. Maureen did call the health department, and they suggested a double-layered quarantine facility for the puppy for six weeks. They also said that to reduce exposure to anyone else in the family, there should only be one person who cleaned the pen and fed the puppy.

When I heard that suggestion, I rang up Maureen. These people were my dear friends and they had three children, two of whom were young. "I can't bear the thought of even one of y'all feeding that puppy," I said. "It's simply too risky. The odds are against you. Please consider allowing me to euthanize the pup."

"Top belongs to Alan," Maureen said. "He will have to make the decision."

I felt sorry for thirteen-year-old Alan. It took me back to a time on the dairy when I was twelve years old. One Sunday afternoon, my dad and I had just finished getting some cattle in, and he began backing out in the old blue farm truck. We felt a bump and in the same instant heard the ear-piercing howl of a dog in distress. I leaped out of the truck. In front of the back tire was Meg, our thirteen-year-old matriarch border collie. Dad pulled her into his arms and carried her to a bed of grass so we could assess the damage. It quickly became clear her pelvis was fractured. This wasn't Meg's first rodeo with a pelvic fracture. She was afraid of thunderstorms and often hid under vehicles, so she'd been hit a few times before. I called several veterinary offices, but none were open for emergencies.

Dad and I knew we couldn't put Meg through another surgery at her age. He handed me an old walnut-barreled .22 rifle from behind the truck seat and loaded it. "If you really want to be a veterinarian, you'll have to do hard stuff like this. I'm going home. You take care of her." He reached down to pet Meg one last time. She wagged her bushy black tail and tried to hoist herself to follow him home, but she couldn't stand. I laid the gun down and sat with Meg, petting her and comforting her, until Dad got past the creek.

I gave Meg one final gentle kiss on the top of her head. "I love you, girl. Thank you for everything." I stood up, grabbed the gun, and cocked the lever. As Meg looked up at me with her bright eyes, wagging her tail, I struggled to sight the gun through the tears welling up in my eyes. I pulled the trigger.

The very act that broke my heart gave her instant relief from her pain. I cried all the way on the long walk home. I set the gun down on the back porch and dried my tears with my shirt collar as I walked into the house. Although we didn't speak, Dad could tell by my puffy eyes the job was done.

Later that afternoon, Maureen called me back and said, "Alan has reached the difficult decision to euthanize Top."

I was proud of the boy and agreed to come to euthanize his puppy. I told her, "I will bring Dr. Kate along to help, since she is also rabies vaccinated."

That afternoon, Dr. Kate and I went into the pen with the puppy to administer sedation. The whole family watched intently from outside the chain-link dog pen. Top began growling and snarling and foaming at the mouth. He looked just like the dog on the front of the health department's rabies awareness materials for kids. He quickly pinned us both in the corner with no escape. Beads of sweat fell from our foreheads as the raging dog stepped closer and closer to us.

In a quiet, calm tone I said, "Kate, on the count of three I'm going to jump on top of him and you jab him with the sedative. One, two . . . three." I jumped on Top and held him down as she administered the sedation in the largest muscle of his rear leg. Top began to seize due to the combination of brain damage and drugs. I continued to hold him down but tried to comfort him through the seizure. Once we regained control of him, Dr. Kate administered the euthanasia solution as the family members watched. The only noise in the still woods was their sniffles as they cried. The puppy became more and more peaceful until he was flaccid.

We removed Top's body from the pen and wrapped him in a blanket that Alan had provided. Dr. Kate and I were so relieved and grateful that none of Maureen's family had entered the pen that day. And we were especially grateful that neither of us got bitten.

That experience taught me more than any veterinary lecture could have ever taught me about rabies. I remember my Eastern European virology professor mimicking a rabid raccoon, with his fingers tightly curled on each side of his wrinkled, grimaced face and his yellowing teeth bared. He told us in his broken English, "If you see an animal look like this . . . run away!" It's a different situation when you're the veterinarian—you mostly end up running toward the bad situation in hopes of making it better. I started out on this career path because I enjoyed bringing babies into the world, but as I matured, I realized it was equally important to be able to relieve animals of their suffering.

I stood at the back of the truck, putting the medical supplies back into the vet box, struggling to get the bottles into their respective holes because my hands were still shaking. Glancing over at Dr. Kate, I noticed the color hadn't yet returned to her face. I grabbed a trash bag from the truck, and Dr. Kate placed the young pup, delicately wrapped in his blanket, into the bag, just to be safe.

"Alan, I know this is hard, but you did the right thing, son," Jimmy said as he handed Alan a worn-out pair of leather gloves.

I carefully placed Top into Alan's arms, thinking about the words from Tennyson's famous poem that my former English teacher used to comfort me after the loss of Meg: "'Tis better to have loved and lost than never to have loved at all." Dr. Kate and I stood beside the truck and watched as the young man walked away from us, carrying his best friend to his final resting place in the woods.

I CRIED ORANGE TEARS

I stared up at the bright lights, and I realized I was being dragged down the hall by two hefty nurses, one on each side, functioning like a team of workhorses hauling a log out of the woods.

The last thing I remembered was writing a check at the doctor's office. How the hell did I land on the floor?

I was hoping to pop into the doctor's office this morning and get an antibiotic that would cure me quickly, since I still had Christmas shopping to do. Several items were missing from Dr. Kate's boys' stockings, including Silly String, slime, bubble gum, and CDs. They'd grown accustomed to getting cool presents from their adopted big sister, and I didn't want to disappoint them.

One nurse put a cold rag on my head, and then both nurses helped me onto the exam table. "You OK, young lady? You passed out at the checkout counter."

When the gruff, middle-aged doctor walked into the room, she told me, "I didn't know what was wrong with you when I first examined you and I especially don't know what this passing out is about, but it's not good. You're in pretty rough shape for a twenty-eight-year-old."

She frantically pulled her glasses from her face and slapped my chart down on the counter. "Would you like to phone a friend to take you to the hospital, or would you like me to call an ambulance for you?"

I opted to call Dr. Kate, who drives much faster than an ambulance. I know my mom, a retired nurse, would have been right there to take me to the hospital herself if she were able. Mom had been mysteriously ill for several years herself, and I wasn't sure she could make the long trip up to see me. Mom had always been so full of spunk, but the fatigue had really set in over the last few years.

At the hospital, I was greeted by a handsome young doctor, with dark red hair and big brown eyes. His shiny name tag read DR. RHETT. The pleats in his khakis, his impeccable two-toned striped silk tie, and his starched white coat suggested to me that he was still early in his career. It was my great hope that he was as good at diagnosing patients as he was at picking out ties.

"So, miss, can you tell me more about this headache you were experiencing last night?" Dr. Rhett quizzed me as he skimmed the notes from the referring physician.

"First of all, sir, I'm a doctor too." Dr. Rhett blushed as he glanced back down at my chart.

"The headache was a skull splitter for sure. I took twelve Motrin and fourteen Tylenol during the night, so I can tell you as a fact it was not responsive to anti-inflammatories. I also have this awful rash around my torso." I lifted my shirt to show him. "Do you think I've done myself in with the Tylenol?"

He paused and shook his head no. "Tell me about how you have been feeling lately."

"Well, sir, I can't remember the last time I felt normal . . . and especially not good. I have been feeling run-down for a couple of months. I had an enlarged, painful lymph node in my groin over two months ago, but the local doctor just brushed it off. I have had infection after infection. First respiratory, then several UTIs. I didn't think much of it. I coach basketball for middle school boys— we all know what germ magnets they are—and work has just been busy and very physical lately."

After hearing my story, he tossed me a paper-thin hospital gown and said, "Get in the bed and make yourself comfortable. I'd say you're going to be staying here awhile."

By the time I changed, the young doctor whisked around the corner with blood tubes and medical instruments. I could tell he must not have been out of school very long. He performed an actual physical exam, complete with palpation. After most of my experiences with doctors lately, I was starting to think only veterinarians did physical exams. I fondly remember one of my veterinary mentors telling me, "Young lady, always, always do a good physical exam. Use all five of those senses God gave you and put all the information together in your noggin, because you know those patients aren't gonna talk." That was some of the best advice I ever received, although admittedly I try to use the sense of taste sparingly.

Upon completion of my physical exam and obligatory bloodletting, he looked up at me curiously. "Your heart is racing and you're burning up. You seem to be extremely painful in your joints. And this rash? I mean . . . for lack of a better word, I'm stumped. I'm going to run your blood while you rest, and hopefully, I can crack this case."

There are 360 joints in the human body, and I know that because every damn one of them was hurting, especially the little ones. I was mad at myself for letting this go so long, but how the hell was I supposed to know I was sick? When you grow up on a dairy, you get up every day and you go to work. It doesn't matter if you're sick or hungover or dying; the cows still must be milked and fed.

As I rustled around in that uncomfortable hospital bed, I couldn't even rest. My heart was about to pound out of my beet-red skin. I felt as though I were burning alive, so I attempted to remedy that by tying the ugly gown in a knot underneath my breasts. When the nurse passed, she whispered, "Dear, you're bordering on indecent exposure with your institutionalized Daisy Duke look."

The older gentleman dying of heart failure in the bed beside me certainly wasn't complaining.

I don't get nervous very often—it's important to be unshakable when you're a field surgeon—but I certainly was now. My background in population medicine wasn't helping. I was certain that if I were a feeder calf being fed for slaughter, the cowboy would have already pulled me, shot me, and dragged me to the dead pile. I just prayed for God to be merciful, and I hoped with everything left in me that my newly assigned doctor was on his A game.

The next morning, lying in the hospital bed watching the sun peek over the Blue Ridge Mountains, I wondered what Dr. Kate was going to do without any help. I remembered she'd worked by herself for fifteen years, so I decided to pick something else to worry about. Right then, my medical ray of hope, sporting yet another pretty tie, bolted through the door as if he were on a mission. He said enthusiastically, "I figured it out. Based on your bloodwork abnormalities, you have brucellosis, better known as undulant fever."

"You're wrong, buddy." I shook my aching head and buried it in my knees. "The cattle don't even have brucellosis. We are a certified brucellosis-free state. So, what are the other differential diagnoses?"

His eyes widened and his smile sank like his shoulders as he stood there speechless.

"Don't you reckon it's time to call in an infectious disease doctor?" I was praying this would only take hours, not days, because I wasn't sure I had days left.

As my thirsty veins sucked down their second bag of overpriced fluids, a nice lady dropped me off a very fancy-looking lunch. She said, "We always do up a real nice meal for our patients who are stuck in here over the Christmas holidays. God bless you, dear, and merry Christmas!"

I looked up from the crowded plate to see a middle-aged man with a dark buzz cut, a mustache, and glasses. He had a stethoscope draped around his neck, and he was wearing a pale pink shirt, white vest, and blue and melon-colored paisley tie. Was this man going to be my savior? Was this what a modern-day knight in shining armor looked like?

The doctor positioned himself at the end of my bed and placed his hands on my feet. "Hey there. I'm Dr. Dan. I'm the local expert on infectious diseases."

"I have two questions for you. Can you help me? And, did you dress yourself?"

He chuckled as he moved closer to me. "Yes and yes." He began to examine me thoroughly and he asked me about a million questions. Right then, one of my mates from veterinary school walked in to visit me. Dr. Meghan's stepfather, also a client of mine, was in the hospital getting a new knee, and he'd told her I was here too.

Dr. Dan pulled up a chair for Meghan and said, "Have a seat, dear. Now, ladies, if Dr. Melinda here were a cow, name a few of the diseases that could fit her symptoms." We felt as though we were back in veterinary school, except if we didn't get the answers right today, it was going to be my ass on the line.

Meghan piped up, "Leptosporosis for sure, and brucellosis fits the symptoms, but it's eradicated so that can't be it."

"And most of the tick-borne illnesses fit, but it's winter and I haven't pulled a tick off for several months," I said.

"Nice work, but you gals have forgotten one important disease. Would it help if I told you that she only has nine hundred white blood cells?" Dr. Meghan and I looked at each other inquisitively. Dr. Dan proclaimed, "Q fever. You know, Query fever. First discovered in Australia in wool handlers." As he proceeded to tell us the entire history of the disease it became evident this man was brilliant. Apparently, these bacteria are commonly found in cattle, sheep, and goats, and a human who breathes in just one tiny bacterium from dust contaminated by these farm animals could become sick enough to die. He explained that, based on my symptoms, he had seven diseases on his list of differential diagnoses, but only two could be real possibilities based on my dangerously low white blood cell count: Q fever and brucellosis. He agreed with us that brucellosis was the more unlikely of the two, but he wanted to do blood tests for both.

As he laid out his treatment plan of three different antibiotics, Meghan blurted out, "Well, Dr. Dan, lucky for you that doxycycline treats all seven of those diseases on your list." I snickered.

I could tell Dr. Dan had been around intelligent women before because her comment didn't seem to faze him. "I hate to do it, but I'm going to have to put you on rifampin until the brucellosis test comes back, and it tends to have a lot of side effects," he explained. I was just delighted somebody had a well-thought-out plan. "You're going to need to wear a mask to prevent contracting any more diseases," Dr. Dan continued. "We're going to keep you here in the hospital for a few more days so you can get your antibiotics intravenously. I will check on you tomorrow, kiddo." He shook my and Meghan's hands and left to finish making his rounds. Meghan gave me a hug and headed back upstairs to check on her parents.

The nurses kept the medicines steadily flowing throughout the afternoon, and I got a new roommate. She was a tiny little old lady with a very wrinkled face. As they wheeled her in, the orderly looked over at the nurse. "This one's a live wire!"

From what I overheard, I realized she was severely diabetic and her blood sugar had reached 545 mg/dL, with normal being less than 140. No wonder she was trying to fight everybody in the room. As nightfall approached, visiting hours were over and the old hospital was starting to get quiet. The medical professionals had even gotten my roommate simmered down with numerous doses of insulin. I was getting bored, just waiting for the evil blood pressure cuff to start blowing up for the twentieth time today. That thing reminded me of doing rectal palpations on the "stale" fat dairy cows in California as a student. Both those cows and that cuff could squeeze my arm so hard I just wanted to scream for mercy. As the cuff started, I smelled something wafting through the open door of the room. It smelled like smoke. Smoke? Hmmm? I was on the seventh floor of this historic hospital, trying to imagine how a fire drill would work when I was hooked up to three IV bags and barely able to walk.

A frantic nurse bolted through the door and shouted, "There's a fire in the elevator shaft. I'm going to shut you all in here. Do *not* open the door for any reason. Stay put."

I found myself wringing my hands. "You're seriously locking me in here with Cray Cray? What if she rouses up in all the excitement?"

The nurse could see how apprehensive I was. "Honey, you do whatever you need to do, but don't you dare open this door. Got it?" I nodded as the door slammed. If that old woman broke bad and started a fight, what would be my plan? If she were a wild cow, what would I do? Tie her up with bedsheets, that's what.

For the next ten minutes, I sat in the bed, staring intensely at my slumbering neighbor. I started to sweat. It was hard to tell if it was from the high fever or from the anxiety, but I noticed something strange. When I wiped the sweat from my brow, the tissue turned orange, bright orange. I wheeled my IV pole into the bathroom, with the door wide open, of course. Looking into the mirror I felt like I was looking at the girl from the Gatorade commercial with bright red cheeks and orange sweat drops on her forehead.

Once the fire scare had simmered down, the nurse came to check on us.

Horrified, I asked, "Why are my excretions orange?" She explained that it was from the rifampin. That gave me some comfort.

As I started to doze off, I prayed I could use this miserable experience to help teach other veterinarians and farmers about diagnosing, treating, and preventing zoonotic diseases. I always knew cows kicked hard, bulls were generally mean, and rickety equipment could hurt you, but I never thought it possible to be taken out by a single microscopic bacterium.

The next morning when I opened my eyes, I thought I was hallucinating. My mother was standing in front of me. "Hey, baby doll. I'm sorry it took me so long to get here, but you know what driving on I-81 is like around the holidays. We've all been worried to death about you! You realize come hell or high water, I'd get here to see you." She stepped closer and took me into her arms and hugged me like she was never going to let go.

"I was hoping I'd get to spend Christmas with you, Mom, but I never intended for it to be like this." I wrapped my bruised arms around her. The tears streaming down my face stained the collar of her white shirt bright orange.

THE BOVINE OLYMPIAN

I picked up the phone and heard the thick local accent of Will, a farmer, rattling a mile a minute about an athletic heifer whose labor wasn't progressing. The veterinary students often ask me if the central Virginia natives are part Cajun because of their accents, which are accentuated when they are excited. Will was calling today instead of yesterday because he and the boys had to get her out of the hundred acres of woods into another pasture so I'd even be able to get near her.

When I arrived, Will took me out to a small patch of woods on the RTV. I loaded the blow dart and walked quietly through the woods until I found my oversize, ticked-off patient. As I walked closer and closer to her, she grew more and more anxious. Finally, she began to run, and the chase was on. She bobbed and weaved through the tall hardwoods like a slalom skier. I struggled to keep her in my line of sight as we neared the edge of the woods. Once she left the woods, I used my last deep breath to propel the tranquilizer dart right into the back of her leg. Sitting on the RTV, I struggled to catch my breath. My stamina was still impaired from my bout with Q fever the previous year.

"It's gonna take about ten minutes for the sedative to take effect," I explained.

While Will and I chatted, the heifer inched closer and closer to a very large pond. "You don't reckon that heifer is gonna go in the pond, do you?" Will asked.

Being the eternal optimist, I replied, "Nah, she's far too drunk to make it that far."

Within minutes the heifer made it to the edge of the water and proceeded to enter the pond. First, her cloven hoof, then her long front limbs, and soon all we could see was her black head. Will and I hauled freight down to the water's edge, but it was too late—she was too far in. By the time she made it to the middle of the pond, the sedative started taking effect. Her eyes started to close and her head dropped. Then bubbles came from her nose as her head went under the water.

Will and I looked into each other's eyes, frozen in astonishment. I couldn't just watch her die, so I did the thing any determined gal would do: started stripping. First the overalls, then the sweatshirt, and finally the boots. I donned a lariat rope around my torso and started swimming across the freezing cold pond. The heifer's head sank lower and lower as I swam faster and faster. When I got parallel to the heifer's head, she took one look at me, and her eyes got huge. I'd seen this look many times before when an animal was about to cross the rainbow bridge. I felt so guilty that I was just seconds too late to save her.

But suddenly the cow's head popped up, and she started swimming toward the other side of the pond. Her athletic forelimbs pulled her through the murky water, one stroke after another, propelling her large body forward. I was hot on her trail and preparing to throw the rope around her when, lo and behold, she put it in a higher gear, like Michael Phelps swimming the last leg of a relay in the Olympics.

The heifer beat me to the other side of the pond and began running across the field. How could this be? It was times like this when I wished I could call Temple Grandin and ask her what to do next. None of her books on humane animal handling ever mentioned ponds.

We were back to where we started except now soaking wet and

cold. Will gave me a lift back to the truck to load another dart. On round two, I shot her with the blow dart while riding beside her on the RTV. Finally, after another jumbo dose of tranquilizer, she lay down.

After nearly an hour in hot pursuit of my patient, I could now do what I was called there to do: deliver her baby. Approaching her vulva, all I could see was the dead calf's oversized head. Every part of the head was swollen; its tongue was so swollen it was sticking out, as was its drunk mother's. With tongues sticking out at every end, the heifer's sole purpose in life seemed to be to torture me. I placed the obstetrical chains on the calf's large feet, nestled under its massive head, and struggled to jack the calf out of her. Once he was out, I gave the heifer pain medicine and antibiotics. I slowly pushed the reversal agent into her bloodstream, and she rose like Snow White after receiving her magical kiss. Off she went, running back into the woods to be alone. I looked over at Will, and we had a laugh.

"Just think, Melinda, if you had ridden a bicycle to shoot her with that dart, it would have been a triathlon!"

When I go to a physician's office, I describe my symptoms in detail, sit perfectly still for an exam, and get scheduled for a multitude of tests and referrals. I have never bitten or kicked anyone in the office or vomited or defecated on their floor. Yet they struggle to get me diagnosed and treated. Meanwhile, a vet might have to do a multi-stage athletic event to even get near their patient, then diagnose and treat them right on the spot—and knows the cost of every service and medication they provide.

DELIVERANCE

*O*ne of my veterinary mentors warned me, "Don't become friends with your clients or your employees." I always thought that sounded so impersonal and quite frankly kind of mean. How do you even do that when your career is your life? I'd been living and working in this community for nearly five years now with no family closer than four hours away. My clients and coworkers had become like family to me, and I wouldn't want it any other way.

This crisp fall afternoon, I had volunteered to go to Wendy's house and help process forty chickens she was planning to put in the freezer. Wendy—owner of Hell, the mule I'd castrated a while back—was a good client who had become a good friend. I knew from the minute I met her that I'd like her. She was petite, with long brown hair and small round glasses, but she commanded the attention of the draft horses that worked for her. When Wendy spoke, the gigantic workhorses listened. She had three lovely children, one with a severe disability whom she cared for intensely and lovingly every day. There was no doubt this woman worked hard day and night.

I had recently been out working on one of the big draft horses and noticed Wendy had one arm in a sling. She explained, "I had an accident on the farm and jacked up my shoulder. I'm so mad at myself. I have children and animals to care for and forty meat birds that should have already been processed. I don't know what I'm going to do."

I was young and single and always looking for an adventure. "Do you need a hand? I'm off this weekend, and I could swing by and help." She hugged me with one arm and told me she'd get our mutual friend Ramona to come as well.

Recently, I had joined the board of the Virginia Veterinary Medical Association, which was a diverse group of veterinarians throughout the state working together to promote excellence in the veterinary community, animal well-being, and public health through advocacy, education, and outreach. In our board meeting, we heard a presentation encouraging veterinarians to practice self-care to improve their mental health. We were astonished to hear about the suicide rate among veterinarians and joked about having no time for "self-care." The self-care tips in the presentation included time off work, meditation, exercise, and good nutrition. I was pretty sure killing chickens on my weekend off would not count. But I've always found joy in simple pleasures and in helping others, and I'm not much into yoga. So I decided to chalk it up as self-care.

Saturday morning, I arrived at Wendy's in my overalls, excited to be just a regular farm gal for the day. Being a veterinarian mostly meant dealing with abnormalities and crises. I missed those days on the dairy when I could just sit on the hill with my braided pigtails and watch quietly as a cow gave birth to a healthy, normal calf. I loved the moment when the dam would heave her strong abdominal muscles and the calf would burst through its sac, hitting the ground while being showered with copious amounts of birthing fluids. It seemed like such a cruel welcome to the world. But then the mama cow would turn around and immediately start licking the baby's head with her rough tongue. The calf would attempt a half-hearted moo, and the bonding process had begun. It was so immediate and beautiful it made me forget about how rugged the birthing process really was.

Wendy ran me and Ramona through her setup and gave us our marching orders.

"Dr. Melinda, you'll be the neck chopper for the day. Just whack the chicken's head off with one fell swoop of the cleaver and put them in the cone to drain, then carry them to Ramona to go to the Feather Pro 2000. Ramona will remove the intestines and cut them up for me to package. Got it, ladies?"

I was seriously impressed with the efficiency of Wendy's setup, even though I'd been cast as the killer.

Our operation was in full swing when a strange vehicle pulled into Wendy's driveway. This was odd because Wendy was far off the beaten path. I was the closest, so I went to see if I could be of assistance. Apparently, if a six-foot-tall, large-boned girl in blood-covered bib overalls approaches your vehicle with a meat cleaver in her hand, it's frightening. Both men gazed at me with wide-eyed, stunned looks on their faces.

"This is like something from *Deliverance*," one man whispered to the other with a look of sheer panic. Then the driver peeled out so fast he threw gravel. Wendy, Ramona, and I all had a good laugh and got back to work.

We got back into our groove, and I left a chicken in the cone to drain while I carried another one to Ramona. When I returned to my station, the cone was empty. Perplexed, to say the least, I started searching everywhere. I walked the barnyard frantically as Ramona shouted, "You OK? What are you doing?"

I explained to her, "I lost a chicken from the cone."

"Let me get this straight," Ramona asked as she cackled. "You *lost* a dead chicken?" She and Wendy were laughing hard enough to pee themselves. I bet Ramona hadn't laughed that hard since she saw me castrate a pig with my teeth at her farm last year.

I looked everywhere for that freaking chicken until there was only one place left to look—the upside-down feed pan near the cone. I figured there was no point in even looking there. How would a half-dead chicken have gotten under there anyway? In desperation, I flipped up the pan and there she was. She immediately started running, even though she had no head.

How was this even possible? Then I remembered what one of my wise professors said in veterinary school: "All bleeding stops . . . eventually." We decided to just wait it out. Sure enough, the bird at last threw in the proverbial towel. Finally, we finished the last bird, and Wendy gave me a few chickens freshly packaged for helping.

When I got back to Dr. Kate's, I offered up an all-natural, local chicken for dinner. Dr. Kate and I frequently enjoyed preparing dinners together; she needed the extra hands, and I benefited from the cooking tips. We were all sitting around the table exhausted from a hard day's work. The boys had been with their father, James, baling straw all day in the heat.

Dr. Kate's younger boy, John, piped up. "Why don't you tell Dr. Melinda what happened today on the straw wagon, Brian?"

"Yeah, Brian, out with it," I said.

"I got bee stung," Brian murmured sheepishly.

Clearly loving this, John asked in a boisterous voice, "And where did you get stung, Brian?"

"In the privates," Brian mumbled. "Dad had to put tobacco juice on it to help the sting."

"On your testicle? That sucks!" I said.

"Damn, son, that's why you don't wear shorts in a hayfield," James uttered in disgust. "How many times have I told you that?"

While we continued to chat on the back porch, enjoying our lovely dinner, Brian said, "This chicken is kind of tough. I like the store-bought ones better."

"Haven't you had a bad enough day already? Do you really want to face the wrath of Dr. Melinda?" I glared at him. "I swear you kids these days don't fully appreciate where your food comes from. Eat the freaking chicken, or you're gonna be needing more tobacco juice for the sting!"

Part 2

Peeling Off the Layers

2008–2011

DRIVING HOME NAKED

It was a chilly Friday night in central Virginia, and everyone was gearing up for the Friday night lights of the local football games—everyone except for me, the on-call veterinarian whose day was clearly never going to end. My thirtieth birthday was rapidly approaching, and I was beginning to understand that the night calls were less taxing than the never-ending days.

Evan, a fun-loving middle-aged farmer from a very rural county nestled in the foothills of the mountains, called to get help for a cow that had just calved and prolapsed her uterus. Knowing how dangerous it was for this vascular female organ to be on the outside of this cow's body, I raced up the road in the vet truck in true NASCAR style. I was hoping if any cops were out, they'd let me go without a ticket since I was on an emergency call. That had worked for me once before when I was headed to a calving.

At Evan's farm, the brisk, cool wind blew bright fallen leaves all around. It was getting darker and colder by the minute.

"Honey, the old cow is pretty weak, but I think she'll be able to stand for you to work on her," Evan shouted as he pushed the patient up the alleyway to the headgate to be restrained.

I washed and scrubbed copious amounts of debris from her huge womb before attempting to push it back in. It was like a bad version of *Where's Waldo* trying to pick out all the dried-up leaves and pieces of hay from in between the fist-sized caruncles, which are normal parts of a pregnant bovine uterus. Once I felt it was clean enough, I started to try and push it back in. As I leaned my chest into it, blood soaked through my clothes like they were a sponge. Within a minute, the blood had saturated my bra and was running down my torso.

"Damn this stubborn thing! It's giving me a fit and a half," I said to Evan. Handling her dirty, bloody uterus was like wrestling an alligator that was half the length of my tall body. I pushed harder and harder.

On one big heave, my feet lost traction. I slipped in a puddle of mud and obstetrical lube. My left elbow smashed into a 4 x 4 post at a very high speed.

"Holy hell, Evan. I think my arm is broken!" I yelled, grimacing.

"Oh crap. I'm so sorry, honey. Maybe we should just shoot her and be done with it?" Evan replied.

When you're a vet, you get the job done before you address your own needs. "Oh no. Hell, naw. I started this job and I intend to finish it. Broken arm or not."

After nearly an hour of pushing, cursing, and slipping, I finally got the whole uterus back in. I looked more like I was saving Private Ryan than a cow. I could feel that my face was dappled with dried blood, extending into my ear canal. The blond tips of my hair were now bright red highlights. The cow was starting to get very weak, weak enough to be a fall risk.

Evan suggested, "Maybe we should open the side to prevent the cow from getting stuck in the metal piece of crap chute." We popped the side gate open. The massive weight of the poor cow fell all the way to the ground on the side of a steep hill, and . . . her uterus came back out.

I stretched my back and wrapped my injured arm with an open roll of vet wrap, attempting to collect my thoughts before tackling this seemingly impossible task once more. I wet a ratty blue surgical towel and looked in the truck mirror while I blotted the distracting blood splatter from the bridge of my nose. I suddenly realized my striking resemblance to Dr. John standing on the back porch wiping the blood from his busted nose. I could hear the voices of him and my father in my head saying, "Young lady, being a large animal vet is a dirty and dangerous job." They had a point, but I would never have made it as a schoolteacher; even my sister, Ann, could tell you, I don't dress well enough.

Back outside, I dutifully knelt behind my patient and used my last bit of water from the truck to wash her uterus one last time. I assumed the combat crawl position and instructed Evan to use his feet to brace mine. With every heave of the massive organ, I could feel the mixture of blood and mud being driven through my thin green overalls into my skin. Finally, I somehow managed to get the uterus replaced once again. I placed a stitch in her to ensure her lady parts stayed on the inside this time.

While packing up my equipment, I could see the cow's muscles begin to tremor and her eyes became fixed. It was clear she was in shock, likely from internal bleeding. Evan and I looked at each other and shook our heads.

"Don't you do it, girl," I warned. Right then, despite all my effort, the old girl took her last breath.

Evan shrugged and said in his slow, calm drawl, "An old farmer once told me, 'If you have 'em, you're gonna lose 'em.' Thanks for tryin' so hard, dear."

I replied, "No problem, man. Now you go on home so I can get out of these filthy clothes. Just leave the gate open for me, please."

When Evan was out of sight, I started removing my disgusting clothing one piece at a time. I braced on the tailgate of the truck with my right hand. My left arm trembled in pain as I struggled to peel off the blood-soaked sports bra. The wet bra rolled up as I pulled it toward my head, making it nearly impossible to get off. I had no water left after cleaning up the cow twice, so I was unable to wash any of the blood off my body. I scrounged up some crinkled Subway napkins from behind the truck seat and desperately tried to wipe off some of the blood, but the lube mixed in with it just made it smear over me even more. I felt like an elephant had sneezed on me. My teeth began to chatter as I stood in the middle of the pitch-black field, stark naked—except for black rubber Muck boots—beside the poor dead cow. I tossed the bloody clothes in the back of the truck and tried to slide my wet rear end into the leather driver's seat. Every push to get in felt like my saturated skin was going to rip off. Finally, I was securely in the seat with the heat cranked up and I was headed home.

By the time I got to the next town, I was parched. My mouth was so dry that my tongue was sticking to the roof of my mouth—even the birdbath in the town square looked like an oasis. But going into a store was out of the question.

"Four large sweet teas, please," I said into the McDonald's drive-through speaker.

"Would you like fries with that?" asked the young woman on the intercom.

"No, ma'am. Just the tea, please." I pulled the truck around to the window to pay. I sheepishly eased my blood-soaked, swollen arm out of the window with the money. The bright overhead light crept up my arm, exposing blood all the way up to my left earlobe. The McDonald's worker on the inside picked up the telephone on the wall and started dialing 9-1—

Before she got to the last 1, I begged her, "Please, please don't call the cops."

She squinted one eye and rubbed her chin, exposing an elaborate wrist tattoo. "Did you kill someone?" she asked.

"Do you think I'd really tell you that?"

My sarcastic answer didn't help the situation. She looked at me even more suspiciously.

"Ma'am, I'm a large animal veterinarian who just finished a very bloody, very difficult job. It was so bloody, in fact, the poor cow bled to death."

The skeptical worker lowered the phone. "Awww, the poor cow."

I continued to plead—she now had a more sympathetic ear. "I'm dehydrated enough to pass out. If you do decide to call the cops, can you at least hand me out some water, please? I will be happy to show you my veterinary license, but that would require me to drop this towel. When I pull the truck up past your window, you'll see the Porta-Vet box on the back of my truck, and you'll know I'm legit."

Cracking a half-smile and shaking her head, she put all four sweet teas in a cup holder so I could reach across and grab them with my right arm.

"Bless your heart, dear. I'd kiss you, but I can't reach you." I gulped down the glorious liquid as if I'd been stuck in the desert for days.

"Ma'am, you get on home now. And for God's sake, don't get pulled over. That would be really awkward."

RUNNING ON FUMES

I sped down the dark, curving country road with my border collie copilot, Dot, delighted to be on my way to my warm bed on this November night. I was also delighted not to be driving home naked, as that could result in frostbite in unmentionable places. Using my knee to steer, I held my frozen hands in front of the hot air blasting from the vents. I found simple joy in the fact that my Robbie Williams CD shimmied out of the sun visor as I went around a sharp curve. I had gotten it many years ago when I was a student in Ireland and could jam to it on the ride home to help stay awake. My last two hours had been spent out in the cold assisting a birthing cow; as I sweated and exhausted myself, I wondered if that was what birth is like for a human. I was glad I wasn't the one birthing the baby. I didn't need a kid at thirty—I had my hands full being a veterinarian.

When I reached the straight stretch of the road, something caught my eye. On a small country road off to the left was a small SUV with its emergency flashers on. On instinct, I turned around. I pulled in behind the vehicle and put my flashers on. A thin young woman bundled up in a tattered winter coat stood there shivering while assessing her left rear tire, which appeared to be flat.

I hopped out. "Hi, I'm Dr. Melinda. I'm a vet just getting done with an emergency call. I saw you were having trouble."

"Ma'am, my baby and toddler are in my car with no heat," she said meekly. "I'm afraid they are going to freeze before we can get the tire fixed."

"Well, we certainly can't have that." I turned my truck on and moved both the plump baby and the anxious toddler into the front seat. The sweet boys sat on either side of Dot, cooing at the pup, with the heat turned up and "Angels" softly playing on the radio.

I pulled off the flat tire and attempted to find the spare. Much to my dismay, I found a spare that was also dry rotted and flat. Right then, a car pulled up and a man's voice asked, "Everything OK, ladies?" After I explained the situation, the nice family returning from a ski trip agreed to take the tire up to their house and fill it with air.

Finally, upon their return, the three of us got the tire on. I loaded the warm children back in their vehicle and started to say goodbye.

The young woman ventured, "Ma'am, I hate to even ask you this, but could you follow me to the 7-Eleven? I'm running on fumes."

When we pulled into the 7-Eleven, I noticed she wasn't getting out of her vehicle. I started thinking about the conversation we had while waiting for the tire to come back. She was out so late that night because she was taking her boyfriend to work. He had a vehicle until he totaled it the week before on a wild escapade. Money was tight, which was why the tires were in such rough shape, and she was out of work with the children. It was at this point I reached into my glove box and grabbed the $100 bill. My dad told me I should always carry one in the vehicle for emergencies. I had never understood why—it just seemed like a good way to get robbed.

I approached the mother's vehicle and leaned into her open window. "I have something to give you, but in return, you have to hear what I have to say." She sat there and listened intently as tears began to run down her thin cheeks. "You need to fill up your tank, then go down to McDonald's and feed yourself and your children. You're a great mother but at the expense of yourself!"

She barely smiled as she accepted my compliment.

I went on, "You're probably tired of listening to my uninvited opinions, but I have a few more things to say. I think your boyfriend isn't much of a man. He seems to be far more of a hindrance than a help. When times get better financially, you really need to get a new spare and a new set of tires."

She sobbed and said, "I simply can't accept the money."

"Sweetheart, I don't think you're in a position to argue." I reached in and handed her the folded bill. She took it and hugged me through the open window.

Months later, after the cold winter was behind us and the summer sun was shining, my veterinary student Jessica and I were headed back toward the office from an exhausting call that involved way too much goat wrestling. Jessica suggested, "How 'bout we stop for lunch at that new little deli that uses local foods?"

We sat down at our table, and a delightful young lady came to take our drink order. When she returned with our drinks, she looked me in the eye and said, "I have an unusual question to ask you, ma'am. Do you by chance drive a white truck with a box on the back of it?"

"Yep, that's me, all right." I wondered if I was about to be towed.

Then she asked, "Do you remember me?"

I stared at her for a moment. Then I realized she was the mother with the flat tire. I stood up, and we exchanged a warm embrace.

"How are your boys doing? I bet they're growing up fast. And is the boyfriend behaving himself?" I asked, dreading the answer.

She smiled from ear to ear. "My boys are doing great—they're growing like weeds—and the boyfriend . . . well, he's no longer in the picture."

When Jessica and I finished our lunch, the owner brought us out a lovely piece of homemade chocolate cake and said he'd heard the story from the waitress. She and I hugged one last time before

Jessica and I went out to the parking lot. I recognized the waitress's vehicle and walked all the way around it.

Jessica looked at me like I was crazy. "What on earth are you doing?"

"Just checking the tires."

"What's the story with the waitress?" Jessica asked. "It must be a good one, since we got free cake."

"It's a long story. But basically, the moral is: keep a $100 bill in your truck at all times."

SPEEDING INTO ACTION

I wasn't going on an emergency vet call when I got the speeding ticket, so I couldn't use that as an excuse. I had no plan for how I was going to get out of it, and my time to go to traffic court was drawing nearer. Whatever happened to karma? Weren't good things supposed to happen to people who tried to do good deeds for people?

Dr. Kate knew a lot about speeding tickets, so I asked her for advice. She was salty because I had been successful at weaseling out of the few tickets I had gotten in the five years I'd been practicing with her.

"You're not as young and cute as you used to be, so good luck getting out of this one," Dr. Kate snarked.

All I knew was that I had to. The ticket was going to cost me a small fortune, one I didn't have. I was already living on a shoestring budget trying to pay back my enormous student loans that were collecting interest every day.

On the Sunday before my Tuesday court date, the phone rang. A panicked man on the other end blurted, "I have a dog emergency."

"I apologize, sir," I began, "but we are a large animal vet service. I'm happy to give you the number of the small animal emergency hospital—"

He interrupted, "My yellow lab, Zeke, is bleeding badly from a deep cut he got while playing around some old farm equipment. Please consider at least helping get the blood stopped until I can make it to the nearest city with an emergency hospital."

His plea was convincing. "I suppose I can do at least that much. Where shall I meet you?"

I pulled into the parking lot of the meeting spot, a law office. I examined the big, sweet yellow dog and decided his laceration was something I could handle right there in the parking lot, so I sedated him. While we were waiting for Zeke to relax, the man and I chatted.

"What do you do for a living?" I asked.

"I'm an attorney. This is actually my office," he said as he held Zeke's increasingly heavy head. My ears perked up, like a dog about to get a treat. Once Zeke was resting soundly, I clipped and cleaned the wound, placed several sutures, and gave him a dose of antibiotics.

The attorney thanked me and pulled out a massive checkbook. To me, it looked nearly as big as the Publishers Clearinghouse check. "Name your price."

I felt my eyes get large. What was it worth to this man for me to save his best friend? I was only used to working for farmers who, in the words of the late John F. Kennedy, "were buying products at retail, selling their products at wholesale, and paying the freight both ways."

I explained to him, "Sir . . . more than money, I really need to get out of a speeding ticket."

"You are aware that I'm an attorney who handles multimillion-dollar accident cases, aren't you?" he explained, loading Zeke into the Mercedes.

"That's fantastic to hear. A speeding ticket should be easy for you."

"Here's what we'll do, young lady. I will write you a check for the price the speeding ticket will cost you. You just hang onto it and don't cash it. I will represent you in court on Tuesday. If the charges get dropped, you tear up the check, and if they don't, cash it and pay the ticket."

"Sounds like a win-win to me, sir. I appreciate it." On the inside I was doing cartwheels as I stood calmly in front of him.

On Tuesday, I walked into general district court dressed to the nines in a sharp black suit with a silky red blouse. I even wore makeup and earrings. This felt so different from my ratty T-shirt and bib overalls. I looked so different that the bailiff didn't recognize me as the woman who rabies vaccinated his hunting dogs. When the judge read my name, my attorney and I went forward, and judging by the sound of things, I figured I'd be cashing his check. We walked out of the courthouse side by side.

I looked over at him. "Thanks for trying, man."

"What do you mean?" He chuckled. "You're off the hook."

I couldn't believe it! I shook his hand. "Thank you again. I knew I picked the right man for the job."

When I returned to the office to shred his gigantic check, there stood Dr. Kate with a smug look on her face. "Not so young and cute anymore, eh?"

"You're so right, Kate," I said with a wink. "Now I'm older and wiser!"

SUPERWOMAN

With each passing day, I got more comfortable with my job, but the thing that was constantly changing during my first six years in practice were the clients. Each day would bring a new cast of characters; every person owned a different species of animal and had unique ideas about agriculture and the world. Since I worked without an assistant for the first several years of practice, I had to train each client (ranging in age from three to ninety-five years old) to be my veterinary assistant in five minutes or less so the animal could get the best care possible. I also had to earn the client's trust to get them to comply with my directions for continued care of the animal after I left. My mother, the nurse, always said, "Being able to get compliance from the patient is what separates a mediocre doctor from an exceptional doctor. You can be the smartest doctor in the class and prescribe exactly the right medications, but if you can't get that patient to follow through at home, you have done nothing."

Some days, earning a client's trust was harder than others. I pulled into the gas pump for fuel, craving a big icy fountain Mountain Dew, when the phone rang. My secretary, Gale, said, "Hey, Dr. Melinda, I just got a call from an old, hard-to-understand farmer calling in to get assistance with delivering a calf. Are you close by?" I wasn't far away, so I sucked down some nectar of the gods and went.

When I turned into the farm, there was an older fellow with long, stringy white hair and an old pair of bib overalls standing by the driveway with an expectant look. I slowed down, and his look turned to confusion. I asked, "Sir, what are you looking for?"

"Why, young lady, I'm waiting on the vet."

After an awkward silence, I asked, "What if I said I was the vet?"

"That's not possible because large animal vets are men."

My eyebrows perked up and the hairs on my neck raised. "Well, I am the vet, and today you're going to have to be OK with that because the only other vet in the practice is also a woman." My tone resembled my mother's in instances where she was forced to use my middle name.

He could tell he'd struck a nerve and quickly began to try to smooth things over. "I do believe girls can be vets. I just haven't ever seen one. I mean, girls should have rights and stuff."

"Buddy, if you want help from me today, you better stop talking and start leading me to a cow!" The whites of my eyes must have been turning red from my rising blood pressure.

In the barn, a huge old Hereford cow was constantly straining and looking hot and miserable. I asked the farmer, "Sir, do you have a headgate or chute or any way to restrain this cow?"

While listening to dozens of excuses, including limited finances and time, for why he didn't have a proper facility, I grabbed a lariat rope from the truck. He and I entered the rickety wooden barn, and I scouted out a post that would be strong enough to hold the massive cow. I roped the cow on the first try because I always rope things better when I'm fired up. This seemed to impress the crotchety farmer, although I wasn't sure if he was impressed by my roping skills or the fact that there was a set of breasts at the other end of the rope. I quickly wrapped the end of the rope around the only solid post in the whole place and started to pull the cow toward me.

The farmer shouted, "Don't get hurt, young lady," as he placed himself between the cow and the side of the barn. She smashed him nearly flat against the wall. "Help . . ." he croaked. I tied the rope off and generously went to push the twelve hundred pounds of cow off him to avoid having to work on him as well. I wedged my big childbearing hips between the cow and the barn and channeled my anger toward saving this undeserving man. Every muscle in my body tightened up as I slowly budged the cow enough to slide the frail chauvinist out of the danger zone.

He half-heartedly muttered, "Thanks."

"Now, could you please stay out of my way so I can finish my work?"

He slithered along the barn wall as I donned a pair of plastic sleeves and reached into the cow's gooey vaginal vault to place the obstetrical chains on the calf's large feet. I placed the handles on the chains and started to pull. The farmer came creeping closer as if he were going to help. Although social cues did not seem to be his strong suit, he began to back up slowly when I glared at him. It was as if I had a superpower to push him backward with my gaze. It certainly worked for my mother when she did it to us!

Finally, I could continue working to help the poor, distressed cow. I grabbed the handles and pulled with all my might—to the point that I fell backward and the huge, wet, dead calf fell right on top of me. The adrenaline pumping through my veins spared me any pain. Approximately a gallon of sweat from inside my obstetrical sleeves dumped into my bra, at which point the cow strained and covered me with several more gallons of birthing fluids and urine. I'm not sure how being soaked with sweat and slime brought my smile back, but it did. I lifted myself off the dusty ground and finished medicating the cow.

Once I loaded the truck, I wrote up his bill. Naturally, he was confused as to why it was so high. I told him, "Sir, not only can girls be vets, they can write high bills for people who piss them off with no proper handling facilities."

It seems hard to believe this mentality about women could exist in 2011. It's true that in 1970, women accounted for only

16.8 percent of all veterinary school graduates, but women have outnumbered men in veterinary schools since 1990. I often think back to a story told to me by my dear friend Dr. Peggy, a brilliant, hardworking veterinarian whom I got to know well through my involvement in the Veterinary Medical Association. She graduated from the University of Georgia in 1975, where there were only seven women in a class of eighty-six students. When her class went to a stable to watch the stallions' semen be collected, she had to wait outside of the barn because it wasn't proper for women to be in the stallion barns. Dr. Peggy showed them! She not only collected stallions in her time as a veterinarian—she charged accordingly for doing it.

SNIP, SNIP

*M*y sister, Ann, always told me, "You'll end up in the cuckoo house one day, mark my words." She just never knew it would be this soon. I had lived in my small apartment in the Cuckoo House for the past seven years. This residence housed five generations of physicians all from one family, so it was only fitting that a doctor would live here and continue the legacy. Occasionally I'd sneak into the one-room doctor's office to the right of the house to admire the old medicine bottles and antiquated medical tools. It smelled as old as it looked, and the rusty sign on the door read, "Closed on Tuesdays and Sundays. If you can't read this, ask the neighbor."

One night, I gazed at the hacksaw hanging on the wall, which was strikingly similar to the one I'd used to cut up the frozen cow corpse as a kid, and I pondered what kind of pain control old Dr. Pendelton used when he performed his surgeries. I fondly remembered Bobby, one of my older dairy farmers, showing me the scar under his jaw where Dr. Pendelton removed his abscessed tooth when he was a boy. From Bobby's account, it sounded like pain control was rather limited. Hopefully, he at least got a shot of whiskey.

Dr. Jane, the first female doctor in her family, and her husband, Dr. Percy, now owned the home. I enjoyed getting to know her and Dr. Percy, who was a past president of the American Medical Association. Dr. Jane and I occasionally got the chance to sit on the porch to enjoy a glass of wine and discuss the trials and tribulations of being female doctors. I once asked, "Dr. Jane, were there many women in your medical school class in 1965?"

Dr. Jane took a sip of her Chardonnay, shook her head, and grinned. "No, dear, there weren't. And I felt like we had to work twice as hard as the men." I knew what she meant, even though our graduations were nearly forty years apart. I don't know if the bar was set higher for women, or if it just felt that way because we were trying to prove ourselves in male-dominated fields. There were certainly more women accepted to doctorate programs when I went through school, but the struggles were very similar. Women's careers were the ones put on hold to take care of their husbands, to birth the babies, and to raise the children. Being a doctor was often the second full-time job women had in our fields.

With dusk closing in, I strolled back around the house to the entrance of my apartment, hoping I was in for the night, when the phone rang. It was a frantic lady about thirty minutes away with a pet goat that was straining to urinate. "It's my little boy goat— he's acting like he's constipated and screaming his fool head off." I could hear the ear-piercing screams of the little buckling in the background. "Something's wrong. He's in a lot of pain. Can you please come help him?"

I assured her, "Help is on the way, ma'am."

It had been a long, hard week of early mornings and late nights, and I was craving a little downtime. So I decided to invite my neighbor to come along. Doris's husband had passed away the year before, and some mutual friends invited us to dinner. Our ages were separated by forty years, but our houses were only separated by a quarter of a mile. We routinely did things together like walk or shoot pistols. We loved nothing more than setting up targets in Doris's yard and challenging each other to a pistol shooting match. This would be the first time I had ever asked Doris to accompany me to work instead of play.

I rang her on the phone. "Good evening, Doris. I know this seems crazy, but I was wondering if you'd like to ride with me down to Gum Spring on an emergency vet call? I could use the company to keep me awake."

"Are you kidding? I'd love it. I could use the company as well." Doris hurried off the phone to prepare for my arrival.

Doris came out of the house sporting old clothes and a bright red plastic scarf tied around her freshly styled white hair. It was just beginning to rain lightly, so she wanted her head covered, like all proper southern ladies do. She hopped up in the truck, smiled, slammed the door, and off we went.

"What exciting thing are we going to do tonight?" Doris asked, raising her eyebrows in anticipation. She loved anything to do with agriculture. She stayed active with the Farm Bureau's Agriculture in the Classroom even after she retired from teaching.

"We are going to see a little boy goat that's having some urinary issues. I hope to God you brought your earplugs."

We had a great conversation about life and love and everything in between, all the way down the road. Doris's presence lit up a dark, rainy evening and made work feel like fun.

Once we arrived, we could hear our patient well before we saw him. "Meeeeh, meeh," he screamed in the distance. I gathered up a few items to stick in my doctor kit, and we followed the screams back to the barn. There he was—all that noise was coming from a tiny little forty-pound goat! He was standing with all four legs spread out and his back hunched, trying like hell to pee.

I explained to his worried owner, "Ma'am, little Bucky likely has one or more stones blocking his urinary tract. If he were to strain hard enough to rupture his bladder, this condition could be lethal for him."

"I don't have a lot of expendable income for a major surgery, but I would like to try something for my tiny buddy." Her dark brown eyes widened knowing there was a glimmer of hope.

"I can do a procedure called a urethral process amputation to give the little guy some relief. If it's successful and you give him some medications and change his diet drastically, we may be able to save him. Does that sound OK?"

Doris listened intently, clearly wondering what role she would have to play in all of this.

"Let's give it a shot," the goat owner said as she gently stroked Bucky's nose.

I heavily sedated Bucky and sat him on his haunches for my lovely assistant Doris to hold.

"Why does he need to be sitting on his butt?" Doris asked.

"It's the very best way to exteriorize his penis." I smiled as I saw Doris's pupils dilate.

"Right . . ." Doris tucked Bucky's haunches securely between her thick calf muscles.

Once his penis was out, all three of us could clearly see the problem. A large stone was stuck in the narrow urethral process that protruded from the end of his penis. Doris and the owner looked at each other as I pulled out a pair of sharp scissors. Snip, snip—and urine sprayed everywhere, on me, on Doris, and painted every wall of the barn.

"Doris, is this the first time you've ever been peed on?" I asked as I mopped up the urine soaking through my clothes.

"Lord, no, honey," she replied. "I had two boys."

We all busted out in laughter. Everyone, especially little Bucky, breathed a huge sigh of relief. From time to time, I wonder why I spent $90,000 and twenty-one years in school to be a glorified plumber, but that's what it took to help this animal feel better.

After finishing up with Bucky's medications and diet instructions, the grateful goat mom wrote me a check and gave me and Doris big hugs. "You ladies have saved the day. I really appreciate you all coming out here in the middle of the night and helping my boy."

When we hopped back in the truck, Doris realized her son Glen had called several times to check on her. When she rang him back, I could hear his loud voice on the other end of the line: "Whatcha doin', Mama?" Doris struggled to explain the goat's medical condition and the procedure.

Finally, Glen stopped her and asked, "How'd you all fix him, Mama?"

"Well . . . we pulled a Lorena Bobbitt on him!"

I died laughing. It's always fun to teach an old schoolteacher something, especially one that was still very active in the Virginia Farm Bureau's Agriculture in the Classroom program. I knew she would be able to pass on that knowledge and passion for her veterinary experience to future generations. And I looked forward to our next adventure together.

NURSING HOME RIDE-ALONG

*F*ranklin was a longtime farmer in his eighties when he had to make the move to Dogwood Village Health and Rehabilitation facility. He became increasingly unstable with his mobility due to worsening Parkinson's disease, and after his sweet wife, Helen, passed away, there was nobody there to stay with him. Franklin was like a grandfather to me; in fact, he was the one who introduced me to Doris. From the time I started working for his daughter-in-law, Dr. Kate, Franklin and his wife Helen embraced me with open arms. They were supportive of me as a veterinarian and a friend.

I knew how much Franklin liked being outside on the farm, and I knew how understandably reluctant he was to leave his home. Sitting on Franklin's front porch, I looked him in the eye and said, "Listen, I promise you, if you go to the assisted living facility I will pick you up every chance I get, and you can ride along with me on my vet calls."

"OK. That sounds nice. I'll go." A tear leached out onto the crow's-feet around his eyes as he squeezed my hand.

I was there every pretty day of the spring, hoisting Franklin's right butt cheek up as he stepped one foot up onto the running board, unsteadily grabbing the "oh shit" handle to pull himself into the truck seat.

Franklin adored our adventures. He rarely got out of the county during his working years because he was always on the farm or playing bluegrass music. He saw areas of central Virginia he'd only heard about, and he loved seeing other people's cows. As his Parkinson's advanced, his dementia worsened to the point that he would ask the same question over and over.

"Melinda, how many cows did they have in their herd?"

"Twenty; he had twenty cows," I stated with conviction, because it was the truth.

"Twenty cows. That's a small group, but manageable."

Five minutes would pass, and Franklin would ask, "Melinda, how many cows were in the last people's herd?" In order to maintain my sanity, I would change the answer each time.

One sunny afternoon, I pulled the vet truck into Dogwood Village to collect Franklin. An elderly lady with iridescent white hair was sitting outside with a stone-cold look on her face. She asked, "Are you a veterinarian, young lady?"

I nodded and smiled. "Yes, ma'am. I certainly am."

"So am I," she said with a serious look. Judging by her age, this seemed nearly impossible. I thought she must just have dementia. There were very few women in veterinary school in the mid-1900s.

The elderly lady asked, "Can I come ride with you one day?"

"I will certainly ask the nurses and see if we can work that out at some point."

Two weeks passed and I hadn't seen the lady again, so I didn't talk with the nursing staff about the ride-along. Before I picked up Franklin for the afternoon, I sat in the parking lot, eating a sandwich and scrolling through my Facebook news feed. An obituary went past, and I recognized the photo as the lady from Dogwood Village. Apparently, I was friends with her granddaughter. Dr. C. A. Hoober was Caroline's grandmother and the mother of two of my veterinary mentors and colleagues, Dr. Pat and Dr. Gillian.

Her obituary highlighted her fascinating life. She was one of only three women veterinary students at the University of Guelph graduating in 1950. Upon graduation, she was accepted to be an intern at the prestigious national stables in England. When the British veterinarians discovered that Dr. C. A. Hoober stood for Cherry Anne, they said they would not accept her for the internship. Following the rejection, she became the first female veterinary intern at Cornell. Dr. Hoober practiced veterinary medicine until she was in her seventies and was still trying to ride along and help until just two weeks before her death.

I still feel guilty that I couldn't get Dr. Hoober in the vet truck one last time. I hope when I'm that age, I'll still be itching to help animals myself.

CRACKING UP

I heaved the large, heavy box containing the electroejaculator into the back of the vet truck and slammed the door as I pulled my fuzzy blue stocking cap snugly onto my head. Breeding season was upon us, and I was off to meet Dr. Kate at a large beef operation to perform breeding soundness exams on several bulls. If our farmers wanted calves to be born in the fall, they'd need to make sure the potential sperm donors could get the job done.

My riding buddy Franklin had passed, and I really missed his company. You'd think the ride home from a job like this with an elderly man might be awkward, but he was a very professional farmer and a gentleman who understood the importance of this task. He would have enjoyed seeing what other farmers valued in a breeding bull, and we'd have discussed it over and over.

Driving up the long gravel farm road, I admired the glistening frost on the barren crop fields that surrounded me. When I pulled in beside the barn, I realized Dr. Kate hadn't arrived yet. It wasn't unusual for her, like most large animal vets, to be late, and I had all the equipment with me. Bert, the farm manager, was there so we decided to get started. Bert was a handsome, mild-mannered young man with a dark, trimmed beard and Wranglers just tight enough to accentuate the Skoal ring in his back pocket.

One after another, we secured the bulls in the cattle chute complete with a steel pipe behind them to keep them from backing up. I measured their scrotal circumferences to make sure their testicles were adequately sized. Next, I performed a rectal exam to make sure their secondary sexual organs were of proper size and shape. Finally, I placed a rectal probe to stimulate the bull to ejaculate. I collected the ejaculate and examined it under the microscope to ensure the sperm cells were motile. Later, I would kill the sperm with stain and make sure the cells were shaped properly. There were several parts to a breeding soundness exam—that's why Dr. Kate and I were planning to tag-team the adventure. After the fourth bull had come through the chute, I was starting to grow impatient. The bulls aren't always excited about getting excited.

When the fifth bull hustled across the scales, the bright red letters read 2,800 lbs. He was like a train barreling toward the front of the cattle chute. It was all Bert and I could do to get him stopped. Bert pulled all his body weight down on the handle of the chute, swinging from the handle like a monkey. The bull's neck was so thick it prevented the metal headgate from holding him properly. I struggled to get the steel pipe shoved in behind him. This pipe is a very important piece of equipment; when placed between a series of backstops, it prevents the bull from backing out of the headgate. Several of the backstops were missing, so I shoved it in the best I could.

This guy was clearly not going to be a willing participant. It was like he'd been paying attention to what was happening in front of him. He refused to stand up in the chute and repeatedly fell to his knees.

"Stand up, bull. What the hell is wrong with you?" I fussed at him as if he understood English. "Stay on your feet. Praying ain't gonna help you." Every time he got up, he'd go back down on his knees again by the time I got to his back end.

In a moment of pure, unadulterated frustration, I kicked his soft, wet nose with my steel-toed boot and shouted, "I said get up, you son of a bitch!" I'd had enough. I decided I'd just insert the probe and turn on the electricity. Surely that would get his attention and get him up on his feet. I securely inserted the probe in his rectum, then placed a collection device on the end of a long stick. I knelt down beside the bull, ready to capture the goods, with my head level with the steel pipe. I manually cranked up the electricity to the probe.

The shocked bull kicked backward with all his might. The steel pipe slammed into my head inches above my right temple. It was like A-Rod had swung a baseball bat at my skull. Everything went dark as I hit the ground.

Bert rushed around to my side of the chute. I was facedown in the dirt, inert and unable to react. He kicked at me a few times: "Doc, you OK? Can you hear me? Please say something. Anything."

Bert started to sob. He must have thought I was dead. I could hear him sniffling, but I wasn't able to speak. As soon as I could, I mumbled into the ground, "I can hear you."

"You can? Thank God." He sobbed even more once he realized I was alive. "Are you OK?" He lay down next to me and rolled me onto my side.

Bert stared into my eyes as he knocked the dust off my stocking cap. He explored every inch of my face with his long fingers. "I heard that pipe strike you. There must be a cut somewhere. Let me pull you up so I can see you better." He got up and reached for my hand.

"Give me a few minutes, please," I pleaded. "I'm not ready to stand yet." I reached up to feel the right side of my head. I was surprised to discover that it was still attached to my body.

After several minutes, I grasped Bert's hand. "I think I'm ready to come up. Go slow, please. I feel very woozy." Slowly and carefully, he pulled me into a standing position and embraced me with his muscular arms. I felt as safe and secure as if I were in the arms of Jesus. I appreciated his compassion so much.

I was so scared I was shaking. Scared of what had just happened to me and scared of what my future held. I was only in my early thirties, just trying to make it. Was there bleeding in my brain? Was I going to die—or worse yet, become an invalid? At least I didn't have anyone depending on me. No children, not even a dog because I was always busy taking care of everyone's creatures.

Bert escorted me to the catwalk of the chute and helped me sit down.

"Thanks for all of your help, Bruce," I mumbled.

Shortly thereafter, Dr. Kate arrived. "Well, what have I missed?" Bert briefly described the incident.

"Do you need to go to the hospital?" she asked.

"No, I think I will be OK." I reached up to rub my head and noticed my skull was changing shape under my stocking cap.

Dr. Kate was not in good humor, and we were only halfway done testing the bulls. She instructed me, "You just sit there while I set up the new microscope, or you can go home if you want." Clearly, she was planning to start counting the semen to evaluate their shape. This news was disappointing. Counting a hundred sperm cells from each bull was going to take forever, and this was something that could easily be done in the comfort of the office!

There I sat, nearly frozen to death, with a headache from hell. My head was swelling so much now I began to wonder why no one else could tell that I was beginning to look like the Hunchback's sister. I realized I'd have to help finish testing the bulls or it would be Christmas before we finished. I really wanted to go home and get warm, but I couldn't remember how to get there.

When bulls six through ten came through the chute, I went through the procedure step-by-step, over and over, until I had collected the last bull. It's fascinating how much muscle memory a person has, even with an injured brain. I helped Dr. Kate pack up the supplies and carefully followed her back to the office. James, Dr. Kate's husband, asked curiously, "Why does your head look so weird?" I was glad someone else noticed. I was beginning to think I was imagining things.

"A ginormous bull kicked a pipe into it during his semen test. It's been a rough day."

He attempted to console me by telling me stories of his past farm injuries. Eventually, I decided I could get home by punching the address on my GPS. I was beyond ready for this crappy day to be over!

Back at my apartment, all I wanted to do was lie down, but every time I tried to get horizontal, it felt like my head was going to literally pop off. My head hurt so bad it brought tears to my eyes. My friend Heidi called to see how my day was going. After I gave her a summary of the day's events, she exclaimed, "Girl, how about I come and take you to the emergency room?" I politely declined. All I wanted to do was lie down. I propped myself up with lots of pillows and dozed off sitting up.

In the middle of the night, I saw a blonde head peer around my bedroom door. I wasn't sure if it was a ghost or an intruder, but I couldn't run away so it really didn't matter. I flipped on the night-light and saw Heidi standing there.

"Hey, girl. Didn't mean to frighten you." In her quiet, maternal way she lifted my chin and carefully examined my strangely shaped head. "After you refused to seek medical attention I got scared and decided to come sleep on your couch so I could check on you."

"Wow. That's super nice. You didn't have to do that, but I sure am glad you're here." I supposed she couldn't let me die; who else would she get to help drag goats and sheep to the inner city?

The next morning, I got up and tried to dress for work. I realized I was unable to bend down without incredible pressure in my head. I had to put my boots up at waist level in order to tie them. It was very difficult to think, and I soon realized I couldn't eat breakfast because I couldn't open my jaw.

Several days passed before I decided to go to the local doctor to get evaluated. I was starting to get very hungry, and I was not sleeping well propped up. After a brief neurologic exam, he said, "Young lady, you've had a severe concussion and I really think you need a skull radiograph, but we don't have the ability to do those here. Come back in three months if your short-term memory doesn't improve."

I decided that going forward I'd take things one day at a time and do the best I could. I had to use the GPS for navigation and dosing charts I had made for myself when I was a young vet to dose animals correctly. For six months, I continued to have short-term memory problems, and I had to sleep sitting up and tie my shoes at waist level. I also realized I couldn't read my piano music anymore. It was a long, scary six months. Every day I hoped and prayed my head would be normal again.

One year after the incident, I returned home to southwestern Virginia for our family Thanksgiving. I was excited to see my family, and I hoped they wouldn't notice any lingering mental impairment. As we sat around the big table, my younger sister, Ann, stared at me.

"Didn't your mom ever tell you that it's not polite to stare?" I said. "Don't worry, there's plenty of baked mac 'n' cheese to go around if that's what you're worried about."

"Girl, you OK? You have blood running down the side of your face." Ann squinted at me, trying to tell where it was coming from.

I wiped the blood away, resumed shoveling macaroni and cheese into my mouth, and attempted to steer the conversation in a different direction. Moments later, Ann looked over and exclaimed, "It's happening again. You should really excuse yourself and figure out what the hell is going on with your head." Ann didn't do blood; she made beautiful wedding cakes and pastries for a living. Bleeding at the table was not ladylike.

I snuck off to the bathroom and locked the door. I traced the bloody path north toward my hairline. My scalp was tender and itchy just above my right temple. My skin felt thin and irritated, particularly in one raised area. I scratched at it until a hard, round white object fell into my hand. What on God's green earth was this? I pondered—then realized it was a small piece of my fractured skull that had finally made it to the surface! It was like getting a trophy for surviving the pipe, but not one I could put on display because it would worry my family too much. I wrapped the bone fragment in toilet paper and flushed it, hoping this experience would be behind me forever.

I knew when I started this career there were dangers involved. I realized I could die doing my job, and that was a chance I was willing to take. Fortunately, over the next year, both the outside and the inside of my head healed up nicely. I began to learn how to anticipate danger better and advocate for my own safety.

TAMPAX FOR THE WIN

"Come quick, Doc," exclaimed Farmer Jim's panicked daughter. "It's 5031. She's had an accident in the free-stall barn and sliced her milk vein. She's bleeding like a stuck pig."

"Hold pressure on the wound," I instructed her. "It'll slow the bleeding until I can get there." I grabbed the truck keys.

I heard the words of my wise veterinary professor once again saying, "All bleeding stops . . . eventually." I hoped I'd be able to get it stopped before the eventual part happened. Months after my concussion, thinking on my feet was still quite difficult. I'd been resorting to a tactic I'd used as a new graduate. While racing up the road, I ran through the scenario in my head of what suture material I would need and how my helpers would need to act as tourniquets to allow me to visualize the gigantic vessel.

Being a bit superstitious and old-fashioned, I was hoping the signs of the moon were in the feet today. I really missed being able to call my grandfather "Pap-Poo" and ask him where the signs were on any given day. The old farmers relied heavily on the *Farmer's Almanac* to instruct them when the moon was in the right phase to do most anything: plant their crops and gardens, wean calves, castrate, dehorn, most any farm activity you could imagine. The theory was that the moon controlled gravity, which controlled the flow of the blood in a living organism's body. For example, if you castrated an animal when the signs were in the feet, the blood would be well below the site where the fresh tissue would be cut, and there would be very little bleeding during the procedure. Tonight, though, nobody chose this, and we were going to have to deal with it quickly and professionally no matter where the signs were.

The farm had festivities underway on this cool spring evening. The smell of grilled steaks filled the air as I passed a surprisingly large white tent strung with white lights in the center of the backyard. Country music was cranking on the stereo as people steadily arrived at the house, which was surrounded by perfectly landscaped flower beds full of blooming peonies. Usually, I'm envious of this kind of celebration because it's hard to always be the passerby, but I was delighted to see this family taking a break. Our dairy clients work twenty-four hours, seven days a week to put milk on our tables and shoes on their children. In my first six years in practice, I'd seen several dairies sell out, which was upsetting because I knew in my heart they would never be dairies again. I have a real soft spot for the dairy farmers—the sights, sounds, and smells take me back to childhood. The faint smell of cow manure being spread on the fields can be off-putting to an average person, but for those of us who were raised on dairies, the twinge of ammonia and hydrogen sulfide is comforting.

When I rounded turn four at the corner of the dairy barn, I spotted a gigantic black and white cow lying on her side, 5031 written on her yellow ear tag, with three young ladies kneeling beside her near a puddle of bright red blood. I jumped out and dashed over to the cow to do a quick assessment of the injury. I had to do a double take to recognize the three beautiful young ladies draped over the cow's huge abdomen as the dairy farmer's daughters. Normally, they run around the farm with hair in a messy bun, wearing waterproof bibs specially designed for milking. This evening, all three had made-up faces and long, glistening strawberry-blonde hair flowing over their shoulders. Luckily, the splashes of fresh blood blended in with the abstract flowered designs on their snazzy sundresses.

"We're in big trouble with our mother," Erin, the eldest daughter, began to explain. "Tonight is the rehearsal dinner for my wedding. But we just couldn't leave our favorite cow up here to die." I assured them I would relieve them so they could go celebrate. I remembered all the years my dad had to miss out on our activities and family vacations because a cow was calving. I didn't even realize until I got to veterinary school that there were drugs to induce labor in animals—in my experience, a graduation or a basketball game seemed to do it every time.

"We tried to follow the advice you gave us to slow the bleeding," Molly said. I lifted Ashley's beautifully manicured hand only to discover a large, blood-soaked piece of cotton with what appeared to be a string attached. Raising one eyebrow, I shot Molly a sideways look. "Ashley had the bright idea to use some ultra-absorbent tampons. Brilliant, eh?" I burst into laughter and shook my head.

As I studied the cow's milk vein to evaluate the damage, I instructed the girls to remove their finely manicured blood-soaked hands from the wound. They eased off the pressure, and the blood began to pour out of the thin wall of the huge vein. I picked up my four-inch curved needle and got to work. It was a race against time. Could I sew fast enough to keep her from bleeding to death? Would my sutures hold well enough to save her?

This blood vessel was responsible for carrying enough blood to the cow's udder for her to produce ten gallons of milk every day. My heart pounded as I furiously and meticulously placed each suture. Magically, when the last knot was tied, the bleeding stopped. I washed the cow with peroxide to clean the copious amount of blood from her underside and treated her with antibiotics and pain medication.

I beckoned the hefty, beer-drinking bystanders. "Yo, fellas, can a couple of you help me push on this cow to sit her up, and maybe one of you can grab her a few buckets of water?" The obedient young men set their cans down and rolled up their sleeves. "Betcha didn't know your groomsmen duties would include rolling cows, now, did you, guys?"

They shook their heads and laughed.

I blotted the splotches of blood off Erin's fair cheeks. "Congratulations on your wedding, dear," I said as she hugged me. "Now please get down there and take the rest of the night off. After all, you girls and a box of tampons have saved a life tonight. Go enjoy yourselves before your mother gets ill with me too. I don't intend to stand in the way of a woman with an agenda."

AN APPLE
IN BACON HOLLER

The bright fuchsia, pink, and white blooms of the peonies lost every petal and shriveled up as the summer heat and humidity descended on central Virginia. The flowers weren't the only things the steamy conditions sucked the life out of in this Piedmont region of the state. The dripping sweat under the band of my sports bra routinely caused chafing to the point of peeling skin down to the second layer. And the poor cows took refuge in any bit of shade they could find from 10:00 a.m. until dark.

I had been working for Dr. Kate for seven years now, and as sometimes happens in long-term relationships, we were at a crossroads. Dr. Kate was looking to slow down after years of on-call emergencies, and her boys were starting to look at colleges. I continued to try to build up the practice in hopes that if I bought it, I'd have enough work to support two veterinarians. Dr. Kate and I were providing veterinary services on six species of animals—cattle, goats, sheep, pigs, alpacas, and llamas—to fifteen counties in our region, but we were getting calls every day to take on new clients. Since I was usually the one who was up for taking on something new, I'd usually handle those calls.

"Come quick, my cow . . . she's choking, and you need to help her!" exclaimed a voice that was gasping for air. On the other end of the line was a farmer all the way up in Bacon Hollow, or as the locals call it, Bacon Holler. I jumped in the truck and headed his way. While driving along the narrow, crooked back roads farther and farther off the main road, I started to wonder if it was wise to go to the legendary Bacon Holler alone. Natives of the area had told me wild tales about the moonshine business that had flourished in the holler for decades. And, of course, along with moonshine come the tales of fights over money, women, and booze that occasionally turn deadly. The locals said you weren't allowed into the holler without an invitation and an escort. What the heck, I was young and single and always up for an adventure. If I survived, maybe I would be able to write a book about it.

I decided to text the secretary in the office an address and tell her to send help if I didn't call in an hour. When I turned onto Bacon Hollow Road, sure enough, there was an escort waiting for me. I followed the small car down a dirt road with a row of dilapidated little houses, their tin roofs two-toned from rust. People sat on the porches, some with cur dogs lying at their feet, blowing smoke from their cigarettes and glaring as I drove by. At that moment, I wasn't sure if I was brave or stupid.

Finally, we got to a cow field with a small pen and broken-down loading chute. There were two other shifty-looking fellows standing guard to make sure the cow didn't bust out. In the pen stood an old black cow with a white face clearly in distress, coughing with her neck extended.

"Any idea what she choked on?" I asked the guys.

One older fellow who seemed to be the ringleader of the group, since he was the only one who ever spoke, piped up and replied, "An apple." The men looked like true country bumpkins in their tattered wifebeaters, one with a cigarette in his hand. I don't think there was a full set of teeth among the three of them. The ringleader stood there staring at me, wondering what a girl was going to do for his cow, while his cronies seemed to be undressing me with their eyes. I felt vulnerable, but I knew my only chance at making it out of this holler unscathed was to appear confident. I tried hard to focus only on the cow. She needed me to be on my A game.

I had the guys slide some boards into the front of the loading chute and push the cow up into it. Then we slid three more rickety boards in behind her. It was certainly not the Cadillac of facilities, but this was *not* the time to discuss proper handling equipment. I climbed up the front of the chute and reached down the cow's throat with my bare arm. As I pushed in farther and farther, she pinched the flesh of my forearm so hard with her dental pad I could hardly stand it. Cows don't have top teeth in the front, but man, did it hurt. When I got to her throat, I was delighted to feel something in my hand. I pulled out half an apple core—but only half. There was only one thing left to do.

I took a deep breath as if I were getting ready to take the polar plunge, and I reached back in, with even more intense pressure from the cow's mouth. Then I pulled out the other half! The cow was so relieved, and so was the ringleader, who shouted, "Thank the Lord." Up to this point he had not expressed much confidence in my abilities.

All I needed to do was a final check. "Guys, do y'all have any tubing I can use to make sure her throat is clear?" They brought me a ratty old five-foot piece of tubing. I passed it down into the cow's stomach and blew on it. Boy, did I get a nasty surprise—the end of the hose tasted like gasoline! I gagged and spit a few times.

One of the guys mumbled, "Sorry, ma'am, that ol' tube might have been used to siphon gas a time or two."

I rolled my eyes and chuckled. "Your reputation precedes you, boys."

When I came back from my truck with the antibiotic and pain meds, the guys stared at my right arm. It was bright purple from my elbow to my wrist; one of the most beautiful bruises I have ever seen. The older fellow asked, "You all right, young lady?"

"I'm just fine, thanks." I attempted to climb up on the side of the loading chute to give the cow her medicine. The rickety boards started to give way. The two creepy silent guys caught me. Each held onto one of my butt cheeks.

"Boys," I said, "if either of you squeezes, I'm going to kick you in the face. We clear?"

They nodded in tandem. Finally, I got the last shot at the cow as she bobbed and weaved to avoid the needle. It has always been an enigma to me how some medical professionals struggle to draw blood out of a human sitting perfectly still with a tourniquet and good lighting.

We released the cow back into the pen to recuperate. I went back to my truck and figured up the bill. "Here's the total, sir. Do you want to do cash or check?"

"Here in the holler, we only do cash." The older man handed me a stack of $20 bills. "Thank ya, ma'am, for the help."

I closed the door and reached for the keys to start the truck. They weren't there. I looked more frantically with each passing second. I always, always leave the keys in the cup holder, and they weren't there, or anywhere nearby.

"What's wrong, little lady?" asked the one who spoke. "You worried about bein' in a strange, faraway place without your keys?"

Right then I spotted the keys peeking out of the floormat, pushed the door lock, and peeled out in a cloud of dust.

"See ya, boys," I yelled through a small crack in the window. The only part of my right arm that wasn't bright purple were my white knuckles clutching the steering wheel. I had survived Bacon Holler.

On my quiet drive home, once the adrenaline rush passed, my arm began to throb. Too often, trying to prove myself resulted in harm to my body. Most of the time I tried to endure the pain quietly, but this time I'd also need to keep my arm covered to avoid ending up in a domestic abuse shelter.

Large animal veterinarians may seem like gluttons for punishment, but I prefer to think of us as having grit. And it's a good thing I do. As people in the mountains of southwest Virginia often say, "If you want to get out of the holler alive, you have to be the baddest ass in the holler."

SHOOK UP

Wrapping up my fair president duties, I tucked the last of the shiny purple Best of Show ribbons into the box and locked the storage unit. The 2011 County Agricultural Fair, which required months of planning and preparation, was over. School was starting, which meant fall calving season was right around the corner. It seemed like the calm before the storm. Dr. Kate told me I could have a day off to recover from the extra work I had been putting in for the last several months, but I didn't know what to do with myself.

I decided to take our eager vet student with me up into the mountains of Greene County to help wrangle some wild goats. Jessica had been interning at the practice for two weeks and was always game for anything, whether it involved veterinary medicine or not. We agreed to try to do something fun on our way back from the call, since Dr. Kate said we could have a light day. We discussed going for a short hike on the mountain trail, then hitting the outlet store to get discounted shoes before stopping at the Mennonite store for freshly made sandwiches. One of the perks of being an ambulatory rural veterinarian is knowing where all the good country stores are.

Driving toward the majestic mountains on the horizon with a clear blue sky as their backdrop turned into driving through a tunnel of foliated trees, as though the mountain encapsulated my vet truck. When we turned onto a smaller road, Jessica glanced down at an alert on her phone. Her Dominion Energy stock had crashed. This was concerning to me because I lived in an apartment only seven miles from the two nuclear reactors owned by the power company. We started to climb the steepest part of the tiny gravel mountain road, and suddenly I felt like I was losing control of the heavy vet truck.

"What's wrong? What's happening to the truck? Are we going to be pulled over that ledge and die?" Jessica glanced over her right shoulder with a scared expression.

"I don't know what's going on. It feels like we have two flat tires or something. I don't even think that's possible." I wrestled the steering wheel, struggling to hold us on the narrow pig path. When we crested the hill, everything seemed fine again. The truck was handling like normal.

We pulled into the goat lady's place. She ran up to the truck, panting. "Did you girls just feel that massive earthquake?"

Jessica and I looked at each other, our pupils dilated like those of a pair of dogs who'd eaten a pack of cigarettes. We got our work done as quickly as possible and headed for home.

Once we got back into better cell phone reception, our phones started blowing up. Suddenly fifty-five people were concerned about my welfare. The text messages flooded in: *U ok? Where were u? U need a place to stay?* Oh hell, why would I need a place to stay? I started to wonder how my tiny second-story apartment nestled at the top of the Cuckoo House had fared in this act of God. Jessica searched the internet for the location of this earthquake and what damages occurred, with no luck. So many people were using their cell phones that all communication was halted.

I decided the best plan would be to get home as quickly as possible. As we sped into the gravel driveway beside the big house, we could see two people standing on the brick walk in Red Cross jackets placing bright-colored tape around the brick patio covered with fallen bricks. When you see the Red Cross at your house, you can rest assured it is not going to be a good day. The workers explained to us that the epicenter of the quake was only one mile from the house, and the limestone mortar holding the bricks together crumbled under the strain. I was imagining how different the story would have been if I'd taken the day off to sunbathe on the patio, and I was glad I didn't listen to everything Dr. Kate said.

"Can I go in and get my stuff out, please?" I begged.

"It's not safe. There are going to be a lot of aftershocks and the structure is unstable. You should enter at your own risk and get only the important things," said the volunteer. Between the intense summer heat and the shock of this disaster, I didn't know how to choose what the most important things even were.

Jessica and I waded through the mountains of bricks to get to the small white door that led up to my apartment. The door didn't open easily, so we kicked it in. Entering cautiously, we were greeted with a stench.

"What on earth is that smell?" I asked Jessica.

"Red wine and tequila, ma'am," Jessica replied.

She was exactly right! I had a small bar that was built into the wall on the second floor. What once was my stairway was now a river of alcohol and broken glass. We picked our way around the shards of glass. We walked into the living room, where my oversized, framed veterinary degree was facedown on my computer. Much to my surprise, the glass wasn't cracked.

I called my friend and coworker Holly to bring some containers to the apartment so I could salvage a few things. Holly, Jessica, and I worked tirelessly, sweating through our shirts while throwing clothes, pictures, and books into plastic containers to haul them out. While I was carrying the third load of clothes across the brick patio, a strong aftershock rocked us. I knew I was standing still, but as I looked down, the patio appeared to be moving. I decided that no material thing was worth losing our lives.

Overnight, both sidewalls of the huge brick house cracked, causing the roof to cave in. In the middle of the night, the expected hurricane blew in from the coast and flooded what was left in the Cuckoo House.

That night I lay in the guest bed at Dr. Kate's, drowning the pillow while I prayed. What was I going to do about housing? I had several house-sitting jobs coming up, so I decided to try and get a few more of those.

My first night of house-sitting—and, more importantly, dog-sitting—was for some dear friends and neighbors, Bill and Cathy, in the Cuckoo neighborhood. It was only one week after the big earthquake, and I was fast asleep. In the middle of the night, I felt their yellow lab Chester's big, wet nose nudging me in the armpit.

"Go away, Chester. I mean it." Less than a minute passed, and Chester nudged me again, this time with conviction and whining. I was getting pissed and tried to roll over to the other side. Chester jerked my bedsheet off with his teeth and ran toward the door. Was Chester trying to be like Lassie? Was he even that smart?

I jumped out of bed and followed him to the back door of the house. He pawed at the door as if I couldn't get it open fast enough, then bolted out to the back part of the yard. I ran close behind. Then came a sudden loud noise, like a massive bowling ball hitting the hardwood and rolling down the lane—an intense aftershock. As the earth shook under our feet, I heard creaking. It came from a massive tree that crashed onto the back porch of the beautiful southern home, landing right outside the window of the bedroom we were sleeping in. I held Chester in my arms, petting him intensely, thanking him for saving our lives.

When was this aftershock business going to end? When was this earthquake going to leave us alone? Thankfully, neither of the nuclear reactors cracked, but people all over the county were struggling with cracked foundations, cracked wells, anxiety, and anxious kids and pets. Students whose schools were ruined were forced to share schools with other students by going to school on alternating days.

Life had changed for all of us.

I had been a rural large animal veterinarian for seven years now, and it was difficult being so far from my family, especially during a natural disaster. I hoped that my connections through my clients and friends in this community would help me to rise above this tragedy and the resulting homelessness. Maybe now was the time to pack my bags and move closer to home in southwest Virginia. After all, there wasn't much to pack.

PACKING FOR SUCCESS

*I*n the months after the earthquake, I realized I wasn't homeless. It was humbling to have so many offers from church friends and clients to stay at their homes. Communities tend to pull together after natural disasters, and ours certainly did.

I decided to stay in central Virginia after the quake, mostly because I didn't want to feel like I was quitting on Dr. Kate or this agricultural community that had been so supportive. Also, the thought of starting over at this point was frightening. I had finally gotten through all the transitions of school and settled in somewhere.

I jumped around from house-sitting job to house-sitting job until my friend and coworker Holly alerted me to a small caretaker's cottage on a big farm owned by a deceased lady. The farm was now managed by a foundation. It was built in 1795, complete with slate shingles and a tiny woodstove. I was glad to finally be settling in somewhere. It had been a rough month, both physically and mentally, trying to balance practicing veterinary medicine and being homeless.

While sleeping one night, I began to hear an obnoxious noise I suspected was coming from the ghosts that had tortured me incessantly since I arrived at the cottage. After fumbling to turn on my night-light, I realized the deafening noise was coming from my cell phone. Dr. Kate and I were trying out a new call forwarding technology so that only the on-call vet received the night calls directly to her phone. So far it was working well, except for the occasional crazy person who would call at 3:00 a.m. to schedule their dog's rabies shot.

I'd specifically set it to the awful default melody old people have on their flip phones so that I could not possibly sleep through any emergency calls. It didn't seem fair; I'd only been soundly asleep for an hour after a very long day.

Tonight, the frustrating person on the other end of the line was a concerned hobby farmer. "Ma'am, I think I have a cow having trouble having a calf or something. I'm not sure because I work full-time and I don't get out here to check these cows until after dark."

I inquired, "So do you check the cows every day?"

"I don't always get out here every single day," he admitted. "I'm kind of new to cows, but they sure do help pay the taxes on this expensive land."

Oh my Lord, if he doesn't care about this cow, why should I? The poor gal could have been lying out there all day pushing. It wasn't the cow's fault she had an idiot for an owner. In my raspy middle-of-the-night voice, I grudgingly said, "It's going to take me an hour to get there. Meet me at the gate so I will know where to turn in." I pulled on some work clothes from the dirty clothes pile. Why on earth would I get clean clothes on?

Speeding along the desolate highway, I cracked the truck window to let the cold air blow in my face and blasted the Rolling Stones song playing on the radio. That was sage advice from Dr. Kate regarding how not to fall asleep while driving. On the long drive north, I had a lot of time to stew on the upsetting fact that there are fewer and fewer "real farmers." The hardworking people who raise our food are getting older, and nobody is replacing them. I'd recently read in a farm magazine that the average age of our Virginia farmers is fifty-nine years old. The young people realize it's hard to make a living in agriculture and are seeking other types of work. The land values are increasing because the cities are closing in all around us. If these land-use tax exemptions didn't exist, even though they seem to attract the wrong type of farmer, would agriculture even exist in this part of our beautiful state? I certainly couldn't afford to let one of these weekend warriors get me hurt—production animal vets like me are getting rarer and rarer too.

Pulling into the gravel drive between the tall weeds, I was greeted by a middle-aged man named Earl. He was wearing a "pretty boy" cowboy hat, the kind whose only practical function is to warn others of serious inexperience.

Earl draped himself over my open window. "Thanks for coming out tonight, honey. I'm sure your boyfriend is missing you. I don't know what's going on with this cow, but I think she probably needs help. She could have been laying out there for a few days." He made several efforts to touch my arm, which sent shivers up my spine and put me on high alert. I started to put the window up, hoping I'd injure his arm, and told him to open the gate.

Once through the gate, Earl said, "I'm hopping in with you to help open gates. Then I can show you where the cow is." I allowed it but didn't have a good feeling about it.

While driving through the field, Earl got very chatty, and I saw him stealthily lock the truck doors. I remained cool and calm. When Earl stepped out to open the next gate, I reached behind me for my pistol bag. I quietly pulled out my trusty .357 revolver, which always had at least two .38 specials preloaded. I slid it under my seat and threw the case in the back just as Earl stepped back into the truck.

We drove farther and farther into the dark pasture. Once again, Earl locked the doors. He inched closer toward me and started caressing my arm. Then his hand groped my right breast. Every muscle in my body tensed. My calf tightened, my foot pressed harder on the gas pedal, and we picked up speed as we crested the hill. Earl must have felt the tension in my body, but he continued to touch me.

Topping the hill, I slammed on the brakes . . . hard enough to dislodge my powerful little pistol from underneath my seat. Immediately, I flipped the interior light on and reached for the gun. "I'm sure glad that thing didn't go off," I said, smiling, "because it's loaded."

Earl's eyes got big, and his demeanor completely changed. He withdrew his left arm from the armrest and slowly reached with his right hand to hit the unlock button.

"Might be time we stop looking for a black cow in the dark, don't ya think, Earl? I suggest you start this wild goose chase again in the daylight with another veterinarian, preferably a male."

Earl agreed. "Yes, ma'am. That would probably be a good idea."

He was well behaved on the silent ride back to his truck. When Earl stepped out of my truck to open the gate, I kept driving, leaving him to hike to his truck. Once I was safely in front of him and headed out of the last gate, I shouted to him, "Since I came all this way tonight, let me give you some farming advice: Don't quit your day job!"

One of my veterinary mentors always said if he hired a woman at his practice, he'd require them to pack a pistol. I'd thought that was overkill. Now I understood. And I'm thankful I heeded his advice.

I'm sure this was one of the many reasons my dad didn't want me to do this job, but I wasn't going to let one creepy predator scare me away. So, I did what any determined woman would do: I bought more bullets and vowed to return to Doris's more often to sharpen my shooting skills.

FEELIN' PEACHY

ortunately, I hadn't had a reason to pull out the pistol for a while, other than burning off some steam with Doris in her yard. With exceptions like Earl, my encounters with farmers were generally very positive. The only thing I knew to do with a negative interaction with a client was to learn from it and put it behind me. Holding onto anger just made me an angry person, and that's not who I wanted to be. I had enough on my plate just trying to navigate life after the earthquake.

One warm spring day, I was preparing to examine a sick calf when I heard the farmer shout, "That calf's gonna die!" He'd driven his four-wheeler up to the passenger's-side door of my vet truck.

When I asked him what he was referring to, he pointed to a small area of watery, fetid, green diarrhea on the ground near my truck. The part he didn't know was that while waiting on him, I hid behind my truck door to relieve my own explosive, cramping bowels.

I blushed as I said, "Well, we better get to work on him quickly." I hadn't been feeling well since I moved to the abandoned farm. Most days were spent trying to figure out if I was sicker than the patients I'd been called to see. That day, I had one last call to do before I could go home for the evening to put my feet up in the recliner in my waterfront cottage.

Annie Rose had called my cell phone and begged for help with her sick cow. It was simply impossible to say no, even though I was running on empty. She is a middle-aged woman who lives with her elderly mother and continues to run the family farm after the passing of her father several years before. She works a full-time job by day and dedicates her nights, weekends, and holidays to farming. In no way is she a hobby farmer like Earl—she is a farmer with two jobs. Annie Rose is the fast-paced, feisty type who doesn't take no for an answer!

When I arrived at Annie Rose's farm, she was leaning out of her RTV, beckoning me toward her. She was dressed in a spaghetti-strap undershirt with a lightweight, unbuttoned flannel shirt overtop. The farther she leaned, the more I prayed the thin straps would hold, as Annie Rose is very well endowed. She glared at me with her hazel green eyes and said, "Load up your supplies and hop in the T-Rex. The huffa ain't lookin' too good."

We took off like a rocket. I was clutching the "oh shit" handle so tight that my knuckles were white. I thought if we hit a groundhog hole, we might take flight. The cows surrounding the down heifer looked scared as we roared toward them. I'd always wondered what it must feel like to cross the finish line of the Daytona 500. Now I knew.

Once my feet touched the ground and I got my bearings, I grabbed my doctor kit and rushed over to examine my patient. The tiger-striped heifer was stretched out on her side, looking up at me with wide, bloodshot eyes. Her rumen, a cow's largest stomach, was steadily filling up with gas as she struggled to breathe. I reached back to grab my bloat needle and saw a small black calf looking at me expectantly. I realized the heifer who was attempting to die in front of us was his mother. I looked into his bright, worried eyes. I think he knew at that moment that I was going to do my best to save his mom.

"Hurry up, Doc! She's gonna blow!" Annie Rose shouted dramatically.

"I know. She's really bloated—you better back up, Annie Rose." It was my turn to bark the orders. "I'm gonna stab her, and it's gonna be nasty."

Standing over her grossly swollen rumen, I raised my right hand, thought of an ex-boyfriend who had pissed me off, and drove the large bore needle through her thick hide at light speed. All we could hear was the sound of air rushing out of the needle as the smell of fermented grass and water filled the air. One of my veterinary school professors used to say, "Everyone measures success differently." For me, this lifesaving procedure was always gratifying. It gave the heifer an immediate sense of relief, and she could breathe normally again.

Unfortunately, the bloat wasn't her only issue. Her calcium was also critically low. I assembled an IV set on a bottle of calcium and slowly ran it into her jugular vein. When the last drop of the sticky solution went in, I removed the needle and placed a halter on the heifer.

I tossed Annie Rose the end of the rope. "Pull, Annie Rose, pull as hard as you can," I pleaded. Together, we tried to pull the thousand-pound bovine up onto her chest. It took every ounce of strength I had left in me to pull; I hadn't eaten food in a week due to my mysterious illness. Feeling faint, I almost had to drop the rope. Then I heard the baby calf cry out loudly. I couldn't let him down—we had an unspoken deal—so I dug deep. Digging deep was part of what made me cut out for this job. Right then, the heifer's weight shifted, and she popped up onto her chest. She let out a huge belch and started trying to lunge forward.

"Lawd have mercy, child, are you trying to kill me?" Annie Rose exclaimed. "You better get that rope off her head before she runs away with it." She peeled off her flannel shirt and began to fan herself with it.

I yanked the halter rope off as the discombobulated heifer rose to her feet. She stood for a few seconds to get her bearings and then slowly walked forward. Her calf dashed over to her excitedly and licked her dry pink nose on his way to the back end to nurse. Annie Rose was delighted. She wrapped her sweaty arms around me and swayed back and forth. It's always rewarding to end the day with a good hug. Since I didn't have family in the area, I didn't get as many hugs as I was accustomed to in the mountains.

We hopped back in T-Rex and zoomed back up to the house. Annie Rose said, "You better come in at least for a minute and see Mama. She needs her hug, and you know she's ninety-four. If you don't come in now, I can't guarantee she'll be here next time."

How could I argue with that?

Upon entering the kitchen, I gave Mrs. Myrtle a big hug and a kiss on the edge of her sparse hairline.

"Good to see ya, sweetie. Pull up a seat and sit for a minute. You're looking a little peaked. You feelin' OK?"

"No, ma'am. I'm not feeling very well, but I'll be OK." I explained that I hadn't been myself for a while. The part I didn't tell her was how long it had been since I'd been able to eat.

The sweet, God-fearing southern lady that she was, she kindly offered, "Let me feed you, dear."

"No, thank you, Mrs. Myrtle. I'd prefer not to eat, but thanks for your concern."

The entire time I was talking, Mrs. Myrtle was reaching up in the kitchen cabinet, pulling out a jar, and putting some fruit into a bowl. In her charming, scratchy voice she told me, "Just have a small bit of fruit, dear. I guarantee it will help you feel better."

Where I come from, you don't argue with your elders. Grudgingly and slowly, I began to eat the peach. It tasted kind of strange, which was concerning because the last thing I needed was more GI drama!

After a few minutes of sitting at the table and chatting, I began to feel woozy and warm. It got a little easier to relax, and I found myself laughing more.

"How you feelin', honey?" Mrs. Myrtle asked.

I told her the truth. "Drunk; I feel drunk."

She bent forward in her chair and cackled. "Well, I'm not sur-prised, sugar. That peach is from the bottom of the moonshine jar!"

Annie Rose began to laugh so hard, the elasticity of her spa-ghetti straps got put to the test once more. I felt my eyes get large. I started shaking my head and covered my flushed face.

Mrs. Myrtle just knew that peach was going to fix me. And I'm sure it would have if I were simply tired and having a bad day.

I sat at the table for several more hours listening to Annie Rose's sordid love stories from the past. Finally, the medicinal peach wore off enough for me to drive home.

Several days passed, with the ill effects of the medicinal peach exacerbating my mysterious underlying condition. One cold, dark night after a long day in the field, I tried to stand up from my hand-me-down recliner beside my tiny woodstove. I realized I was too weak to pull the handle of the recliner hard enough to get out of the chair.

I rang my friend Holly to rescue me from the chair and give me a ride to the emergency room so that I could get fixed up before work the next morning.

Upon my arrival at the ER, the doctor grilled me about what I'd been drinking. He quizzed me about my hydration status, my water source, and my line of work. I soon figured out where his line of questioning was going. I didn't tell him about the medicinal peach.

"Has the well water been checked since the big earthquake?" he asked.

"No, I don't think so," I said.

"Sometimes wells can crack after a natural disaster and E. coli gets in, especially if there are animals around," he explained.

I made a quick phone call and discovered the well had not been checked. E. coli rose to the top of the differential diagnosis list.

The ER doctor started me on antibiotics, gave me some IV fluids, and told me to take it easy for a few days until the antibiotics took effect and I got rehydrated. Naturally, the next morning, I replaced my tea with Pedialyte and jumped in the truck to fulfill my duties to the animals and clients I serve—while praying nobody would spike my fruit!

Part 3

Wearing Many Hats

2012–2021

NEW DIGS

"Just come and look at it, Melinda." Judy turned on her charm to persuade me to check out a potential new residence. "Holly told me your other place is haunted, and I can promise you, the only ghost this house has in it is the Holy Ghost. My father built it just before he passed, and my stepmother is moving to another state."

It never hurts to look, right? Never mind the fact that I had no money or that I had finally made peace with the ghosts that haunted the little cottage. They tried really hard to run me out of there, between the bed-shaking and turning the radio on in the middle of the night, but they didn't realize what a stubborn individual they were dealing with and finally became resigned to the fact I wasn't leaving. Even ghosts can learn that persistence pays.

But I was ready to leave the cottage, and it was time for me to buy the business from Dr. Kate, so I needed a place to put it. Previously, we had worked out of Dr. Kate's basement, and that obviously wasn't going to work anymore.

The long gravel drive to the one-story brick rancher was lined with scrubby cedar trees. I hated working on cows under cedar trees because the prickly cedar pieces got into my bra and could ruin even the best of days. But then Judy and Dick invited me in through the attached garage. Wow! It was unfinished, but what a perfect room for a little vet clinic, with drawers and shelves aplenty.

"This is a sturdy house, Melinda—steel-framed. You don't see that much around here." Dick began to walk me through the house as he talked. "My father-in-law always was a little quirky, and he demanded I weld a steel frame for this house. But I promise you one thing—it's not gonna blow down. It's rated for one hundred miles per hour of wind, and I know what a fiasco you've had with weather disasters recently."

"If I can get a mortgage, I'll take it." My heart raced, and the wheels in my head turned at light speed. My chance of getting a mortgage with all those student loans was probably about as good as that of the half-dead cow I saw yesterday with gangrenous mastitis nursing another calf.

Wait, had I just bought a house? It checked all three boxes for me: no ghosts, perfect room for a vet clinic, and braced for acts of God. The past year had been such a difficult one for weather, it truly seemed like the end of times. If Pap-Poo were still alive, I could have asked him to remind me about all the signs from the book of Revelation, like the one-hundred-pound hailstones and the lake of fire and sulfur—he knew them all.

In April of 2011, just four months before the earthquake in my county, a powerful tornado swept through my hometown of Glade Spring, leaving an eighteen-mile path of destruction. I had driven down to the demolished town a week after the event to help pick up the pieces, and I didn't even recognize it as home. The homes of friends and loved ones, businesses, and churches were destroyed. Nary a tree was left standing anywhere. I gazed down the road that led to my old elementary school, and I could only see tents in yards where homes had once been. Smoke filled the air from burn piles and small campfires. It looked like a scene from the Civil War.

I will never forget standing at the top of a hill with my uncle Freddie on his sixtieth birthday as we stared down at what was once his home and small farm. He held an old black-and-white photo in his hand. "I have worked for sixty years to make this a nice home for us. Now look at it," he said. "Hellfar, one hellacious storm, and I have lost everything. The house is destroyed; the barn is gone . . . completely gone."

"But you did get a ratty boat randomly in your front yard; there's that." I tried to get him to smile. With an encouraging tone, I said, "You, Aunt Vickie, and your critters survived. All the rest of it can be replaced."

He cracked a half-smile. "You're right, kid."

My sister, Ann, and I soon realized that picking up shingles and debris wasn't going to be enough. Together, with numerous family members and good friends, we organized a large-scale fundraiser in which all proceeds would go to the victims of the Glade Spring Tornado. We called it Operation No Place Like Home. In a way, it was the first introduction to running a business for both of us, although neither of us aspired to do so then. We'd always worked for other people and so had our parents; we didn't feel we were business-savvy enough to be in charge.

On the day of the fundraiser, hundreds of people were lined up to come through the gate. The sky was overcast, with a few sprinkles of rain here and there, while the sound of our buddy Josh cranking out Garth Brooks tunes blared over the loudspeakers. The smell of freshly grilled hot dogs and hamburgers filled the air as person after person bid on the silent auction items and bought T-shirts. After twelve straight hours on our feet, we looked more like defeated contestants in a wet T-shirt contest than proud public servants.

Our friend the CPA suggested waiting until all the mail-in donations came in to tally up the money we raised. I'd sent out a letter to my veterinary clients before the fundraiser describing the situation in my hometown and told them any help was appreciated. Numerous clients made substantial financial contributions to the fundraiser. Some of my clients bought up items on sale—toiletries, cleaning items, and the like—and sent them with me every month on my trip home to give to a family in need.

One client put $1,000 in cash in my hand and instructed me to take it to a small business owner. I handed over the cash to a local shop owner and said, "My farmer client wanted it to go from one small business owner to another, so here you go, buddy."

The recipient couldn't believe that a perfect stranger would help him get back on his feet. With a single tear coming down his cheek, he said, "You and your client have restored my faith in humanity and given me a reason to keep going."

I was so impressed that my veterinary clients would invest in my community in this way. It made me want to work even harder for them and the needs of their communities. The final total from the one-day fundraising event and all the donations was just over $30,000. We were overwhelmed with joy, and we knew these hard-working, resilient people would overcome their misfortune.

The next year of my life, after both the tornado and the earthquake, was spent restructuring. I had been in practice long enough that I was beginning to get itchy to do things my own way, and I was getting tired of paying into the black hole called rent.

Helping Ann organize the fundraiser showed us both that we were more capable businesswomen than even we were aware. I was at ground zero again, and it was high time I started investing in myself. Dr. Kate was getting older, and she had been making noise about selling the practice to me. I was young and eager enough to want to grow the practice further. Looking for a more permanent home started to become a priority.

I was so lucky that Dick and Judy started neighbor-shopping on this sweltering summer day. Once I found a mortgage lender, I purchased a chain saw and some painting supplies and began preparing my home for a business. During the coming months, I worked on animals by day and the house by night. There wasn't much money left over on payday for anything other than an additional can of paint, so I was fueled by only one meal per day, unless a client gave me fresh eggs or a pack of ground beef. Despite being exhausted and hungry, I was proud to be climbing the ladder with the work of my hands and the sweat of my brow.

VIRGINIA CHAIN SAW MASSACRE

*N*ever underestimate the power of a chain saw and a few cans of paint. It's like the redneck version of *Extreme Home Makeover*. After a couple of months of hard work and determination, I'd transformed my little one-story brick rancher into a proper veterinary clinic. The small, attached garage, once uninvitingly lined with bare Sheetrock and a concrete floor, was now coated in warm vanilla paint. A cashmere-scented candle filled the air to dissipate the fresh paint smell. Medicine bottles neatly lined the shelves, organized by the ailments they cured. Thousands of needles and syringes were stacked on a tall wire rack in order of size, from the tiny tuberculosis needles to the "holy hell, what on earth do you stick with that?" needles. The small, shiny autoclave that looked like it belonged in a museum was perched between the microscope and the jar of dog treats used to reward compliant canine visitors. Boxes of powdered milk and gallon jugs of obstetrical lube filled the tall wooden shelves, and a long white plastic table sat in the middle of the floor to serve as an examination/surgery table. It wasn't perfect, but it was mine.

Holly helped me get through the transition of buying the practice and moving it to its new location, but she had expressed interest in changing jobs once I was standing on my own two feet. It was time to start building my team. First, I'd need a vet, since I'd bought a two-doctor practice and I was growing weary from being on call for emergencies 24/7. I decided to ring Dr. Lesley, who was practicing in New Zealand. Dr. Lesley and I had gone to veterinary school together and she was exactly what I was looking for: young but experienced, eager, capable, and hardworking. How would I ever convince her to leave New Zealand? I had been there for one summer as a student and I'm the one who recommended she go there. The people were nice, the scenery was gorgeous, and there were more cows and sheep than people.

But I knew if I didn't ask, there was a 100 percent chance I would never get to work with Dr. Lesley, so I picked up the phone and dialed the never-ending number.

"Hi, Les. It's Melinda. How are ya, girl? How's work?"

"Hey, chica. Sorry, I'm a little groggy—it's two in the morning here. Work is going well; it's just full throttle. Last weekend on call I did eight calvings. My arms were like Jell-O. How are things with you?" Dr. Lesley said, sounding exhausted, but happy to hear from me.

"Oh dear, I'm sorry about the late-night call. I forgot to do the math. I was too nervous," I replied.

"Nervous—why are you nervous? Is everything OK?"

"Everything is fine. I just bought this practice from Dr. Kate and I'd really love it if you'd come back and work with me. Just think, you'd be close to your family. Your Gran would be so happy. What do you say?" I wiped my sweaty palms on my dirty jeans and awaited her response.

Dr. Lesley replied, "Sounds like an exciting possibility. Let me ring you soon when it's not the wee hours of the morning. Talk soon, promise."

After Dr. Lesley thought on it for a few weeks she rang back and said, "I'd love to work with you. Remember, I told you at my graduation party that one day we'd work together. I think we'll be a great team. It will be a bit before I can get back because I have to work out my contract."

"Great! That sounds lovely. I'm so excited. We are going to be a kick-ass team. Now get some sleep, gal, or you're going to be dragging tomorrow." I couldn't believe she said yes. I felt as lucky as the squirrel this morning whose tail only got brushed by the large vet truck tire.

I knew it would take a few months to get Dr. Lesley back to Virginia from halfway across the world. Just knowing it was going to happen gave me the motivation to keep hustling and get our other team members in place.

Another important piece of this puzzle would be finding a good receptionist. This wasn't going to be a run-of-the-mill phone answering job. My person would need to be able to calm panicked animal owners, take clear directions, and dispatch us to the farms in an order that made geographical and medical sense. I heard through the farmer grapevine there was a young lady who lived in the next town looking for a job closer to home, so I gave her a buzz.

"Hello, Savannah. This is Dr. Melinda from the Vet Service. I heard you might be looking for some work."

"Yes, I am looking for a veterinary receptionist job and I really need to be closer to home," Savannah stated in her sweet southern accent. "I'm tired of driving to the city to work at the cat care clinic."

"If you can put up with those cat people, I know you'd do great here. We're way more laid-back than them. We can teach you everything you need to know about the big animals—just come with a good attitude and a sense of humor." I was delighted to have found a qualified and nice person to fill Holly's big shoes.

While driving into town to dump trash and fetch the mail from the post office, I was fantasizing about how nice it would be to have a veterinary assistant on our team. I had worked nearly ten years without one, and my body was feeling the effects. I was pretty sure I couldn't afford one, but if they improved the efficiency of the practice, wouldn't it be the right thing to do? Just as I turned the sharp curve into town, I had to slam on the brakes, narrowly avoiding the back end of a dump truck. I crept behind the truck, stoplight after stoplight, through the tiny town lined with light posts, each bearing an American flag. By the third light, I peered through the cloud of thick black exhaust into the driver's-side mirror of the truck. The reflection in the mirror was familiar. It appeared to be Christina. Christina's parents owned a beef cattle farm on the lake.

I honked my horn and motioned for her to pull over. She obediently guided the dump truck off the road, because she was raised to obey her elders too. Christina leaned out of the truck window, with her long muscular arm and the messy bun preceding the rest of her. She pushed her bedazzled sunglasses up on the top of her head and peered at me curiously with big brown eyes. As I approached her window, I hollered, "Christina, honey, what are you doing driving a dump truck?"

Christina shouted over the idling engine, "Well, I just graduated from Tech a few months ago and I needed money, so I'm working for Dad at the moment."

"A smart gal like you with an animal science degree should be working with animals. Don't you agree?"

Christina raised her dark eyebrows in curiosity. "Yes, I'd much prefer the animals."

"Well then, be at my place at eight sharp on Monday. You'll be a fantastic addition to my team." I knew Christina was the real deal ever since a few years ago when I saw the ladies at the county fair trying to get the thick black grease out from under her fingernails so she could compete in the beauty contest.

Several months passed with the Veterinary Service fully staffed. On a manic Monday morning, Savannah was running late for work, driving like a madwoman down the little country road to the vet clinic. She had already gotten herself, her kiddos, and her husband ready for their day, and now it was time to come help her vets get their days sorted. Speeding past a little abandoned white cinder block building, she glanced in the rearview mirror and saw the blue lights.

Savannah obediently pulled over to talk to the officer. She was calm and cool on the outside, but she was seething on the inside. Finally, she snatched the ticket out of his hand and jerked her sunglasses back down to hide her disgust.

The way Savannah stomped through the door with her long blonde hair swinging, it was easy to tell she was a woman on a mission. She looked like somebody had pissed in her Cheerios for sure. Savannah went off on a rant: "Y'all won't believe it. There was a freakin' cop hiding behind the tree line at the little white cinder block building, and he busted me for speeding."

"Sorry, girl. Maybe we'll get lucky and one of the lawyer's dogs will need stitches soon?" I gave her my condolences and some pointers on getting the ticket reduced. God knows we large animal vets get plenty of speeding tickets and know about every trick in the book to get out of them.

Around lunchtime, I called to check in with Savannah. "Where to next, boss?"

"Nothing new, just proceed to the next farm on the schedule. One quick question, though: Could me and Christina borrow your chain saw during our lunch break?" Savannah sounded desperate.

"I reckon. Tell Christina it's out in the shed. I don't know what you girls are up to, but please be careful."

When I got back to the office from my calls, Savannah and Christina were sitting in the office, giggling. I asked, "Why did you lovely ladies need the chain saw?"

Christina began explaining, "We had to take care of some business." Christina, like Savannah, was in her early twenties. She was smart, strong, and had grown up around her father's excavation business, so there was no piece of equipment she couldn't run, and no job was too big. "After I heard Savannah's heart-wrenching story of the speeding ticket, we devised a plan to make sure that SOB could never hide behind those bushes at that abandoned building ever again."

The girls waited until the cop went to lunch and moved in. Savannah stood guard at the road sporting her blue blockers and holding her lit Marlboro between her finely manicured fingers. She stood guard while Christina wreaked havoc on the line of shrubs that provided a blind for the cop. Christina worked diligently. After she finished, it looked like Edward Scissorhands had been there. The girls exchanged a high five and hopped back in the car to return to work as though nothing had happened.

When I heard the story, I did what any smart woman would do. I googled "How to remove fingerprints from a crime scene." Then I wiped the chain saw down with rubbing alcohol and a lot of elbow grease and never said a word to the girls.

CATS:
THE OTHER RED MEAT

"**E**xcuse me, sir, did you say fifty-one cats?" Savannah scribbled notes as she twirled her long blonde locks. "OK, sir, we should be able to take care of that." By this time, her conversation had drawn us all to the office, like bugs to the neon bug zapper. Dr. Lesley, Christina, and I hovered, waiting for Savannah to hang up so we could get the scoop.

Finally, she hung up. She turned to us and said, "Y'all won't believe this!"

"Believe what?" Christina blurted, throwing her hands in the air. "Out with it. You're killing us with suspense."

"This dude two counties away has fifty-one cats. He needs them rabies vaccinated at his place, and he needs them done by Monday of next week or else."

"That's a lot of pussy," Dr. Lesley said. She and Christina doubled over in laughter.

I asked, "And why, pray tell, did we agree to this, Savannah?" I did poach Savannah from a cat-only veterinary practice, but we were large animal veterinarians—we couldn't afford to be getting bitten and scratched by a bunch of ill-behaved felines.

"He sounded pretty desperate, and I kind of felt sorry for him," Savannah said defensively. "And think of the money. You gals can do it. I have faith."

Dr. Lesley and I talked it over and decided to tag-team this project, since handling cats can be difficult and their bites are nasty. Dr. Lesley and I trusted each other implicitly, and that was critical when our safety was at stake. Christina was young and didn't have much cat experience; we were afraid that if a cat tried to bite her, she'd throw it through a window.

Dr. Lesley and I engineered our Monday to meet up at my place for our after-hours cat-wrestling experience. We thought it wise to put it near the end of the day in case we needed an adult beverage afterward.

Dr. Lesley and I pulled up to the house. The brick rancher generally appeared unloved, with its front stairs falling off. The large, attached sunroom had all the windows spray-painted black. In the garage was a broken-down bright purple SUV with expensive rims. Were drugs involved in this situation? I try to be a good Christian and not judge, but I watch too many police shows.

Walking toward our truck was a white guy of moderate height and hefty build with a brown mullet and dark transitional lenses. He had the Texas state trooper look, complete with a tattered Metallica T-shirt, camouflage cargo pants, and black boots. "Afternoon, ladies. The name's Sean. Thanks for helping me out. We'll start with the colony of female cats, then move to the males, and finish with the nursing females," he stated matter-of-factly.

Nursing females? In our neck of the woods, there's typically nobody breeding cats on purpose!

We attempted to keep open minds and started filling syringes with the watermelon pink vaccine. I stuck cat after cat with the vaccine while Dr. Lesley clutched their scruffs with her small, strong hands. Her grip was so powerful that every knuckle on her right hand was turning white over her exquisitely defined metacarpal bones.

With each cat we vaccinated, I scribbled their name on a small notepad stashed in the chest pocket of my coveralls.

"Sir, what is this cat's name?" I asked.

"Ummm, Cookie."

"Cookie? Are you sure? I feel like this is the third female cat named Cookie." I was beginning to smell a rat. Sean seemed to be making up the names as he went along; Buttercream, Cinnamon Stick, Pumpkin Pie, Sugar and Spice. Most of these cats, who seemed to be named after Yankee Candles, acted as if they'd barely experienced the human touch.

Eventually, we moved onto the back deck of the house to the pen of male cats; Dr. Lesley and I marveled at just how large these cats were. Maybe he was justified in calling a large animal vet? The necks of the intact male cats were massive, with sharply defined muscles that seemed wider than the base of their skull. It was going to be extremely difficult to restrain them. Of course, it was my turn to hold the cats for Dr. Lesley. After about six cats, my hand started to cramp.

The male cat pen was complicated to work in because there were two stories, complete with a large metal pole extending from the roof to the basement. Occasionally a cat would descend to the lower level before we'd gotten it vaccinated. I leaned over to Dr. Lesley when the owner was off chasing a cat and whispered, "Do you reckon the cats are firefighters or strippers?" She cackled as she shook her head.

Once we finished the males, Sean went into the creepy room with the spray-painted windows and, one by one, brought out the nursing female cats. It was clear by their mammary development these ladies were nursing several litters of kittens. After vaccinating the third nursing female, I blurted, "Why are you so desperate to appease animal control? What's going on here?"

He sheepishly began to explain. "Well, I'm in a bit of trouble with animal control. It all started with the snakes."

Dr. Lesley and I looked at each other. I couldn't restrain myself from asking, "And where do the snakes live?"

"Would you ladies like to see them?" he said. "They're in the basement."

A tiny voice inside me was urging me to skip the viewing of the snakes. I ignored it and went into detective mode. "Yes, sir, we'd love to see the snakes."

Dr. Lesley elbowed me in the gut and gave me a sideways glance. Sean led us to the basement. We walked into the first room and saw tall metal shelves on every wall containing hundreds of uncapped Rubbermaid containers. Duct tape on the containers stated how many male and female snakes were in each. Before following the owner into the next room, I whispered to Dr. Lesley, "Take some pictures while I distract him." I was certain this would be the part where we ended up on an episode of *Dateline*.

The snakes in the next room were much larger and more beautiful. They were ball pythons. The one on the farthest wall was bright shimmering yellow and was thirty feet long. While surrounded by robust reptiles, I did what any good southern woman would have done. I asked in a sweet, innocent tone, "Why are ya raising snakes?"

Our mysterious new acquaintance replied with a dejected expression, "Selling snakes on the internet used to be a booming business. Nowadays lots of people are selling snakes online, and it's not nearly as lucrative."

Dr. Lesley entered the room gazing around like a kid at Epcot Center as I asked, "Any chance we could handle the snakes?" Dr. Lesley glared at me as if she were using lasers coming out of her pupils to slit my jugular veins.

"No, ma'am. That's probably not a good idea since we have the cat smell on us." At that moment, all our questions were answered. I suppose I had never really thought too hard about cats being used for food. We got our money in small, unmarked bills and got the hell out of Dodge. As we predicted, we needed several adult beverages when we got back to our office.

NINE LIVES

"*A*aaaahhhhh! Ahhhh! Help! Please help me!" All of us working around the cattle chute instantly stopped what we were doing to try to figure out where the screaming was coming from. Had someone gotten injured? Were the cows escaping? What was the problem? We quickly discovered the screaming was coming from Pops, who was standing at the back end of the cattle chute on this sweltering Independence Day. He was holding his hand over his left ear, screaming more and more loudly. Dr. Lesley and I ran to him to try to assess the situation while his son Charles called 911.

Pops, the seventy-five-year-old patriarch of this large-scale beef operation, had worked hard all his life to provide for his family and keep this farm going despite a series of farming accidents. Several years ago, he had been electrocuted while carrying an antenna across a cornfield from one house to another. At one point a tree fell on his leg (already with impaired nerves from the electrocution) and broke it. One of the scariest episodes was when he had silo-filler's disease severely affecting his lungs from a grain bin encounter gone wrong. Many farmers aren't lucky enough to survive the dangerous fumes of nitrogen dioxide. In agricultural areas, firefighters often go through special training to attend to farmers who are trapped in grain bins to give them a better chance of survival. And through the years, just like on many farms, several cattle had run Pops over. He never complained about his bad luck; in his strong, quiet way, he got up each day and went back

166

out to do his work. Farming is consistently in the top ten most dangerous occupations in the world, and many people take that for granted.

What was the issue with Pops today? How many lives could he possibly have left? I started quizzing him, trying to get a clue about what was happening, and he just continued clutching his left ear.

He began to cry, bent over at the waist, and wailed, "Help me! Please help me!"

The wailing turned to silence as he started falling. I managed to catch him just before he hit the ground. I braced his distressed body in my arms. "Pops, where do you hurt?"

He was crying so hard that he was jerking. "My ear, my ear . . ."

I looked over to Dr. Lesley. "Run to the truck and get the longest pair of hemostats you can find from the cold sterile pack. Hurry."

Dr. Lesley was an avid runner, so she was back in record time with the hemostats.

"Reach in there and see if you can pull something out," I ordered. I wasn't usually quite so bossy, but Pops was a father figure to me and I just couldn't stand seeing him in so much pain.

Within seconds, Dr. Lesley hoisted a tiny, evil Japanese beetle from deep inside Pops's ear canal, complete with blood on his spiny short legs. Dr. Lesley's smile was so big I think she may have blinded drivers on the road with her ultra-white teeth. Pops finally breathed a sigh of relief, and his crying turned into laughter as he watched her examine the beetle.

About then, the rescue squad arrived. Out in the country, we are dependent on volunteer rescue squads, but for farming accidents, we are even more dependent on veterinarians. The boys from the squad gave Pops a once-over and congratulated Dr. Lesley on saving him from the beetle.

When we finally got enough internet service to consult Google, we learned that a Japanese beetle can claw through the human eardrum in twenty to thirty seconds. This has happened to other unfortunate people that weren't lucky enough to be standing beside a veterinarian. Vet Service—1, Beetle—0.

We did what any good God-fearing vet would do: we gave Pops hugs and kisses, finished working the cows, then took the evil little bastard home and put him in the freezer, in case we wanted to have him crafted into the bottom of a shot glass!

Eight years later, Pops was spending his Fourth of July out in the tractor feeding cows when he suddenly developed intractable stomach pain. As the day went on, the pain worsened enough for his wife, Betty, to take him to the emergency room. Once the doctor looked at the images, he gave them the awful news nobody wants to hear. Pops was diagnosed with stage four pancreatic cancer. How could it be possible for this dear man who had been like a father to me to have a terminal diagnosis? Maybe they were wrong and he'd just swallowed a beetle?

Although he was shocked and upset by the diagnosis, Pops accepted it with the same strength and dignity he'd accepted all his misfortune through the years. He decided to come back to the farm and live out his last few months. Rather than wallowing in sorrow, Pops wanted to celebrate life while he was still living.

On the night of the party, strings of bright white lights were draped through the walnut trees in the front yard of the big farmhouse. The smell of freshly cooked barbecue filled the night air as people continued to pour in. Little girls in sundresses twirled around and around on the dance floor as the DJ played Red Steagall's "Somewhere My Love." Pops sat in his comfortable lawn chair in the middle of the front lawn, wearing his Quaker Hill Farm hat and greeting over five hundred of his favorite people. The entire yard was filled with a community of people that had one thing in common: their love and respect for Pops.

WATER BIRTH

*E*very deafening raindrop smacking onto my windshield was more and more irritating. The poor windshield wipers just couldn't work any harder. As a farm girl, I understand the importance of rain, but I remember Grandma McCall telling me, "Too much of anything is not a good thing."

It was the wettest fall Virginia had experienced in over fifty years; it had rained nearly every day for six straight months. The ground was so saturated the pastures had turned from green grass to brown mud. The farmers couldn't get a second or a third cutting of hay, which the cows would need to survive over the winter. Most of the farmers couldn't even harvest their small grains this year. The fall cows were starting to calve, and checking cows had become an exercise in mud bogging. The pitiful little soaked calves only got refuge from the rain by poking their heads under their mother's flank to nurse. The last time I'd seen this much rain, I was a student in Ireland. If this is what it takes to get grass that green, then count me out!

Decked out in every piece of rain gear I owned, I headed out to deliver a calf for a young guy named Ronnie who had a cow having trouble birthing. He rented a small farm in a beautiful area in the foothills of the mountains of Greene County. Ronnie, the cattle trader, was quite an animated character. He had short blond hair and strutted around with a chew of tobacco in his cheek and his chest poked out like a banty rooster. When I arrived, he explained,

"Honey, I don't have no catch pen here, and I ain't building one 'cause it's rented land. I think I can sneak up and slip a rope on her, though." I had been practicing for ten years now, and I'd heard that many times. Rarely did it ever work out as the confident farmer predicted.

Ronnie grabbed the lariat rope and started to prowl along the tree line in the direction of the cow lying quietly under a dilapidated walnut tree. When he changed his trajectory and started walking toward the cow, her eyes got big, and she jumped up and bolted—the look I see every month when my border collie realizes I have flea preventative in my hand instead of a treat. I shook my head, knowing what could have been an easy job had now turned into a rodeo. Not to mention that my truck was probably going to get stuck in the mud again today and we'd have to find a tractor to pull me out.

I finally had saved up enough money after buying the vet business to buy a brand-new work truck for myself. After just a few weeks in service, "Big Red" had mud in every possible orifice, and the flimsy plastic around every tow hook was cracked from being rescued repeatedly by tractors. The soles of my recently purchased Muck boots were being held together with duct tape from traipsing through quagmire after quagmire. One of my older farmers said to me, "Young lady, I'm going to give you a little extra cash to put toward a new pair of boots." Who knew a few pieces of duct tape were better than a GoFundMe page?

I wondered where the spastic cow would end up. She was on high ground when we first approached her, but now her only choice was to go in or near standing water. Not this again!

"Ronnie, man, is there any way we can keep that crazy hussy from going into the pond?"

With a thin stream of tobacco juice running down his lip, he explained, "Oh, honey, that is not a pond. It's a big-ass dip in the land that fills with water during flood seasons. The old-timers say sometimes the water would freeze in here in the winter, then they would chip ice out of it and sell it to people in Charlottesville."

Well, guess where the cow went . . . right out in the middle of the big-ass depression full of water! How is it that pregnant women can barely stand up from the toilet in their third trimester of pregnancy, and cows turn into superstar triathletes? I started to strip off my outer layer of clothing and kick off my boots. Much to my surprise, Ronnie started to strip, too, except he was taking off his jeans. *Oh, dear God, not his jeans!* The only lucky break I had all day was that Ronnie was wearing underwear, and fortunately they were ugly boxer shorts instead of whitey tighties. He hiked up his T-shirt into a crop-top formation, baring his snow-white, fuzzy belly.

I grabbed a rope, placed it over my shoulder, and went boldly forth into the great flooded unknown. Ronnie followed as I waded carefully through the waist-deep murky water. I could feel lots of objects touching my bare feet. Some were squishy and some were hard. I tried not to dwell on what each object might be. I thought this might be God's way of getting me back for making fun of my sister for cringing every time a piece of seaweed touched her ankle at the beach. Everything I stepped on made me wonder more and more about when I had my last tetanus shot.

When we finally made it to the buoyant bovine, Ronnie slipped the rope around her neck. I moved around to her back end and reached inside of her to see if I could feel the calf. As I expected, the calf was dead, but I told Ronnie, "We need to get her out of this germ pool so I can attach a calf jack and get this calf out of her."

Just then, a neighbor came driving a tractor across the field. He was a small-framed, middle-aged man in bib overalls and dark glasses, but to me, he was a knight in shining armor. The neighbor stopped the tractor and watched as half-naked Ronnie stood on the solid ground trying to pull the cow by the rope as I swam behind her, pushing her. He exclaimed, "What in the Sam Hill is going on here?"

"Sir, can you please bring that tractor closer so we can tie the cow to it and pull her out of the water?" I shouted to him. He nodded. We finally got the patient to the mushy ground by the edge of the water. I fetched my trusty calf jack from the truck and carefully attached it to the back of the expectant mother. I placed the obstetrical chains attached to each foot of the calf into the hooks of the jack and begin to click the ratchets. One foot advanced, then the other, slowly and meticulously. When the cow would strain from a contraction, we used the long arm of the calf jack as a lever, pushing down toward the ground to help gently stretch her vaginal tissue. The calf's head began to appear through her vaginal vault. The black tongue was sticking out of the lifeless, oversized baby. Patiently, I continued jacking while instructing Ronnie to lever the jack: "Up, now down, up, down, up, now down, hold it, good." You'd have thought we were starring in an exercise video. Ronnie did bear a striking resemblance to Richard Simmons with his crop top and super-short boxers—all he was missing was the headband.

Once the hips came through the pelvis, I jacked the remainder of the calf out onto the ground. Ronnie pulled the calf jack away from the cow and tossed it to the side while I got the cow a dose of pain medication and an antibiotic. As cattle veterinarians, we pride ourselves on using antibiotics judiciously and making calculated decisions to ensure we're using the appropriate one. We are working on the public's food supply, and we take that responsibility seriously even when it seems like we're doubling as rodeo clowns. I wasn't even sure what the appropriate antibiotic choice would be for having an arm shoved up your womb for that long in a glorified swamp. The cow was clearly pissed off, but she was too tired to fight. I finished treating her and released her from the rope.

I met Ronnie down at the gate to collect my earnings, wondering how on earth I'd ever charge for such an ordeal. While I was figuring up his bill from inside my truck, I could see him out of the corner of my eye, peeling his wet T-shirt off. He carefully tried to position himself in my line of vision. He approached my open window shirtless, drying his hair with a hand towel. He handed cash through the window to pay his bill and winked. "You could follow me to my place and get out of those wet clothes if you want."

"I don't think my boyfriend would like that too much, so I'm going to pass on your kind offer." I tried to be polite while containing my laughter.

The dejected Ronnie replied, "Well, hon, if you change your mind, just let me know."

On my way home, there was a beautiful rainbow forming over the mountains. I peered over my shoulder. Lo and behold, the end of the rainbow appeared to be directly over Ronnie's ice pond. But I knew there was no pot of gold there.

COLD HANDS, WARM HEARTS

*I*magine being so cold that you would consider urinating on yourself to warm up? Here's a pro tip . . . it works for exactly twenty-five seconds. I wasn't quite that cold on this winter day, but I was plenty cold. I had just walked back into the office to warm up and grab a bowl of soup. It was the coldest winter I had ever experienced in central Virginia, and we were now three long months into this relentless deep freeze.

Dr. Lesley started her veterinary career in North Dakota before relocating to New Zealand, so she shared several tidbits of wisdom for surviving the cold. The night before, when the temperature fell below zero, she suggested we plug the block heaters in on the trucks and that we leave the diesel trucks running all night long so they wouldn't freeze. If there were a middle-of-the-night emergency, we certainly wouldn't want to be held up by struggling to get a truck started. She also bought us a box of hand warmers to put in our pockets to help prevent frostbite. Sliding my numb fingers into the pocket with the hand warmer reminded me of getting into the car warmed by the blazing sun after swimming in a cold pool all day. The glorious warmth had a way of providing instant comfort.

While standing in the kitchen opening my can of soup, I overheard my new secretary, Debbie, on an interesting phone call. When you're the business owner, you have to give the verdict on how to handle the strange clients and the unusual requests. After owning the business for three years, I was starting to get more comfortable with the decision-making, even the strange ones. Debbie hung up and shouted, "Dr. M, that call was from an older gentleman named Brother something. He sounded very distressed, and he needs a call back from you ASAP."

We only have one client who goes by "Brother." Brother Giovanni is a self-professed Franciscan monk and has lived with his flock of goats in the wild for many years. His business is land clearing—he and his goats move from place to place, clearing land sustainably. Brother G pitches a tent and goes everywhere the goats go. He truly lives off the land. I had known Brother G for several years because he had cleared land for some of my clients. I'd even provided medical care to a few of his goats. One sweltering summer, when Brother G was having some health issues himself, I begged him to leave the goats and go to a hospital. He told me he had a pact with God, and part of this was that he would live with the goats to the end of his life.

Uncertain of what to expect, I picked up the phone to return Brother G's call. The voice that answered was frail and shaky. "Dr. Melinda, thank you, dear, so much for returning my call. The goats and I are in dire straits. I don't know what to do, and I need your help," he pleaded. "The goats are dying, and I'm afraid pretty soon I'm going to die too."

"Listen, Brother G, I know you have a pact with God and all, but would you consider coming to my house where it's warm?" I begged. "I'd hate to see anything bad happen to you."

"There's nowhere for the goats to go. I simply wouldn't feel right leaving my family behind to die. Is there any way you could help me stop the goats from dying?"

Dr. Lesley happened to walk into the office still bundled up in her winter gear. I told her, "Before you get too comfy, hop in the old truck with no vet box."

"The old truck? What's up? Is everything OK?" Dr. Lesley obediently climbed into the front seat and slammed the squeaky door.

"We're going on a mission to save some lives. Both human and animal."

We stopped at Goodwill and bought several sets of long handle underwear, two sweatshirts, one heavy winter coat, and two pairs of gloves and socks. Next, we went to the local feed store and bought a new pair of insulated Muck boots. We had the guys in the warehouse fill the bed of the truck with straw, hay, tarps, and goat feed. Then, we drove around Hardee's and got a large combo burger meal with a hot coffee and a piping hot apple turnover. Finally, we headed out by the lake to find our struggling friend.

Upon our arrival at the farm, we saw Brother G's old jeep tracks in the snow. We followed the tracks down the hill through nearly two feet of snow.

The first thing we saw was a large pile of deceased goats. Most appeared to be very old and thin, along with a few mothers and young babies. Finally, we got to one rickety small tent. When I peeked through the door, there lay Brother G curled up asleep among several large goats, some dead and some still living. We took a good look around the camp and evaluated the two shelters that had been damaged by the heavy snow.

Dr. Lesley and I just looked at each other. We literally couldn't believe what we were seeing. My heart hurt so much.

"You're sure he won't leave here, right?" she asked.

"Girl, have you ever tried to talk anybody into breaking a pact with God? He'd listen about as well as the horse ladies when you tell them not to get any more horses. It's seriously easier for us to just repair these shelters. Let's just get to work." I started by dragging the goat carcasses to the dead pile. Brother G roused upon hearing the commotion.

Every time we started pulling another corpse to the pile, Brother G would tell us the goat's name and a bit about their personality.

"Such a shame about Milly. She was such a gentle soul . . . and a spiritual leader in our community. Only one of her babies survived. I named him Isidore, from the Greek meaning *strong gift*." I could tell seeing these lifeless bodies stacked on a funeral pyre had caused enough traumatic emotional stress to break his heart. It was as if he'd lost a significant portion of his family over the past few weeks.

Next, we repaired the two large tent structures. We worked together to clear the snow from the tarps, then pulled them tight and reinforced them at the base. We toted bale after heavy bale of straw through the deep snow and filled the inside of the shelters. Just an hour ago, these shelters had looked shabby and abandoned. Now, with some slight modifications to the tarps and a deep bed of golden straw, they nearly looked inviting.

Finally, we needed to address Brother G's tent. We used shovels to clean out the soiled goat bedding. Buck ass has a distinct odor that doesn't belong where humans reside, and Brother G had plenty of buck goats because he didn't believe in castrating them. Next, we spent some time repairing the holes in the tarps and hanging new tarps so that no snow could get inside the shelter. We bedded the entire back area with fresh straw that he and the goats would sleep on, diligently keeping it away from his propane burner in the front of the tent.

Once we completed all the shelter preparation, we strategically placed flakes of nutritious green hay in several areas throughout the shelters and poured heaping mounds of textured grain on each flake. Neither Dr. Lesley nor I was a good cook, but today we felt like we'd prepared a meal fit for a king. When we allowed the goats access to the shelters, we each policed a shelter to ensure the goats wouldn't hurt each other fighting with their long, curved horns. They wouldn't intentionally hurt each other, but they were very hungry, and their instinct to fight for survival is strong.

After getting the goats situated, we helped Brother G get into his new winter gear and placed the extra clothes in his jeep. I always wondered what it would feel like to be Santa Claus. And Dr. Lesley made such a cute elf. Brother G's eyes lit up, pulling the corners of his lips up toward his ears as we pulled out each piece of apparel. I thought of how some children rolled their eyes when they got clothes for Christmas. I guess they were fortunate enough to have never been cold. Brother G exclaimed, "Ladies, I'm seventy-five years old, and I have never had such a nice, warm pair of boots in my whole life."

While we cleaned up our mess and tied up a few loose ends, Brother G sat in my warm truck with the heater blasting as he chowed down on his meal and sipped warm coffee. A man who just hours ago was experiencing hopelessness and disgust was now content and filled with gratitude. "You girls are my angels. I promise that God will protect and provide for both of you for all your days on Earth. I can't thank you enough for what you've done for me and my family today."

"We're glad you reached out to us. The bad weather is supposed to continue for at least another couple of weeks, so we'll be checking in on you all every few days. If you get in a bind and can think of anything you need, please call us." I hugged him, holding my breath to prevent inhaling too much buck ass odor. Dr. Lesley did the same; she always said the odor burned the inside of her nose.

I peered into the rearview mirror to watch our smiling, frail friend in his tall black boots waving goodbye.

PLEASE,
NOT ONE MORE VET

While driving down a long stretch of road, I dialed up Robin for a status check on how things were going at the Veterinary Medical Association. Being on the executive board was a new responsibility for me. I joined the board in 2009 but had been newly elected to this leadership position in 2015, and I wanted to do my part to make the organization successful.

Robin, the lead administrator of the organization, is usually chipper and upbeat. She is the lady who makes us think everything is OK, whether it is or not. Today, her tone was somber.

"Is everything OK, Robin?" I didn't know what else to do but ask.

"Well, Dr. Melinda, I just received some very bad news. Dr. Day passed away today."

We had both worked with Dr. Day on the board for several years. He was only in his early forties. "What do you mean? What happened?" I pulled the truck off the road so I could process this information. My mind had been so foggy lately, and I was exhausted all the time. Normally, multitasking was my forte, but not these days.

"He took his own life. I'm so sorry to have to tell you this, dear." Robin was sobbing.

I laid my forehead on top of the steering wheel, my mind blank. A more appropriate response to the news would have been to cry, but I was too numb for that. I refused to believe it until I got to that next meeting and the chair beside me was empty.

Dr. Day was a very put-together, respected, successful professional. I went over our last conversation. I must have missed something, some warning sign. We were sitting at the hotel meeting room stuffing our faces with lovely spring mix salads slathered with balsamic vinaigrette, likely to disguise the lack of vegetables, discussing his recent trip to Prague. I remember how jealous I was hearing about the good food, fine wine, and interesting sights he and his fiancée had enjoyed. For the life of me, I couldn't recall anything at all being wrong. He and I had snickered at the concept of self-care when it was brought up. His life sounded perfect. And his treasurer's reports at that meeting were right down to the penny.

I had recently read a report in the *Journal of the American Veterinary Medical Association* that veterinarians were 2.7 times more likely than the general public to die by suicide, but it didn't seem very real to me, since I didn't know any vets who had committed suicide. Something I did know well is that we have a lot of risk factors for suicide, including long work hours, never-ending practice management responsibilities, high student debt, poor work/life balance, and access to euthanasia solution.

After the untimely death of Dr. Day, many of us involved in organized veterinary medicine began to work together to create resources for our colleagues, including our veterinary technicians, staff members, and their families. Our organization spent a decent amount of money on an employee assistance program. The managers of this program were required to send us a monthly report on its use. Each month that the fatality report was zero, we felt like the money had been well spent. Our organization also pooled our resources to create an endowed scholarship for one veterinary student in our state each year to honor the memory of Dr. Day. The passing of Dr. Day was a tragedy, but knowing that there was at least one veterinary student a year who would not have to struggle with finances for most of their life was comforting.

Around the same time in 2015, other veterinarians were being called to action. While perusing social media one night, I stumbled upon an online organization working to help prevent veterinary suicide called Not One More Vet. I immediately joined so I could read the tales of woe from twenty thousand other veterinarians around the world. I was incredibly saddened yet comforted to think we weren't alone in our struggles. Some had issues I was all too familiar with, and some were facing issues I'd never even considered. For instance, cyberbullying: Why on earth would a person completely dehumanize another human being in such a brash, public fashion? And why would a compassionate professional take these words so personally they would consider ending their own life? This is not something I had to deal with much, working mostly on animals who were eaten if the outcome was substandard. After reading story after story of compassionate, hardworking veterinarians, some of whom I knew personally, being punished for outcomes beyond their control, I remembered Dr. Marie in veterinary school teaching us about the human–animal bond and how pets were becoming a bigger part of families.

On the dairy, our working border collies lived outside. Under no circumstances were we allowed to bring a dog in the house. But it was clear that times were changing. I fondly remember Dad allowing us to bring a litter of puppies into the living room one winter. He'd just had his second back surgery, and this litter of puppies required bottle feeding. The only way my mother could manage to care for him and the puppies was to have them at his bedside. My sister, Ann, and I loved helping bottle-feed those fuzzy, plump babies, and Dad would quickly correct us if we were doing something wrong.

The more I pondered the human–animal bond, the more I could see that some humans were bonded to their animals more than they were to their family. Pets seemed to love their humans more unconditionally than some of their family members. I vividly remember going into an elderly gentleman's home to euthanize his dog. He sat alone in the chair in the cool, dark house with his old small brown mixed-breed dog curled up in his lap.

"Do you live alone, sir?" I asked, glancing around the empty living room.

He looked up at me from the chair with glassy blue eyes. "Yes, ma'am, it's just me and Buster. My wife died a few years ago and I have a daughter, but I haven't seen her in several years. We had a disagreement, and she has never come back home, not even when her mother passed. All I have is Buster, and soon I won't have him either." My heart ached for him.

EXPECTING
THE UNEXPECTED

*T*he fluorescent lights shone in my face as I lay stretched out in the dentist's chair, wearing my insulated overalls speckled with cow manure. I meant to pull them off in the parking lot, but I rushed into my appointment late from an emergency veterinary call. I barely remembered the days when I could schedule an appointment and make it on time wearing clean clothing. I knew Katie, the dental hygienist, wouldn't care. She was used to the aroma of animal feces from her sister, Dr. Lesley.

I was grateful to be in a warm place where I could lie down for a bit. The peace and quiet were just what I needed after the stressful birth I had just assisted. That mama goat screamed so loud when my hand entered her vagina that my ears were still ringing. I tried to make the experience as pleasant as possible; I was very gentle and used obstetrical lube and everything. Some procedures just can't be sugarcoated.

Katie entered the room as though she were walking on air, chatting about her upcoming wedding to her partner, Angela. "How have you been doing? Are you taking good care of my little sister? She said y'all have been busy lately." Katie placed the bib around my neck and smiled.

"Yes, we have been busy, considering it's still technically winter. Usually the birthing season starts closer to the spring, but not this year. They are running us ragged." I tried to get my sentence finished before she started working in my mouth.

"Chica, we need to take X-rays today. No chance you're pregnant, right?" She placed the awkward film cassettes in my mouth.

It was a reflex to blurt out, "No, of course not," but this was the first time the question ever resonated with me. Katie started snapping the X-rays. Was there a chance? There wasn't a chance of rain today, but it rained. There was a chance I'd make it to my dentist appointment on time, but that was a bust. I had been feeling so rough for the past seven weeks, but I just thought the cold winter and the physical nature of my work were wearing on me as I approached forty years old. I was extremely tired and very moody, and even the thought of eating made me nauseous.

As Katie scurried around working on my teeth, all I could do was stare into the bright light she'd pulled down close to my face. This is how a deer must feel right before he gets hit by a car. I could hear Katie talking, but I couldn't process her words. I was racking my brain to think where the closest pharmacy was. When Katie finished, I hopped out of the chair, gave her a hug, and thanked her. I was hell-bent on getting an answer to the question that she had just made me ans wer. And when a southern woman is hell-bent on something, the best thing you can do is to stay out of her way.

I jumped into the vet truck and hauled ass to the tiny pharmacy a few buildings down on Main Street. It took me a bit to find the aisle with the pregnancy tests, but I wasn't about to ask. No way on earth. I also purchased some completely random items, including a pack of gum, a newspaper, and a Mountain Dew (because I was pretty sure it would be my last one for a while).

"Do you have a restroom, sir?" I asked the oblivious male clerk, trying to remain cool and collected.

"Yes, ma'am. All the way in the back to the left. Have a good day, ma'am." He began to check out the next customer.

The instructions that came with the kit seemed so complicated.

I reckoned those must have been written by a man because a woman would have a simple three-step picture guide. She would have realized how high the stakes were for getting a quick answer to this life-changing question.

Once I had completed the test, I waited the longest five minutes of my life. Most of the women I had sat with while waiting on this result were brimming with excitement at the thought of getting a positive. I, on the other hand, was scared to death.

When the timer rang on my phone, I looked down to discover what I had feared the most: two pink lines. How could I have let this happen? I was a reproductive expert, for God's sake!

But all experts are human beings. And why was I so scared? I wouldn't let a two-thousand-pound bull intimidate me, so why should I let these two measly pink lines?

Over the next couple of days, I kept my secret in order to process it. I decided to share the news with Dr. Lesley because I had to tell someone before I exploded. She had a level head and a big heart. Our line of work requires handling reproductive hormones and large animals who kick and have unpredictable behavior, so I would definitely need her to know about my condition so she could help protect us. I called her in a shaky voice and asked her to meet me at a restaurant near her last call.

"Everything OK? You sound upset," Dr. Lesley said.

"I got some news that I need to share with you," I replied while speeding along.

At the restaurant, Dr. Lesley greeted me with one of her famous super tight hugs, and we sat down. "I don't even know how to say this, so I'm just gonna say it . . . I'm pregnant." I leaned my elbows on the table and put my face in my hands. "Your sister helped me come to this realization."

"Holy balls, Melinda. I thought you were going to say you had cancer or something. Congratulations! That's way better than cancer." Dr. Lesley smiled so big I was nearly blinded by her pearly white teeth.

"Well, now that you mention it, a fast-growing mass grows inside of you until it begins to compromise the function of your organs, like your bladder and lungs, so I'd say there are some striking similarities." I shook my head, closed my eyes, and took a deep breath.

"What did Lewis say? Have you told him yet?"

"No, hell no, I haven't told him." I nibbled on the pub mix the waitress had placed on the table. "I don't know how to tell him, so I'm still devising a plan for that."

Lewis and I had been dating for nearly seven years. He was a good-hearted, hardworking farmer. I felt sure that after he got over the shock factor, he'd be excited about the news and we could iron out the details.

I had so much to figure out about how this baby was going to fit into my life. I certainly wasn't the first pregnant large animal veterinarian; this was not uncharted water. Dr. Kate, and other mentors, would be able to offer advice to help me stay safe and comfortable in the months ahead. I decided my first steps would be to make an appointment with an obstetrician and to try and change my attitude from apprehension to excitement, since I firmly believe everything, and I mean everything, happens for a reason.

BOOTY BLING

"Come quick, Doc, the old cow has thrown out her womb!" Annie Rose exclaimed on the other end of the line. Being a thirty-seven-year-old pregnant veterinarian, I felt a new sense of kinship for those words. I was certainly no spring chicken—the OB doctor preferred to use the phrase "advanced maternal age"—and I spent nearly every day devising tactics I would employ to keep my own womb from falling out. Dr. Lesley kept a pretty good eye on me, but she simply couldn't be everywhere, so our trusty veterinary technician K.P. would often come with me to make sure I was behaving myself and to help do the heavy lifting. K.P. was excellent at keeping things orderly; she always looked professional with her clean coveralls and her dark hair pulled back in a ponytail through her ball cap.

It was the last week of April, and the spring calving cows were in the full swing of birthing. Annie Rose met me at the driveway of the house, out of breath from worry.

"Follow me. The ol' cow is in the back forty." Secretly, I was delighted not to have to ride in the RTV—my unborn child would have brain damage for sure. Fluid is a good shock absorber, but there wasn't enough fluid in the human body to save the baby from riding across the groundhog holes in the cow pasture at eighty miles per hour. K.P. and I followed Annie Rose through pasture after pasture in the dirty maroon vet truck until a large black cow came into sight. Her dark silhouette stood out starkly against the beautiful white dogwood buds at the edge of the woods. The cow was desperately licking the lifeless calf lying on the ground in front of her. Her bloody womb protruded from her rear end. To say the cow was not having a very good day was an understatement.

"You want me to load a dart for her?" K.P. asked from the passenger seat. K.P. isn't a pessimist; she's a realist. She'd worked around animals most of her life, and she knew how unpredictable their behavior could be, especially when they weren't feeling well.

"Yeah, I reckon. God knows I'm in no shape to chase her down. I'm supposed to have my four-month OB checkup today. They probably wouldn't be favorably impressed if I came in with a cast." There was a day I would have roped that cow and tied her to a tree, but now there was another human being to protect; I had an obligation to safeguard my baby just like that mama cow had to protect hers.

Leaning over the tailgate and reaching up to the top drawer, K.P. resembled a bartender mixing a cocktail for the cow. She'd pull one milliliter of sedative out of one bottle, place it into another bottle, and shake it. She placed the two parts of the blowgun together and looked up in confusion. "Why is your blowpipe bent?"

"Well, when I was younger and faster, I shot a dart at a crazy heifer in the middle of a field from twenty feet away," I explained. "The part I forgot was that the truck was sixty feet away and the sedatives take ten minutes to work. When the heifer came running at me full throttle, I had no choice but to clock her over the head with the blowpipe. Dr. Kate wouldn't let me get a new one."

K.P.'s eyes were wide as she handed over the fully loaded blowgun. "Just to be safe, why don't you shoot this cow from the truck window?" she suggested.

As we inched closer to the cow in the big truck, she popped her head up and stared. I drew a big breath, further compromising my diaphragm, and blew forcefully into the pipe. It was a direct hit on the first attempt. The flying potion popped the cow in the hindquarter, causing her to go into a tailspin. Her massive, bright red uterus flopped from side to side so hard I was afraid it might fall off.

K.P. and I smiled at each other. I immediately backed the truck down the grassy knoll to give the cow some time to calm down and allow the high-powered sedatives to work their magic. Our moment of silence was interrupted by the obnoxiously loud ringtone of my cell phone. Normally I wouldn't try to answer a call out in the middle of a field, but I was expecting critical test results.

"Hello, can I help you?" I answered the phone in a gruff tone.

"Yes, ma'am. May I speak with Dr. Melinda? We have some results from her MaterniT 21 test," the polite lady said.

"This is she." My hand began to quiver and my heart rate steadily increased. "What did you find out? Is everything OK with the baby?" The more anxious I became, the more sedate the cow got. I watched as her head dropped and she started to drool profusely.

"Yes, ma'am. I am happy to report your baby does not have any genetic defects. And by the way, it's a girl. Congratulations." I could imagine the lab tech smiling warmly through the phone. K.P. overheard the conversation and grinned as she patted my arm.

As the cow plopped down on the ground, I decided I better not even try to process this news right now. K.P. and I hopped out of the truck and started gathering our supplies. The cow was sitting on her chest with her womb strewn out behind her, large enough to fill a five-gallon bucket. The intensely red mass was covered with fist-sized dark red meatballs called caruncles where the placenta had been attached.

"Annie Rose, can you help us pull this cow's feet straight back behind her, please? We need to put her in the frog-leg position." I hustled around to the opposite side of the cow.

Once the feet were positioned correctly, I carefully lifted the uterus up as K.P. slid a two-foot-long plastic tray underneath, propped evenly on the cow's pointy hocks. Dr. Kate always felt it was easier to get the cow's womb back in when she was positioned this way. I administered a spinal epidural and began the tedious job of cleaning up the cow's filthy uterus, while K.P. counted out the small metal hog rings we'd need to stitch her closed. The hog rings were designed to be placed in a pig's nose to help keep them from rooting, but large animal veterinarians use them for a multitude of tasks.

I felt like the pieces of debris covering the uterus were breeding as I scrubbed them. It seemed like a never-ending task. Finally, I peeled the last piece of the fetal cotyledon from the fleshy maternal caruncle so that all the afterbirth from the calf would be removed before I replaced the vascular organ. The corrugated, red caruncle closely resembled one of the intricate corals I used to see scuba diving. Staring at it, I wondered if I would ever get to scuba dive again.

Once the large, shiny womb was properly prepared for reentry, I handed Annie Rose the cow's tail to hold to the side. I sat on my knees behind the cow and began to push. While struggling to push, I chanted silently in my head: *What comes out must go in; what goes out must go in.* The progress was so slow that it was depressing. After fifteen minutes of hard pushing, I shouted to K.P., "Would you stand behind my feet so I will have something to push against? My feet are sliding."

"You got it." K.P. dutifully positioned herself behind my dirty Muck boots. I lay down behind the cow with my baby bump dragging the bare ground. K.P. held her position as my weight pressed hard against her strong ankles and I belly crawled to propel the uterus steadily back into the cow. Suddenly, our progress came to a screeching halt.

"Annie Rose, pull the plastic tray out," I barked.

"You sure about that?"

"Pull it. My boobs are hanging up on it and I need to get my body closer so I don't lose my progress. We're on the home stretch—just remove the freakin' tray!" As the tray slid out from under my incredibly tender breasts, a cool, moist sensation filled my midsection. Apparently, my whole body was going to have to support the weight of the remaining bloody, heavy uterus now. It was rather convenient to have a belly shelf to help push against, but it did put me pushing from a steeper angle than I was used to.

I continued to thrust forward using K.P.'s feet for leverage until the entire uterus was back inside the cow. I held it in with one hand while I laid my head on the cow's nasty rump in pure exhaustion. The feeling of the blood soaking into my ear, face, and hair didn't even faze me. Once I caught my breath, I continued to turn the entire length of the uterus right side in so it would stay in the cow. One of my vet school professors said the old vets used wine bottles for this task. I always suspected those vets just drank the wine to help them get through this tough job and then said they needed the bottle.

"Are you really supposed to be doing stuff like this in your condition?" Annie Rose asked as I placed hog ring after hog ring parallel to both sides of the cow's vulva.

"You mean making a cow's rear end look like a millennial at a nightclub?" I asked, and at least K.P. cracked a smile.

"No, silly girl. Replacing a cow's womb when you're knocked up?" Annie Rose, who didn't have children, was suddenly becoming very maternal. Comments like this were exactly the reason I had kept my condition a secret up to this point. Now the belly bump was giving me away, and I was forced to hear my clients' opinions. Some were ecstatic, some were concerned about the welfare of the unborn child, some were concerned I wouldn't be able to do my job, and some were upset that I wasn't married. The most maddening comment I would occasionally receive from my male farmers was, "Aren't you supposed to be a reproductive expert? How'd you let this happen?" Those words not only insulted my intelligence, but they also grated on my increasingly sensitive nerves.

"All I ever heard that doctor say was not to lift over twenty pounds. He never said a thing about pushing or pulling." I neatly threaded the thick white string through the pig rings until the cow's vulva looked like the top of a Converse sneaker.

Annie Rose snickered as she shook her head of tight, curly brown hair. "You ain't right."

K.P. drew up syringe after syringe of medicine for the dozing mama cow. I slowly administered the last dose to reverse her sedative. Within a minute, the groggy cow was up stumbling around.

"You're gonna need some clean clothes if you're going to the doctor this afternoon," Annie Rose said, looking at my blood-soaked shirt and wet, muddy jeans. "Do you have some in the truck?"

"I'm fresh out. Would you happen to at least have a T-shirt I could borrow?"

"C'mon up to the house. I can hook you up with some clean clothes, and you can say hi to Mama."

At the little brick farmhouse, I stripped off my blood-covered T-shirt and jeans on the porch. By the time elderly Mrs. Myrtle got to the door, I was scantily clad in my underwear and socks with my large, tight, red-tinged belly front and center. She said, "Good to see ya, honey. It looks like you're having a rough day."

"Yes, ma'am, I am, but please don't feed me any fruit today! I'm expecting a baby." I knew consuming fruit was encouraged for pregnant women, but not the kind from the bottom of Mrs. Myrtle's jar.

"Congrats, sweetheart. That's wonderful news. I'm sure Annie has some clothes you can borrow."

Annie Rose came around the corner and beckoned me to enter the house. She had an armful of clothes. "There's a washrag and towel for you in the bathroom. Get washed up and changed," she instructed and pulled the door closed.

I strutted into the kitchen radiating the essence of Irish Spring, sporting a bright red book fair T-shirt and faded black jeans with bedazzled rear pockets. The last time I saw anything bedazzled, it would have belonged to my sister, Ann, in middle school. I generally shopped for work clothes at Goodwill and was no-frills, but beggars, especially blood-covered ones, can't be choosers. I gave Annie Rose and Mrs. Myrtle each a big hug.

"Thank you, ladies, for the use of the clothes. I better hustle to my doctor's appointment. Be sure and check on the cow a bit later, Annie Rose."

I used the steering wheel to pull my tired body back into the truck seat and sped off to avoid being late for my doctor's appointment. As I drove down the long stretch of road, the Dixie Chicks song "The Long Way Around" came on the radio. Its lyrics made me think about those who had told me that being a large animal veterinarian was "not women's work" and how "awfully hard it would be for a girl." My quivering muscles and sore chest wanted to agree with them, but my heart said no. I wasn't going to let a big belly and a little fatigue fulfill their prophecy.

STUCK

I was hitting a breaking point. Everything I did required a lot of extra effort. I was seven months pregnant in the first week of August, and the blazing heat was getting to me, although I think I was twenty degrees hotter than the average American on the inside. I hadn't had a good night's sleep in nearly four months, between the carpal tunnel and the inability to get comfortable in any position. No clothes fit anymore; my belly needed its own zip code. It was impossible to wear coveralls. Plus, there was no such thing as maternity coveralls, so I was stuck with oversize T-shirts, baggy gym shorts, and rubber boots with the tops turned down to accommodate my leg swelling. Professionalism was out the window; on one occasion, I was dressed so poorly that a euthanasia client denied me access to their house because they thought I was a homeless person seeking shelter. And to top it all off, a few nights before, I'd nearly burned my house down after setting a plastic cutting board on the stove burner thanks to "pregnancy brain."

I had been called by a farmer named Andrew to see a steer that was severely lame in his foot. I was not looking forward to treating a lame animal because that usually involved tranquilizing the animal and working on it on the ground. Getting to the ground wasn't too hard; it was the getting up part that was becoming impossible.

When I opened the truck door, I spotted my crippled patient in a pen on the other side of a large concrete feed bunk. The bunk was deep with tall sides to hold feed for the cattle, and it had several large-gauge cables above it to keep the cattle from jumping over it and escaping. I was fascinated by this creature that got around worse than I did, so I decided to get a closer look by climbing over the bunk.

I had always wondered if those cables worked. Now I knew.

"Come quick, boss! She's stuck," Reggie the trusty farmhand yelled to Andrew, who was climbing out of the beat-up farm truck. Andrew hurried around the truck to save the trapped heifer. Instead, he found me, with my hugely pregnant body officially stuck between the side of the feed bunk and the lowest cable.

Andrew's eyes were so wide his pupils were fully dilated. "Are you OK? Hold still and we'll get you out."

"I'm fine. Just please help me get out of here soon because it's getting harder and harder to breathe." I did some Lamaze breathing to stay calm. Even though my birthing class wasn't supposed to start until next week, I'd looked ahead at the material because that's what Type A people do. Reggie climbed up on the side of the trough and pulled the cable up with all his might as Andrew clasped my hand firmly and pulled me. Once I was free, we all chuckled.

"I just wanted to have a closer look at his foot before I gathered my supplies. I'm not used to the beached whale physique just yet. Thanks for saving me, guys."

This poor crippled steer was getting the B team today. To prevent taking extra steps, I decided it would be wise to fire a dart into him from the outside of the pen. Once he was in a deep sleep, I loaded the supplies I needed into my trusty plastic carrier and instructed the boys to help me get through the trough without getting stuck. Judging by the massive swelling in the lateral claw of the calf's hoof, I determined he had septic arthritis from a deep puncture wound. I turned to Andrew and said, "There's only one option. I need to surgically remove the infected claw."

"Are you up for it?" Andrew looked at me skeptically.

I may not look like the surgeons on prime-time television, but one should never underestimate the ability of a pregnant woman with a scalpel. "Yes, sir. I may need some help to do the sawing, but we'll get it off." I tied the calf's feet six ways to Sunday and placed a copious amount of numbing into the affected claw. Sweat poured into my eyes as I began to cut through the skin to get to the necrotic bone. Once I had outlined my target with the scalpel, I carefully placed the cable wire into the cut, attached the metal handles, and began my free cardiac stress test. I fully intended to pass the bulk of the sawing off to one of the boys, but watching that infected bone come off was so gratifying I just couldn't stop.

After five minutes of intense work, we achieved success. I placed a medicated bandage on the bloody stump and gave the steer massive amounts of painkillers and antibiotics before waking him up. The gentlemen lifted the cables for me once more to get back to the truck, proving that chivalry was not dead in Orange County.

Later that evening, I kicked up my tired, swollen feet and sank into the recliner. As I leaned back, I heard a loud crack from deep inside the chair. It's a sad state of affairs when an inanimate object gets tired of supporting your pregnancy. Aimlessly staring at the television, I felt something wet between my legs. Oh great, was I now losing control of my bladder? How was I going to make it eight more weeks with incontinence? Things seemed to be on a downward spiral.

I was so restless I nearly wore a hole in the chair squirming around. The only thing that was more uncomfortable than my body was my mind. I felt like an old cow nesting in the straw, anxiously preparing to birth her baby.

After I wore myself out with worry, I fell asleep in the chair and was awakened by a sharp pain in my abdomen in the wee hours of the morning. *I must have worked too hard in the heat today and got dehydrated*, I thought. Another hour passed, and the pain became more and more intense. I decided to get up and walk around to see if that would help. My loyal border collie, Cap, scratched at the arm of the chair. I presumed he needed to go out for a pee break, but he seemed anxious in my presence.

When I stepped outside the door to let him out, I felt my Croc fill with copious amounts of liquid. Oh my God! Was I in labor? I was supposed to have two more months to prepare.

THE RECEIVING END

*A*t 4:45 a.m., I rang my neighbor and faithful friend Deb. "Come quick. I need a ride to the hospital. I think I'm having the baby." I also called Lewis, the baby's father, and instructed him to meet us at the hospital.

Upon my arrival at the hospital at 5:00 a.m., the tired nurse took me back and phoned my doctor. After careful examination, the doctor looked at me intently and said in his stern Russian accent, "Yes, young lady. You are in labor, but we can't deliver this baby here. The baby is too premature. You're going to have to go to the university hospital, where they have a neonatal intensive care unit. We're going to give you a shot to help develop the baby's lungs and another shot to try and stop your labor. An ambulance will arrive for you momentarily."

When I felt the sharp point of the needle enter the tense, contracted head of my triceps muscle, I just knew the medicine had about as much of a chance of stopping my labor as one strand of barbed wire fence had of stopping a hobby farmer's bull. My contractions were getting more and more painful and closer together. I looked up at the nurse, grinding my teeth. "You better tell that ambulance driver to put it in high gear."

When the two EMTs pushed me into the ambulance, one jumped in the driver's seat while the other one started strapping down my arms. I went from feeling like an excited expectant mother to feeling like a suspect in custody for a crime. I don't even tie goats down this much for abdominal surgery.

"Sir, please don't strap me down. I will lie still, I promise."

"Sorry, ma'am. It's the rule. As fast as we're gonna have to drive you, you'll be thankful for it. We don't want no babies being born in the Band-Aid box." He tightened the straps over my ankles.

"Not my feet! No, please no. I need to bend my legs, sir. These contractions hurt so much. Please, I really need to bend my legs." It became clear that my desperate pleas were falling on deaf ears.

Every contraction was more and more intense. I wanted to writhe in pain, but it was impossible, so I just pulled my feet back as hard against the straps as I could. I pulled back so hard that I felt like the circulation was being cut off to my feet. My body was exhausted, and I did not like what I overheard. "We're here, but we're gonna have to take her in from the underground entrance because of the construction. We'll have to unload her in the rain."

When the medic in the back loosened the straps, I couldn't figure out whether I wanted to kiss him or kick him. I think he realized that possibility existed, so he didn't remove them completely. He threw a white sheet over me and said, "Apologies in advance, ma'am. It's pouring rain. You're gonna get a little wet on the way into the hospital."

A little wet? As we call it in southwest Virginia, it was a toad-strangling rain. I couldn't see it, but I could feel it. Within seconds, the sheet was custom fitted to me. The metal frame of the stretcher hitting the door jarred my tense body.

"Boys, could you pull the sheet off?"

"Are you claustrophobic, ma'am?" the taller medic asked.

"Hell no, I'm not claustrophobic. Isn't the morgue at the bottom of this hospital? I don't want to be mistaken for a bloated corpse!"

After the men wheeled me into a room and moved me to a bed,

a young man wearing a starched white coat approached me. "Hello, ma'am. I'm a medical student here at the university, and I'm going to do an internal exam on you." He began to put warm lube on his gloved fingers.

"Like hell, Doogie. Listen, buddy, I'm all about teaching students, but not today. Go get the big boss. I'm going to push this baby out now!" His face turned as white as his coat and he ran out the door to get help. Within thirty seconds, there were fourteen people around me: one doctor to deliver the baby and thirteen specialty nurses and doctors to attend to baby girl. Modesty had officially gone out the seventh-story window.

"Can I have an epidural or some pain medicine or something? Anything?" I begged the doctor conveniently positioned between my bent legs.

"No, dear. You can't have anything," she said with a flat affect; empathy wasn't in her vocabulary.

"Seriously, I'm not like my clients at the hippie commune who birth in livestock tubs of warm water. I'm all about Western medicine. Please, can I have anything?" I tried to muster up a tear, but I was too dehydrated from all the sweating.

"You're too far along now. You're just going to have to do it the old-fashioned way. When I tell you to push, you push hard and push silently. It helps the push be more forceful." I was relieved that Lewis was there with me so I could squeeze his hand while I pushed. At this point, the doctor just sat there in a supervisory role, holding a white towel and instructing me to push. When I deliver calves, I wear plastic sleeves up to my shoulders and lie on the ground among the birthing fluids, working my muscles to the point of exhaustion from turning and pulling the baby. I could hear my dad in the back of my head saying, "Who's the dumb one?" I channeled my frustration with this backward situation into the pushing, and it seemed to help. With each intense push, I squeezed Lewis's hand hard enough to allow him to share in the pain of childbirth.

I spent the next thirty minutes working harder than I ever had before. It was more painful and grueling than any job I had ever done on the dairy, in veterinary school, or as a veterinarian. But my whole life had trained me to dig deep, and I knew this was the most important work I would ever do. With one final push, I heard a loud, shrill cry, and I knew at that moment she was worth every second of agony. I wanted to kiss her head just like I'd watched the mama cows do immediately after they birth their babies. The doctor congratulated us and tilted our slimy angel toward us to sneak a peek before the thirteen-member team whisked her away to the intensive care unit. The situation was simply too critical to sneak a kiss.

Boy-o, this was certainly not how I envisioned motherhood. This day was supposed to happen on a beautiful fall day at the end of September 2016. I intended to be swaddling my big healthy baby girl against my half-bare breast at the newly built hospital complete with tasteful decor looking out onto the Blue Ridge Mountains. This is exactly why I don't do selfies for Facebook. There I lay looking like a horse that had been rode hard and put up wet, getting sutured from the damage of the early birth, while my baby that was the size of a Chihuahua was undergoing lifesaving procedures complete with catheters and breathing tubes on a different floor of the hospital.

After a few hours, the doctor allowed me to walk upstairs scantily clad in my hospital gown to the neonatal intensive care unit, dragging my IV pole. Lewis and I stopped at the mandatory hand-washing station at the NICU entrance. I grimaced as I scrubbed my hands, which were sore from the multiple needle sticks earlier in the day. Nervous about what was on the other side, I pushed open the large double doors and saw row after row of tiny plastic incubators.

Much to my surprise, there were no babies crying, only incessant beeping from the equipment. Every incubator contained a struggling premature infant attached to several monitors, with tubes coming out of nearly every orifice. As I walked slowly past the incubators, I noticed the beautiful hand-crafted signs attached to the outer end of each box. Each sign had the name of a baby— some mundane, some unique, and some longer than the baby. It was clear by the bright colors and patterns that these signs had been made by creative, hardworking nurses to give the tiny infants an identity. Eventually, I got to a box with no sign, just the word "Kangaroo."

I turned to Lewis, confused. "Who on earth would name their baby Kangaroo?"

"Honey, Kangaroo is the maker of the box. She's ours. We just need to give her a name." Lewis shook his head and smiled as he pulled the gown back up on my shoulder.

"Oh my word! She's ours? She is so tiny and so beautiful. We need to give her a name, right now. And she needs to be named after strong women because she has to be a fighter." I felt negligent for having this baby lie here with no name, but I'd been sure we had eight more weeks to work on this project. "Our grandmothers were strong, hardworking farm women. Grandma Mary and Grandma Lucile were two of the finest ladies that ever existed. Why don't we name her after them? Maybe we can just call her Lucy?"

"I agree. Let's do it," Lewis agreed wholeheartedly. He loved his grandmother as much as I loved mine.

Peering in at the four-pound, ten-ounce infant covered in soft brown fuzz, I knew my most important job now would be to instill the morals and values handed down to me for generations into this baby girl.

GOT MILK?

I'd been pumping breast milk for my sweet Lucy for eight long months, and I'd decided to stop. Pumping milk for a baby takes a special kind of dedication. Women who pump exclusively are required to do so every three hours, day and night. Many times, there is no privacy or quiet place to do this in a work environment. I remember seeing a picture on Facebook of another female vet with a breast pump attached under her surgery gown while she performed lifesaving surgery on a dog. In my line of work, I had to figure out how to pump and drive using a pump that plugged into an inverter. Initially, I was proud of myself for figuring out how to perform my motherly duties while in constant motion. After all, I had driven home naked several times; driving around only half-naked should be a breeze.

One day while I was pumping and driving on the interstate, a jacked-up, pimped-out truck started to pass me. The truck vaguely reminded me of one I'd seen in a parking lot recently with large brass truck nuts dangling from the hitch. When the guys went in to buy beer, my vet student and I promptly banded the nuts with a castration band.

I wasn't worried about the young guys passing me because I was sure they couldn't see anything too revealing. The passenger's eyes got wide, and he nudged his buddy and pointed at me. When I heard the loud noise of their redneck chariot hitting the rumble strips, I realized they could see a bit more than I thought. I grabbed a towel to throw across my bare chest and laughed harder than I'd laughed for months.

It felt good to laugh, even if for a moment. It made me feel like my old self. For months, I had struggled with postpartum depression. My thoughts were consumed with guilt—guilt about everything. I felt guilty for having the baby early, for not being able to stay home with her, for not being happy at what should have been the happiest time in my life, and for not being mentally clear for my patients and clients. My muscles were so incredibly tense that when the chiropractor tried to loosen my shoulders up with an acupuncture needle, he inadvertently collapsed my lung. The landmarks for his incredibly long needle were distorted enough that it pierced my left lung, requiring an ER visit that I had neither the time nor the money for. I just couldn't seem to get myself back on track. My mom was living with me to help take care of Lucy, and in her quiet way, she looked after me as well. I had to take one day at a time and pray that time would heal me.

It had been a tough spring so far, filled with too much work, not enough help, and barely any sleep. This was part of the reason I was less than thrilled to get a call from one of my least favorite clients. Dr. Kate and I had decided years prior that Bob shouldn't have cows anymore. Today, he called me out for a cow with a prolapsed vagina. Prolapsed vaginas usually happen just before the cow has her baby. They are unsightly, but easy to fix—if, and only if, you have a way to restrain the cow!

When I pulled in, I asked Bob, "Where's the cow?" He pointed to a huge open field. I could see the back end of a black cow running in the opposite direction with her prolapsed vagina bouncing up and down with every stride. It looked just like a basketball bouncing on the hardwood. I was simply in no mood for a rodeo. I hadn't gotten more than three hours of sleep at night for over a year. The process of drying up my milk production was incredibly uncomfortable and did nothing to improve my demeanor.

Bob could see my look of disgust as I watched the cow running away. I lectured him about his lack of a facility to restrain the cow as I loaded a tranquilizer into my blow dart. I jumped in my pickup and hauled freight toward the fleeing bovine. While speeding up to the cow, I leaned out my window and fired a shot. It was a direct hit to the flank; I always shoot better when I'm mad. Hitting the cow with the dart was perhaps the only thing all day that had brought me any joy.

Because of the incredible amount of adrenaline pumping through the cow, I had to shoot her a second time to get her to succumb. Once the cow was fast asleep, I used a foot rope to tie her foot forward to keep from getting decapitated. I gave her an epidural to numb her delicate peroneal tissue and cleaned the tissue with warm, soapy water. The tissue had been out for more than two or three days, as evidenced by its lacerations and swelling. For the best chance of replacing the vaginal tissue, I was forced to lie facedown on the ground behind the cow. As I eased myself down, my engorged breasts pressed firmly against the hard, drought-stricken ground. The intense pressure and pain brought tears to my eyes.

I started to lubricate the tissue and push it back into the cow. Bob asked, "How long is this going to take?" That was the *wrong* question at that moment.

Grinding my teeth hard enough to crack a filling, I explained, "If you had a proper cattle handling facility, Bob, it would take about fifteen or twenty minutes, but without that, it's gonna take me at least forty-five minutes." Since I was having to do this grueling task, I used the time to lecture Bob on topics related to the proper care of cattle. The topics included but were not limited to the importance of checking cattle at least once a day, having proper handling facilities, and getting rid of cattle that have chronic health problems. Bob looked like a schoolboy being lectured by the principal. He made excuse after excuse as to why his cattle affairs were not in order—the same excuses I'd been hearing for fourteen long years. In some ways, my lashing out felt cathartic.

After I placed the stitch in the cow to hold in her vaginal tissue, she stood up. My breasts were as thankful for the relief as the cow's vagina was.

As we headed to Bob's house so that I could get paid, I remembered what one of my old vet school professors once said: "If you have to do an awful job, charge enough to make sure you enjoy it!" I wrote the man a hefty bill, hoping to dissuade him from ever wanting to own more livestock, and he apologized for his lack of facilities once more. He gave me some fancy European chocolate, hoping to make my day better, but there are some things chocolate just doesn't fix.

PULLING IT TOGETHER

*A*s I rocked my fussy baby back and forth in the half-broken recliner, I was startled by the obnoxiously loud *ding, ding* of the driveway alert. The broken chair was the least of the many frustrations I had these days. The baby was colicky and had never slept well, I continued to struggle with postpartum depression, and trying to balance running a business and raising a baby was starting to feel like I was an amateur firestick juggler on *America's Got Talent*.

With Lucy on my arm, I headed out through my small garage, which was currently functioning as my vet clinic, to see who our after-hours visitor was this dark, cold evening. I cautiously cracked the door. I didn't see anyone in the span of the floodlight. Did the crappy driveway dinger misfire? Was I going crazy?

"Sorry to disturb you, ma'am, but aren't you the vet?" a deep voice cried out from the darkness. This burly young man was unfamiliar. He appeared to be in his early thirties with dark hair and a dark beard, dressed like the lumberjack on the Brawny paper towel package.

I looked at him skeptically. "Yes, I am a vet. What do you need, sir? Dog medicine or something?"

He replied, "No, I need you to help me. I had an accident with a chain saw and I'm in need of some stitches. Can you fix me?"

"I doubt it, buddy, but show it to me in the light."

He slid his right hand just inside of the bright floodlight and began to unwrap the dirty, blood-soaked towel from around it.

I have seen more than my fair share of blood and gore, but this wound made me vomit in my mouth a little.

I stared into the gaping, jagged wound extending across the top side of his hand with blood oozing out of every severed vessel. "Nah, man, you don't need a vet—you need a hand surgeon. I'd be happy to give you a ride to the hospital. Just let me pack up the baby."

He rewrapped the wound and hung his head in obvious disappointment. He began to walk back toward his truck. "I'm not going to the hospital. I will just manage it the best I can. Sorry to bother you, ma'am. You and the baby have a good evenin'."

"Come on, man, don't be like that. If you don't do something soon, you're either gonna die from blood loss or infection. You're too young to die!"

It was clear my message was falling on deaf ears. "I hope it's a quick death," he moaned. The truck door creaked as he began to pull it closed.

"All right already, get your stubborn ass in here and sit down in this chair. I can at least clean it up for you."

I placed the baby on the floor in her bouncy seat while I pulled up two chairs to the end of the long plastic table. I dare say nobody has ever gotten more use out of a plastic Walmart table than I have gotten out of the one in my makeshift vet clinic. The word "multipurpose" doesn't even do it justice; from C-section to euthanasia to diaper changes, it had seen it all. I draped some clean towels across one end of the table and sent the man to the sink to start scrubbing the wound.

My nervous subject sat down at the end of the table and began babbling baby talk to Lucy. She was grinning as she gazed up at this silly man with a shiny dark beard. I could tell he must be a father. It was comforting in a way because the possibility still existed that I had invited an ax murderer into my home. I set two shots of Woodford Reserve in front of him and instructed him to drink up.

"Ma'am, I don't drink."

I said, "OK, think of it as your anesthesia." He knocked back those shots like a sorority girl at happy hour.

While we waited for the alcohol to kick in, I began to quiz him about who he was, where he was from, and how he found me.

"People call me Moe. I'm actually your neighbor, just tucked back in the woods. I have seen you working on my next-door neighbor's cows, and you seem to have a good reputation around here."

"How'd you manage to nearly cut your hand off with a chain saw?" I asked.

"I'm a logger, been logging those woods in the mountains since I was a young boy. It's a dangerous business. Even the best of us can have an accident." It was clear the redneck anesthesia was taking effect. This initially shy, quiet fellow was becoming chatty, and his cheeks were flushed. As he got calmer, baby Lucy grew increasingly fussy.

I drew up the syringe full of lidocaine while I bounced Lucy's chair with my foot. "Last chance to go to a human doctor . . ."

He just shook his head and snickered.

I aggressively scrubbed the slightly less intimidating laceration and started to inject the numbing agent. I began to quiz my buzzed friend about why he was so afraid of going to the hospital.

"When I was a young teen, I worked alongside my best friend in the woods, day in and day out. We loved our jobs, being outside every day and running those big saws." I thought that all sounded lovely and thought perhaps he was too drunk to understand my question.

"Then one day there was an accident, a very bad accident." After a long pause he continued, "A large tree limb fell across my buddy. He was trapped and screaming. I had to go a long, long way through the woods to find help. When we got him free, I performed CPR on him all the way to the hospital. He never got to come home. I was devastated. I'm haunted sometimes by the sound of those beeping alarms and even the smell of the disinfectant they used in that emergency room."

Holy crap. Here I was just thinking he was refusing the emergency room because he didn't have health insurance or something. My heart hurt for him. I had finally gotten the gash clean enough to suit me and opened my surgery kit. Lucy started to sob, as if she understood the story she'd just heard. Moe volunteered to hold her. I lifted the sweet baby up and sat her on his knee. The more he bounced her, the more contentment they both seemed to find. I donned my pearly white sterile surgery gloves and got to work. As the point of the needle entered his pale skin, he winced.

"You know, if you'd gone to a real hospital, you could have gotten real pain medicine."

"Did you hear me complain?" he asked with a half-smile.

One stitch at a time, I pulled the jagged edges of the wound together until I placed the last suture. I looked down at the finished product. "I hope you weren't planning on being a hand model."

"It's a work of art. Thank you so, so much! What do I owe you?"

"You crazy man, the only thing that's more illegal than me performing surgery on you is me taking money for it. You don't owe me a thing. But you do owe it to yourself to get some professional help to work through the trauma you experienced. 'Cause I sure as hell ain't doing no heart surgery on this damn plastic table!"

SEIZING THE DAY

*I*t started as a halfway decent day with some hope of getting finished before the early November darkness set in. My veterinary student Maria and I scarfed down our Subway sandwiches and discussed fun things to do if we finished early. That is, until our laughter was interrupted abruptly by a phone call from the police.

"Sorry to bother you, ma'am, but I'm going to need you to meet me out here at this farm. We have a bit of a situation," the officer explained.

Once I get called to a crime scene, there is no opportunity to leave until the job is done, no matter how long it takes. "How bad is it?" I asked with hesitation.

"You don't even want to know. Just come as quickly as you can. I'll text the address. If you say what I think you're going to, we will need every bit of daylight that's left." I could hear the disgust in the young officer's voice.

When Maria and I arrived at the farm, we were greeted by a tall, dark-haired officer dressed in a pleated forest-green uniform with ANIMAL CONTROL written on the sleeve. It was only his second week on the job, and he didn't know how to handle this complex situation, but he knew for certain he needed a veterinarian.

"I was called here because there was a goat loose in the middle of the road, so I hopped out of the truck to put the goat back in, and out of the corner of my eye I saw a dead goat. At that point, I started looking around, and every place I looked there were more animals and more problems. I fear there may be animals inside of that single-wide trailer, too, so I called the magistrate to get a search warrant. Would you like the tour of the rest while we wait?" He squinted his eyes with a nervous half-smile. It was like a toddler asking if you want to see their poop. Hell no, nobody wants to, but if you're going to clean up the mess, you're going to have to look.

"I reckon. Let's start with the goats and you can trace your path of everything you've found so far, then we'll call for some deputies. Were you able to find who owns the property?" The three of us entered the dry lot where the goats were located as we talked. There appeared to be about forty goats in the lot of all shapes and sizes. Several appeared to be severely lame, with their cloven hooves twisted around like a witch's fingernails. A few of them were so crippled they were three-legged lame.

Walking into the barn, I spotted a pile of bones with a shriveled-up two-tone hide underneath. Near the bone pile lay a white doeling, dead in lateral recumbency. Based on the lack of decomposition, she hadn't died very long ago, unlike her herd mate. Examining the deceased bodies, the human side of me hoped their deaths weren't prolonged or agonizing, but the crime scene detective in me had to start looking for clues, both from the corpses and the environment, that could tell their stories.

The goal in these animal cruelty cases wasn't necessarily to get justice for the deceased animals—it was to be able to stop any further cruelty to the living animals. In thirteen years of veterinary practice, I'd seen more of these cruelty cases than I ever imagined possible. Most cases involved owners suffering from mental illnesses that resulted in the neglect of the animals. Occasionally there would be a case involving cruel intent, even torture of an animal. These were the ones that scarred my mind with images that I could not unsee. Those are the cases I will never understand.

"We have identified the owner of the property as a seventy-seven-year-old woman named Jane, but we haven't been able to locate her at this point. Shall we head to the next collection of animals?" The officer led us around the barn to a chest-high, dilapidated wooden hutch with a blue tarp over the top. As he began to pull the tarp back, I could feel every muscle fiber in my back shorten. There appeared to be four separate compartments, with mesh wire covering the front entrances. Maria and I pulled open a small wooden door to discover upwards of twenty furry guinea pigs.

Maria continued to open doors. I was impressed with her desire to keep looking ahead.

"Whatcha got behind that end door, chica?"

"Behind door number four, you'll never believe it, wait for it . . . there are at least twenty-five more inbred guinea pigs with freaky eyes and funky skin. There must be close to one hundred pigs in this hutch! It looks like there may have been an attempt at population control before the boys chewed through the wooden dividers." She shook her head as she closed the last door and pulled the tarp back down.

The officer led us to a large grassy area with fifty or more decrepit wooden hutches interspersed with small wire cages stacked on top of one another. Some of the cages contained a pair of rabbits, while others contained single chickens. The common theme among this critter shantytown was the copious amounts of feces filling the bottoms of the cages, some to the point that the animal could barely stand. There was also a lack of apparent food and water. Maria attempted to count the rabbits and chickens but grew tired once she got to fifty.

"I'm afraid to ask, but what else is left to look at, Officer?" I pried Maria away from the cage with the large gray floppy-eared bunny because I could see the thought bubble above her head: her, cuddling the bunny on the couch in her college apartment, watching Netflix.

"There are just a few more spots around the house here. A few larger chicken pens, one lean-to shelter off the side of the barn with

a bunch of random bird species, and a few cats in cages in a barn."
We followed him, dutifully glancing at each set of animals. The poor
cats were in varying sizes of wire crates with a scant amount of food
and filthy water. I realize many cats have what's known as "resting
bitch face," but these cats appeared destitute. Maria extended her
hand toward the cage in a friendly gesture, and one small cat hissed
as it arched its back and retreated to the far corner.

"Well, sir, I have seen enough to say with certainty that these
animals need to be seized. File the charges for animal cruelty based
on deplorable living conditions, inadequate shelter, and apparent
lack of food and water. We also need to locate a place we can take
all these animals and a group of volunteers to help move and care
for them. We're going to have to get going before we run out of
daylight." Even I thought my orders seemed impossible.

"Would you like a million bucks and a massage too? Just kidding, I will get right on it, ma'am." The young man chuckled as he
walked away to start dispatching help on the radio. Within minutes
we had the chief animal control officer on the scene. He was depu-
tized and had more access to resources. I explained to him what we
were going to need to go forward with the seizure.

"You know, there's a group that recently formed in our county
that's dedicated to emergency preparedness, response, and management of emergency types of situations for pets. CART, for
Community Animal Response Team. Last I heard, they had a
bunch of animal-loving volunteers. Let me give their leader, Donnie, a buzz." The chief was proud of himself for coming up with
such a brilliant idea, and I was proud of him too.

"Great idea, sir, but first we need to figure out where we're
going to put them. I'm not even sure how many animals there are,
but there must be at least five hundred."

His eyes widened, and a blank look came across his face. Then
he said, "What about the fairgrounds?" He looked surprised, as if it
had come out of someone else's mouth.

"If you weren't married, I'd kiss you!" I said. "Call and get us permission to use the grounds, and see if you can get the CART team leader here. We're about to put this operation into a higher gear. Somebody should probably call the sheriff and tell him what we're up to as well." I picked up my phone to start organizing clients and friends with livestock trailers to help haul the animals into town.

Within two hours, the deputies had placed crime scene tape around the property, and we had twenty volunteers from the CART team on-site. The volunteers listened eagerly to their leader, Donnie.

"Thanks for coming out today, team. We have quite a large-scale seizure that needs to be executed. This is Dr. Melinda. She's the veterinarian in charge. You need to take instruction from her, and we need to work efficiently so we can get these animals out of here and get them to the fairgrounds before darkness closes in on us. I'm going to turn the floor over to her now so she can give us our marching orders."

Looking around at the volunteers, I could see their eagerness to start helping these animals. I had done enough of these animal seizures that I dreaded the work that lay ahead of us, but I knew that would be my little secret. Dread does not boost morale.

"Good afternoon, folks. Thank you all so much for coming. I'm going to be brief in my comments because we need to hustle. I have a few people coming with livestock trailers to do the transporting. We will need a few people to go to the fairgrounds and start preparing areas to put the animals." I began to roughly sketch out the layout on a piece of cardboard. "One main area for the goats, one for the pocket pets, and one for the birds, please. Another group will need to stay here and help identify and load animals. We'll need one scribe, one person to tag animals, a few to hold animals, and several to assemble and carry crates to the livestock trailers. Everyone that will be dealing with the animals must wear gloves, and if you enter the bird areas, please wear a mask. We need to work hard and fast and keep excellent records, as this will be a criminal case."

Everyone scattered like a pack of rats. My team consisted of Maria, two animal control officers, a criminal investigator with a very nice camera, and four CART volunteers. I couldn't figure out why the criminal investigator looked so familiar—then it hit me. When I noticed his eyes, I remembered the last thing he'd said to me: "Ma'am, do you realize how fast you were going?" It was Officer Love, or as I liked to call him, Officer Where's the Love? I tiptoed around him, wondering if he was still bitter that I had sutured my way out of his speeding ticket by fixing the lawyer's dog, but he didn't seem to recognize me. Today, he seemed to be as thankful for my veterinary skills as I was for his law enforcement knowledge.

We decided to start working through the goats and get them out of the way before nightfall. I had euthanized a few of the most crippled goats earlier in the day to relieve their suffering, so only the sound goats were left. I had also called my dad, who happened to be visiting, and asked him to bring our loyal border collie, Jessie, to help herd the goats onto the livestock trailer for transport to the fairgrounds. My faithful friend Ben had the long trailer backed up to the entrance of the pen.

"Away to me, Jessie." My dad instructed Jessie to make a sweep to her right around the tightly knit group of goats. Once she positioned herself behind the goats, she stealthily weaved back and forth a few steps at a time to work the goats toward the trailer entrance. One of the CART members standing near the trailer door shouted out, "What do you want us to do?" He had never seen a herding dog do the work of three humans.

In between shouting orders at Jessie, Dad replied, "Just stay out of the dog's way and shut the trailer door when the last goat steps on."

If every task ahead of us were this easy, it would be smooth sailing. I patted Jessie's muscular shoulder, and dust flew up with every touch. I always admired the dedication, intelligence, and strong work ethic of our border collies. One time when I was home at the dairy on a college holiday break, Dad and I had to go back to the house and get Katch to help us pen a group of Holstein heifers. Katch was a twelve-year-old border collie that was partially retired due to lymphoma that was infiltrating his nasal passages. That day in the cold rain and mud, we turned Katch out to work his magic. Within ten minutes, all the cattle were penned, and Katch was in the back of the truck, licking my frozen cheeks. The border collies taught me more about handling livestock than anyone in my life. Looking into Jessie's bright eyes, I wondered how she would feel about herding guinea pigs. Since I was personally responsible for the welfare of these animals, we opted to excuse Jessie for the day and continue the wrangling only with humans.

Just as I pondered how well things seemed to be going, I heard some commotion coming from the driveway of the trailer. A petite older lady with salt-and-pepper hair in a messy bun on top of her head was climbing under the crime scene tape. Two deputies were trying to stop her, but she appeared to be a woman on a mission. The chief came over to us and said, "Uh-oh, looks like the owner is home and she is pissed."

I did understand the shock she must have felt. She had just gotten home from work to find crime scene tape wrapped around her home. I had the same experience on the day of the earthquake; the difference for me was that there was no alleged crime committed on the other side of the tape. I could barely hear her words, but it was clear she was pleading her case to the sheriff.

I decided it would be best not to involve myself in the owner's predicament and just keep plugging along with my team. We had no time for drama. Next, we moved to the rabbit and chicken village. Maria pulled on shoulder-length black gloves that were sturdy enough to withstand bites. With her long, glistening curly locks and athletic build, she could have passed for a dominatrix. I was privately delighted to have a young, limber person on my team who could bend at the waist and reach to the back of the rabbit hutches. We had developed quite an efficient routine. Maria pulled them out, I did a brief exam to make sure there were no glaring health issues, the young animal control officer recorded them, and Officer Where's the Love snapped a photo with their identification number. Once they were official, Rebecca, a leading CART volunteer, would put them in a cage and hand them off to two other CART volunteers to be carried to the livestock trailer. This routine went on for hours until darkness descended on us.

There were two bright sides to the darkness. One was that we got fresh CART volunteers who had just gotten off work, and the other was that the criminal investigators were able to get us some very nice lights. As the deputies began to set up the lights, Maria stretched her long, slim torso through the small hutch door to pull out the final rabbit. When I reached down to grab the animal out of her gloved hands, I noticed it seemed to have a very long tail. Maria jumped backward and tossed the mysterious, furry creature into the air. "Oh shit, it's a rat!" She tried to catch her breath as we all laughed. We decided at that point that we all needed a short break to regroup. I looked across the yard and saw my parents and Lucy pulling in. It was so comforting to see their smiling faces.

I stretched my tired arms across the bright yellow crime scene tape to clutch my darling baby Lucy from my mother's arms. I kissed her soft round cheek while seeing the flashing blue lights of the police car reflected in her crystal blue eyes. She was only a year old and didn't know her mother should have been home hours ago to tuck her in and sing her lullabies. We were just overjoyed to see each other despite the time of day, temperature, and wildly strange circumstances. Mom hugged me and handed me an extra-large fountain drink. With hugs from my family and an icy Mountain Dew, I could persevere even through the most grueling of jobs.

"Dr. Melinda, the sheriff is looking for you." One of the deputies beckoned me back to the scene.

"Be right there, Officer." I gave my sweet girl a rapid series of kisses all over her chilly face and gently handed her back across the tape, this time to my dad. I thanked Mom and Dad for coming by with my girl. Dad wasn't always there to tuck us in because of work, but he and Mom wanted to be sure I got to say good night to my baby, despite my work, and for that I was grateful.

"Be careful, baby. You know there are jobs out there that don't require police to be involved," Dad said as he opened the door of the white Acadia to drive Mom and Lucy home.

I rolled my eyes. "Yeah, yeah. I know. Don't worry about me. Everything is under control here." I turned to walk away. Dad finally had some scrap of tangible proof that my job could be dangerous, and he was going to make sure I heard about it.

When I walked back up the slight incline from my brief visit with Lucy and my parents, I was stopped by a newly arrived CART volunteer. "My name is Gary, ma'am. Where would you like me?" He gazed at me with kind eyes.

"Glad you're here, buddy. Grab the other end of this heavy peacock cage and help get it to the stock trailer, please. Everyone's back is starting to wear out."

"Yes, ma'am." Gary lifted the end of the cage as a deputy turned on another set of professional-grade lights. Illuminated by the bright lights, Gary's shiny silver hair and beard sharply contrasted the brilliant blues and greens in the peacock's feathers. These were the first bright colors I had seen since I'd arrived at this shit show. It was hard to appreciate the colors of the other animals from the dusty, drab, manure-filled environments we hoisted them out of.

We decided the guinea pigs would be the last creatures we would deal with, since it was now approaching midnight. Several of the pigs had injuries to their eyes and legs from fighting. Some had crusting and bleeding skin lesions from their unclean living conditions. One small tri-colored female needed to be euthanized due to painful bilateral corneal ulcerations rendering her blind. I cupped her in my large, cold hand and carefully injected the euthanasia solution into her heart. I could feel the life exit her tiny, fuzzy body. One of the CART volunteers looked over and asked, "Does that ever bother you to put animals to sleep?" She had a sympathetic expression on her face as she gently placed her hand on my shoulder.

"Not really. As veterinarians, we are called to relieve animals' suffering, and sometimes the only way to do that is through humane euthanasia." I got this question from clients occasionally, and I never knew if this was the answer people were expecting.

When we'd loaded the ninety-first guinea pig into its carrier, we could barely hold our eyes open, and we feared the fatigue would lead to a recordkeeping error. Maria and I had been working on this project for twelve straight hours with very little food or water. The chief announced, "Why don't you all go home and get a few hours of sleep. I will leave two deputies here overnight, since it's an active crime scene. Let's meet back here at daylight and get the remainder of the animals out. We should have the search warrant for the residence by then. Thank you all for your hard work today."

Falling into bed, I realized that lying flat felt so good that I might not be able to even fall asleep. I reached over and rubbed baby Lucy's back while she slept peacefully. I prayed that at the end of this epic debacle, I wouldn't end up with a living room full of guinea pigs and rabbits.

AND A PARTRIDGE
IN A PEAR TREE

Beep, beep, beep—the obnoxiously loud alarm alerted me that it was 5:00 a.m. I reached over to hit SNOOZE but remembered that was not an option. I turned back over, kissed Lucy's warm round cheek, and hoisted my tired legs from the bed, being careful not to wake her. I had hours and hours of work left to do to get the rest of the animals away from the crime scene, and the overnight deputies needed relief. Maria and I pulled on our stocking caps, jumped in the truck, and cranked up the heater. We drove through Hardee's to grab some sustenance for us and the deputies before we returned to the scene. We had gone nearly thirty-six hours without food. "We're getting a freaking biscuit before we go back to that mess no matter what. My chiropractor told me last week that you can't take care of anybody else unless you take care of yourself first. That may be the only glimmer of wisdom you get from me all day, Maria, so don't forget it."

We pulled in, carting our bag of greasy biscuits under the crime scene tape. The warm biscuits brought a smile to the exhausted deputies' faces. I called Donnie to see how things were going at the fairgrounds, since I hadn't been there yet to check.

"Hi, Doc, things here at the fairgrounds are going well so far. We were able to get some livestock panels from a neighboring county to build a pen for the goats, so please just send me some dimensions so we can get that built and get them off the trailer today," Donnie recapped breathlessly.

"We also lucked out and got a hundred more crates from another CART group. We made a pocket pet area in the old bingo building and we're currently using the pole barn for the birds that are here so far. What else do we need to do?" Donnie was in his element. He was always on the move and had an infectious passion for helping animals.

"Get some money from the county and send someone to purchase feed today and make sure we have enough feed pans and water bowls. I expect we'll be sending at least another one hundred birds by lunchtime today. We almost sent you a rat yesterday, but Maria let it get away."

"A rat? Thank God you didn't. Some of the volunteers already think the guinea pigs are rats." Donnie snickered and took a sip of his coffee.

"Seriously, though, thank you for your hard work and leadership," I told him. "Please thank the other volunteers as well and tell everyone I will be there to check in once I have wrapped up here." It brought me comfort to know things were going well on the receiving end.

I gathered the fresh set of volunteers and officers who had just arrived on the scene. "This morning, we need to work through the rest of the chickens and the random assortment of birds so that we can get them on their way. A lady from the Humane Society is coming to get the cats to take them to the shelter. And I will need to be notified once the warrant has come through for the trailer— whatever the hell is in there will have to come out too."

The young animal control officer, a CART volunteer, Maria, and I entered the lean-to shed with two nets among the four of us. The floor was covered in dust and piles of putrid bird manure. It was mass chaos, with doves flying around in every direction, swooping past our heads, which were skimming the decrepit tin roof. We could barely see through the thick cloud of dust the birds were stirring up. The way I had it figured, we weren't coming out of that death trap without either tetanus or salmonellosis. I'm glad nobody was filming us, although watching six-foot-tall, out-of-shape white people try to catch wild birds with nets would be a good reality television show. After twenty minutes of struggling, I started to get the hang of the net. I remembered an interview I saw with Loretta Lynn. The interviewer asked her how she learned to shoot so well. She replied, "I was hungry."

I was hungry, too, hungry for this seizure to be over.

We finally got the last of the random birds captured before we started on chicken duty. We handled so many skinny chickens that I never wanted to see another chicken again in my life. At least the chickens were less loud and obnoxious than the geese.

As we loaded the last chicken into its crate, the chief came to find me. "Hey, Doc. Do you want the good news or the bad news first?"

"Is there any good news? If so, let's start with that."

"We got the search warrant for the single wide." He smiled as he pointed to the residence.

"And the bad news?" I raised my dusty eyebrows and leaned toward him.

"Well, that means you have to go in there. Don't worry, we ordered you and your vet student Tyvek suits and respirators because one of the deputies peeked in the door to make sure no people were there, and he said you were going to need them. And, oh yeah, the other bit of bad news is that the property owner's family has called the news stations to say we're bullies for picking on an old lady." He covered his large forehead with his hand as he looked down.

I rolled my eyes. "Well, shit. Bullies? Really? Any idea when the suits will be here? Maybe we can get in there and get the animals out before the news crews arrive."

"They are coming with the suits now, so you lovely ladies go ahead and suit up, and we'll send an officer in with you. Good luck." The chief raced off.

"Maria, you don't have to go in there if you don't want to. I'd love to have your help, but I will understand if you say no. I promise I won't fail you." I didn't want to go alone, but I didn't want to be part of the reason a young vet burned out too soon.

"Are you kidding? I can't wait to see what's in there. I haven't ditched you yet and I'm not going to now." She smiled as we pulled on the bulky white Tyvek suits. A deputy handed us the respirators just as a sharp-dressed news reporter came crawling through the crime scene tape with a cameraman on her heels.

"Ma'am, you're not allowed to be in here. Do you understand this is a crime scene?" The stern deputy stared at her, and she slithered back under the tape.

Walking up the rickety steps to the trailer door, I began to get nervous about what we might find inside. Did someone live here? Were we invading a person's home? And was all this ghostbuster apparel necessary? I cracked the door and quickly wished for a respirator upgrade. Mine had already let in the foul stench.

On my first step through the door, plywood cracked as my large boot plunged through the floor. The deputies had said the owner told the sheriff she'd broken her leg this summer and that's why she was so far behind on her animal care. Maybe she fell through this very floor? I turned to Maria and pointed at the hole so she knew to avoid it. Stacks of boxes, newspapers, and magazines nearly six feet tall on both sides of us filled the entire room. On the far wall was a picture of the owner with her husband and children in a fancy oval frame. The family in the picture looked happy and vibrant—much different than now. We followed the extremely narrow path toward a red glow coming from the kitchen area. Inside the kitchen, there was one group of baby turkeys and one group of baby chickens in small, filthy pens under heat lamps. When I turned around, I saw Maria pulling open a door on a small incubator. The smell of rotten eggs filled the air. There appeared to be at least one hundred eggs in the incubator that had rotted.

"C'mon, Maria. Don't open anything. You're going to make the officer puke in his respirator. Turn around and let's go look in the back bedrooms."

We tiptoed down the narrow hall, anxiously praying we wouldn't fall through the floor. We entered a small, dusty room with nearly twenty parakeets in at least ten birdcages. The remainder of the room was filled with bird feed sacks and trash. These birds were vividly colored, small, and chatty. Most were pale blue and white, with a couple of beautiful yellow and green ones as well.

"Ladies, the rest of the residence is clear," the young officer said through his mask. "Let's get some cages for the birds and get the hell out of here. I can't take it much longer." I could tell this job was above his pay grade.

While handing the last birdcage out of the narrow door, I heard a noise that sounded like a motor running above me. I looked up and spotted a small drone capturing footage for the news. I hung my head to hide my face. I was trying to stay out of the public eye to protect my family's safety.

The newly elected sheriff gave one reporter a guided tour of the crime scene in his crisp white uniform. The only other person excited to speak to the reporters was Jane's grandson, dressed in his stained wifebeater and baggy jeans, describing how unfair we were being to his grandmother.

And with the news crews came nosy passersby. "Any chance I could get one of those goats y'all took for my granddaughter for Christmas?" Oh my Lord, what is wrong with people?

I couldn't take much more of the crime scene, so once the last birdcage was loaded, Maria and I shoved cold pizza into our mouths and headed to the fairgrounds. I was mentally and physically exhausted, wondering how much other work was stacking up on me while I was dealing with this damn zoo. Speeding down the unmarked road, I tried to imagine how the CART team got all those guinea pigs and rabbits shoved into the bingo building. What in the hell were we going to do with forty-one goats, ninety guinea pigs, twenty-seven rabbits, nineteen parakeets, seven cats, seven guinea fowl, eleven geese, forty-seven ducks, two hundred twenty-seven chickens, thirty-seven doves, one peacock, and one pheasant?

GUINEA PIG
REFUGEE CAMP

"Five hundred and fifteen? Here at these fairgrounds? Are you serious?" I shuddered at the thought of how we were going to take care of all these critters. And how long would we be responsible for them? This could go on for months if Jane didn't surrender the animals in court.

Donnie explained, "Yep, I'm serious. The cats are at the shelter, but everything else is here." He lit another cigarette. "It will be OK, Doc. Since the news broadcast, my phone has been ringing off the hook. Some people want to volunteer, some want to donate food and supplies, and some want to adopt animals. Go with my wife, Rhonda, and she'll show you how we have everything set up."

Rhonda had bags under her tired eyes from being at the fairgrounds for forty-eight straight hours. She tucked a bottle of Mountain Dew in her back pocket and lit another cigarette as she headed toward the bingo building. "Follow me, dear. I hope you're happy with the setup. We have rabbits on the left side and guinea pigs on the right. All are in individual cages with fresh shavings and clean water. The parakeets you sent this morning are down at the end in the birdcages you sent them in."

"Wow, you all have done an amazing job with these little guys. And by the sounds of the whistling and munching in here, they are pretty comfy." Rhonda and I turned to walk out the door through the center aisle of the fairgrounds.

"The french fry building is currently our center of operations. We figured that would be best since there are lights, a bathroom, and a heater in there. Then the goats are over here to the right by the baseball field." Rhonda took a swig of Mountain Dew before taking another drag from her cigarette.

The large pen made of heavy-duty livestock panels was built surrounding a stationary livestock trailer so that the goats would have shelter. The small herd of goats was happily munching on a fresh bale of green hay one of the volunteers had just tossed over the panels. Several five-gallon buckets filled with clean water stood near the front of the enclosure.

"And now to the poultry palace . . . brace yourself. We're doing the best we can in here. It's a work in progress. We're getting tight on space in this pole barn since you sent the rest of the birds. Do you have any ideas?" Rhonda pulled her ringing cell phone out of her pocket and carefully extinguished the last bit of her cigarette.

Several volunteers were working fastidiously in the poultry palace. "Hey, gang. Thank you all for being here," I told them. "I was thinking to make a little more space, we could move the geese, the ducks, and maybe the turkeys outside of the barn by the fence. Do y'all think we can make that happen?" They agreed and immediately began to think of what building supplies they'd need for the project. There were chickens everywhere I looked; some cages still had multiple birds due to the cage shortage. I instructed the volunteers to separate the birds if they started fighting, and Rhonda and I headed back up toward the french fry building.

"Donnie, you and the CART team have done a fantastic job," I told him when I saw him. "I'm lucky to be working with such a motivated bunch of compassionate, hardworking people. I plan to be here at least once a day and on weekends to personally check on every animal. In the meantime, if anyone notices anything that needs medical attention, please just call me."

"Well, Doc, there is one more thing." Donnie set his cigarette in the ashtray as he reached for his clipboard. "We're going to need individual medical records on all of these animals to meet the standards of care."

I winced as I thought of how many hours this was going to take. "Of course, no problem. I've gotta do that for my records anyway, since they will be subpoenaed to court next week." I reached for a Mountain Dew from the cooler.

"And the standards of care dictate that the records must be made within forty-eight hours of the seizure." Donnie squinched his face as if he'd told his mother he'd had a fender bender in her new car.

"Within forty-eight hours? We're already past that. It's gonna take me forty-eight damn hours to do physical exams on all these animals." I placed the palm of my hand into my tense forehead. "Well, if that's what must happen, then we'll make it happen. Do you have some volunteers that can help me now, and we'll start with the goats since I'm most familiar with them?"

"I think the powers that be will be lenient on the timeline since we have over five hundred animals, but I do think we should start today. Since it's been on the news, there's a good chance someone might come to check on us." Donnie lit another cigarette.

A team of six volunteers (including my former coworker Christina and her husband, Ben) and I worked diligently for nearly four hours through the group of goats. I decided since we were handling them, we'd just go ahead and vaccinate them, deworm them, and trim their feet. Once we finished with the goats, we moved over to the poultry palace to start processing chickens. Christina said, "You know, Dr. Melinda, we could *actually* process the chickens, and we could all take some home for the freezer. We'd sure have a lot less work to do."

"Sugar, you're not wrong, but you better hush your mouth 'cause some of the volunteers are from the Humane Society. Now let's get to it, or we're gonna be here all night." Once we got a system developed, I could examine one chicken a minute. With nightfall rapidly approaching, it was starting to get very cold—after all, it was the first week of December. I noticed several male volunteers had arrived wearing tool belts to put up plastic windbreaks for all the animals. They had just gotten off work and come over to lend a hand. Boy, was I happy to see them! I was worried about the animals being cold since many of them were in substandard body condition. I'd been very anxious ever since I had Lucy, so it was nothing new, but the thought of anything being cold under my watch was driving me crazy.

"Why don't you go get some rest, Doc?" Donnie suggested. "I will stay here and help the guys winterize. Maybe we can work on the pocket pets tomorrow?" He grabbed a piece of cold pizza and left the office.

I cracked the window in Big Red and cranked up the volume on my new Maren Morris CD. While driving home, I started thinking about how I'd organize tomorrow and I came to the realization that I didn't actually know anything about a guinea pig, or a rabbit for that matter. I was used to treating cows with needles that were longer than the guinea pigs. What the hell was I going to do? I was supposed to be the animal expert in this epic cluster.

I decided the wise thing to do would be to ask for help. After all, I'm a woman, not a man. I turned down the radio and called my dear friend and colleague Dr. Kelly. We had gotten to know each other through our work with the Veterinary Medical Association. Dr. Kelly had owned a practice for many years in the city but would work on any creature great or small. I once met Dr. Kelly and her young associate to help them dart elk. I felt like I'd brought a knife to a gunfight. They had a dart rifle, and I had a blow dart. I looked like Xena: Warrior Princess minus the princess out there crouched behind a tree, stalking those massive male elk. We got the job done in record time.

"Siri, call Kelly." I used Bluetooth because I was way too tired to be fumbling with my phone.

"Hello. Dr. Kelly speaking." There was a bit of trepidation in her voice, as if she feared I might be a telemarketer.

"Hey there, Dr. Kelly, it's Melinda, and as much as I hate to say it . . . I need a huge favor."

"Anything for you, dear. I saw your big animal seizure on the news tonight. What a disaster." Amid clanging noises, Dr. Kelly explained she was unloading the dishwasher.

"I hate to have to ask, but tomorrow I have to medically evaluate a slew of guinea pigs, rabbits, and a few ornamental birds, and to be quite honest with you, I have no clue what to do. Any possible chance you could pop in and help me tomorrow morning? I realize it's super short notice." I tried to accentuate the desperation in my voice.

"I'm supposed to go get a Christmas tree with my family tomorrow, but you know what, we'll get the tree another time. I'll come. Just name the time."

"Oh my gosh. Thank you so freaking much! Could we start at 8:00 a.m.? I love you; you're the best."

I was relieved to my core, and hoping and praying Dr. Mark and the kids wouldn't be mad at me for stealing her for the day.

Early the next morning, I hauled in another bag of greasy Hardee's biscuits for Dr. Kelly and my team of volunteers. Donnie had put some heaters in the bingo building for the comfort of both the humans and the animals. I was fascinated watching Dr. Kelly handle the small fuzzy creatures. The amount of information she could ascertain from one tiny rodent was incredible. She prescribed ointment to soothe their scabby skin and drops to heal their painful eyes. I felt like I should have gotten continuing education credit just for being in her presence.

We worked for several hours until our legs wore out from standing on the concrete. I gave Dr. Kelly a big hug and thanked her profusely as she left.

"Let me get this straight—eighty-five out of the ninety freaking guinea pigs are knocked up?" Ashlyn, one of the teenage volunteers, shouted from across the aisle of the old bingo building.

"Bingo! No pun intended," I said. "That means we need to put the guinea pig adoption process in high gear, or we're going to have to call *Extreme Home Makeover* and ask if they do guinea pig editions."

"Wonder if they actually would do home makeovers for animals? Has anybody checked that out?" Ashlyn desperately consulted Google on her phone.

"Thanks for all your help today. I need to go tend to all the other animals so I can get home to put up the Christmas tree." I headed back to the office to drop off a stack of medical records taller than the camel I had seen last week at the Nativity scene.

Driving home, I wondered if my baby girl would be awake, and I fretted over when I'd ever get time to prepare for Christmas. When I walked into the house, Mom plugged in the small Christmas tree she'd just assembled while baby Lucy and Cap the border collie sat on the floor staring at the tree, both chewing on bright red Santa ornaments. Lucy lit up like a Christmas tree herself when she saw me. She raised her arms, creased with fat rolls, to signal me to pick her up. This was the most relaxed I had felt in a week. My heart rate lowered, and I breathed a sigh of relief when I discovered everyone was happy and content at home.

"How are things at the fairgrounds today, baby?" Mom asked as she placed the angel on the top of the tree.

"You don't even want to know. We discovered that we have eighty-five pregnant guinea pigs." Cap's ears became erect, and Lucy began to clap her hands.

"Don't you dare bring a damn guinea pig in here for Lucy's stocking." Mom made a point of peering around the side of the Christmas tree so I could see the glare in her eyes.

"Aw, c'mon, Mom. I'd never put a guinea pig in her stocking. It would hold at least six . . . Just kidding, Mom, please don't throw an ornament." I kissed Mom on her forehead, and Lucy and I headed to bed. When my head hit the pillow, I realized that even in all the craziness of the week, I had so much to be thankful for this holiday season: a beautiful baby, supportive parents, a phenomenal team of volunteers, a dedicated staff keeping my business running, and some kick-ass colleagues and friends.

THAT'S A WRAP

*E*very light post held a brightly lit wreath with a large red bow in preparation for the town's annual Christmas parade. Smoke from woodstoves filled the air as warmly dressed adults and children lined Main Street in anticipation of seeing all the floats that preceded Santa Claus. The CART members, sporting their navy-blue hooded sweatshirts with yellow letters, were putting the finishing touches on their decorated gold truck. Participating in the parade was a spur-of-the-moment decision, so the team decided to use Mary's dog Jake in the truck, since he howled on demand and we thought that might help us get some donations.

While putting the finishing touches on the float, Bekah, a dedicated CART volunteer, shouted to Donnie, "You know how people throw candy from floats at parades?"

Donnie replied, "Yeah . . ."

"What if we tossed guinea pigs into the crowd? Or chickens?" Bekah chuckled and nudged Mary with her elbow.

Donnie shook his head with a smirk on his face. "Let's get it together, gang. The parade is about to start. Everybody be nice and we might get some donations to help take care of our refugees."

"Now that the float is all ready, I'm going to walk back down to check on that little brown goat," I said. "One of the volunteers said she seemed off. I'll see you all back down at the fairgrounds. Howl pretty, Jake." I began my short walk down the crowded street.

As I entered the pole barn we referred to as the poultry palace, I realized Martha, one of the dedicated CART members, had made a makeshift pen at the end of the barn out of straw bales and bedded it with fresh straw. Inside the plush pen was the small brown goat with long, curving horns and a tiny, wet brown baby. What? I didn't even know she was pregnant. How could I have missed that?

Who am I kidding? I didn't even realize *I* was pregnant for quite a while. I just thought I had overdosed on vitamin D and was tired from working hard.

"Check it out, Dr. Melinda. We have a new baby," Martha said, carrying a bucket of water for the mama goat. "I know we don't need anything else to take care of, but it ought to boost morale."

The new mom steadily licked the baby's head and body in between her cries. At the goat's rear end, another bulging fluid-filled sack was gradually appearing. I pointed this out to Martha: "And it looks like we're about to have another new baby as well. Can you grab a heat lamp and get it hooked up? We'll also need to go to the cauldron and get some warm water for the mother to drink to help her pass her afterbirth." I opted to stay with the mother in case she had any trouble. She was doing such an awesome job giving birth that I just propped myself against the bale and silently observed. I remember one of my wise veterinary school professors saying, "Sometimes all the animal needs is a good ol' dose of benign neglect."

With every exhausting push, the mother cried out more and more. The slimy infant became more visible with every strain, until *plop*—it hit the soft straw and shook its head so hard its wet ears flapped. The mother swung around and began aggressively licking her new brown and white baby. I enjoyed watching this beautiful, normal birth. It seemed like ever since I became a veterinarian, all I did was assist with difficult births, usually involving a dead baby and occasionally a dead mother. Nine times out of ten, I was forced to decide if the mother or the baby was more likely to survive before proceeding with the birthing. Making life-and-death decisions was always, always heart wrenching.

I made my rounds to check on the 514 other animals. With eighty-five pregnant guinea pigs, there was a good chance this wouldn't be the only birth today. The sick animals were in an isolation area in the upstairs fair office, and they all still needed their eye drops and antibiotics. Once the parade crew made it back to the fairgrounds and admired our new arrivals, I looked over to Donnie in sheer exhaustion.

"I'm heading out for the night, man. The mom and babies are sorted. The sick animals are tended to. I need to go home and kiss my baby and prepare about a zillion pages of medical records for court tomorrow," I said.

"Good luck tomorrow. We're rooting for you. I hope to God she comes to her senses and relinquishes those animals. Thanks for everything, Doc." I could see the dark circles under Donnie's eyes even through the clouds of cigarette smoke he blew.

I used my cell phone flashlight to walk to the truck and saw a small car slowing down outside the fairgrounds gate. An older man with a raspy voice blew smoke out of the cracked window as he shouted, "I'm still looking for some goats for my granddaughter for Christmas. You ready to give me some?"

"Dude," I called back, "you might as well go to Walmart and get her a present. These goats are not leaving here. This case is still in court. Unless you're here to volunteer or drop off supplies, you need to move on." I was tired of people who just wanted free animals.

The next morning, I kissed sweet baby Lucy's soft, fuzzy head and tucked her snugly into the bed with my mother. I felt so guilty for having to leave her every morning. Some days the guilt took up all the space in my mind.

I made it back to our fairgrounds refugee camp by daylight. Donnie and Rhonda were smoking cigarettes while lighting the fire under the cauldron so the morning chores could commence. Out of the corner of my eye, I saw a truck pulling in. A small, energetic blond lady hopped out.

"Hi, Dr. Melinda. I'm Dr. Nikki. I've brought a truckload of animal feed and supplies from the northern part of the state. How else can I help?"

"Wow, Dr. Nikki! That's fantastic. Any chance you'd want to advise me on treating a few guinea pigs and a rabbit with an ear infection?" No matter what type of veterinarian she was, she'd be more qualified than me to work on those pocket pets. Dr. Nikki followed me up the old wooden stairs. As we opened the door, a CART volunteer yelled, "Dr. Melinda, there's someone here to see you over by the poultry palace."

I left Dr. Nikki working in the sick ward and headed to the pole barn. I was greeted with a warm hug from my office manager, Debbie. The fresh scent of floral shampoo from her dark curls was the best thing I had smelled in days. Between the aroma of chicken feces and not having time to shower for nearly two days, there was nowhere to go but up.

Debbie was a certified wildlife rehabilitator, and she had come to give me advice on the wild birds. "See here, this pair of doves need a perch in their cage." She bent down and threaded a long, thin stick across the middle of the cage. Both doves immediately hopped up onto the perch and looked more content than they had since their arrival at the fairgrounds.

Debbie had a way of comforting nearly any type of creature. She once had a young beaver named Fuzzbucket that stayed in a playpen in my garage and got bottle-fed throughout the day while Debbie worked in the office.

"Dr. Melinda," one of the CART volunteers called out, "come look at the concession stand building. You'll never believe it." I hoped there was not another disaster around the corner. When I entered the building, it was nearly full with animal feed, shavings, hay, straw, and supplies.

"Wow! This is incredible. Where did it all come from?" Being well supplied gave me an incredible sense of security.

"People are continuing to see our story on the news and in the newspapers. Nobody likes to see a hungry animal," Donnie replied. He tossed another fifty-pound feed bag on the stack.

"Dr. Melinda, you have a visitor at the entrance gate," Mary said with a huge smile.

At the entrance stood my mom holding baby Lucy. Sweet Lucy reached out her chubby arms and babbled "Ma-ma." She was dressed so warm there was no denying she had a grandma who was also a nurse.

Mom reached over to kiss me on the cheek. "How are you doing, baby doll? I just thought you'd want to see your girl and show her those cute baby goats you texted me. We brought you a turkey sub and some fries—they are in the car. Don't let me forget to leave it."

"Thank you, Mom. You're a lifesaver. Let's go see the babies." I gave Lucy at least ten kisses on our short walk to the pole barn. When we got to the goat pen, I sat on a bale of straw on the perimeter of the pen with Lucy on my lap. The red light from the heat lamp shone in her crystal blue eyes as she watched the tiny, fuzzy goat kids vigorously nursing their mother. Once the pair finished, I picked up the little doeling and sat her on my lap. She let out a scream that seemed larger than her lung capacity, and Lucy jerked backward. I sat the baby goat back down and hugged Lucy to ease her fear. I walked Mom and Lucy back out to the car, kissed them goodbye, and picked up the food Mom brought me. I hated to see them go, but I had important work ahead of me.

I could barely even eat because I was so anxious about the court case. I prayed Jane would do the right thing and surrender the animals so we could start adopting them out to permanent homes. If she decided to fight the cruelty charges, we could spend months in the courts with appeals and continuations. I simply couldn't bear the thought of being responsible for these animals until spring. We would run out of feed and volunteers.

Right then, Donnie strutted into the office. "Great news, she surrendered the animals," he announced.

"All of them?" I asked in disbelief.

"Yes, ma'am. All except two little birds." The CART volunteers cheered and gave high fives as Donnie talked. "We can officially start calling the rescue organizations and making a plan to wrap up Operation Noah's Ark."

Since Jane peacefully surrendered the animals and because of her advanced age, the judge did not sentence her to any jail time, only community service. He allowed her to own the two birds she requested and no other animals. Still, I knew the public was going to be outraged. Some people wanted to see her in handcuffs being carted off to the slammer. They didn't believe someone could be so cruel to so many animals and get away with it. The part that they couldn't see was this compassionate older lady who worked as a full-time caretaker for elderly people day in and day out until they passed. Jane had broken her leg in the summer and gotten behind on her animal husbandry. It wasn't that she didn't have a heart; it was that her heart was larger than her means. She was trying to take care of too many things all at once.

As a veterinarian, I had seen several animal cruelty cases that involved ill intent, like the guy who killed a geriatric cow by beating her to death with a claw hammer or the young couple who watched a dog starve to death on their bathroom floor. This wasn't one of those cases. I was certainly not happy with Jane when I was at the crime scene trying to rescue all those animals in the cold and dark, but it's not my job to judge people, only to help make a bad situation better.

In the weeks to come, one rescue organization after the next came to take our critters. Who knew there was a bona fide guinea pig rescue organization? Or a waterfowl rescue? Martha from our CART team had a farm in the county and decided she'd like to adopt the mama goat and the two kids, which she named Donnie and Rhonda. She vowed to tame them so they would be good public relations mascots for our CART team.

When we loaded the last chicken onto the trailer to send with the waterfowl rescue group, the fairgrounds were empty. A single tear slid down my face from a feeling somewhere between joy and exhaustion. A fresh set of volunteers came in to start the labor-intensive cleanup and disinfection process, which continued for weeks.

In the months to come, the goat kids, Donnie and Rhonda, quickly outgrew their mother and became popular at community events. Our CART team developed a sense of camaraderie that was unmatched. We received many awards from several organizations for our handling of such a large-scale seizure, but for us, it was never about the awards.

While parking at the community building to attend the county's volunteer awards ceremony, I spotted Jane leaving the building wearing a tattered, thin hoodie. She must have just completed her community service for the day. On my way home, I stopped at the local feed store and purchased a beautiful purple fleece-lined hoodie and a bag of bird feed. I knew she was staying at my neighbor's house on a caretaking job. When I was sure her truck was gone, I left the hoodie and bird feed for her on the porch. When you spend your days caring for animals, it's always good to remember that people are God's creatures too.

SPIN CYCLE SÉANCE

*I*f my hands weren't moving, something wasn't getting done. Being the single mother of a two-and-a-half-year-old and running an overbooked, full-time business was enough to make even a sane person crazy. I had owned the business now for nearly five years, and when Lucy turned two, Lucy's father and I started with a new split custody arrangement. It was an adjustment for all of us, and I really missed that little rascal on the days she wasn't with me. My solution to this complicated situation was to do more veterinary calls on the days I didn't have Lucy so I could spend more time with her when she was here. On the dark, lonely nights, I jotted down my veterinary stories, hoping that one day they'd bring joy to someone who needed a hearty laugh or some inspiration.

One busy spring day packed with vet calls, I swung by the house to see if our man from the bank had come by to set up our new remote check depositing system. Debbie and I were looking forward to new technology that would help us run the business more efficiently. Operating a business in a rural area is difficult for many reasons, most of them related to the internet working only at a turtle's pace and only on sunny days. I opened the door from the garage clinic to enter the house when the smell hit me: vanilla, Christmas tree, mango, cashmere truffle, with the essence of rottenness. There were candles burning on every conceivable surface of the kitchen, the living room, and the dining room. The wooden laundry closet doors in the hallway were wide open, as was the lid to the front-loading washing machine. In the office, across from the laundry closet, I heard snickering. Dr. Liz was a middle-aged English veterinarian, who now lived in central Virginia and helped do some overflow calls during the busy season.

"What in the Sam Hill is going on around here? Is it someone's birthday or are we having a séance? And for God's sake, please say the guy from the bank hasn't come by yet?" I wound my tangled hair up in a tight bun and raised an eyebrow at them.

Debbie spun around in her office chair. She ran her hand through her tight, dark curls and grimaced. "Well, the bank dude hasn't been here yet, which is good because all morning I kept smelling a strange smell, a really nasty smell, but I couldn't tell where it was coming from. A little bit ago I went to move the overalls and surgical towels from the washer to the dryer, and there it was."

"There what was?"

"There's no easy way to say this, so I'm just going to say it. The rotten testicles—they were stuck in the rubber lip of the machine." Debbie could see the look of disgust on my face.

"I know, girl. I vomited in my mouth a little, too, then called Dr. Liz in to remove them." Debbie had a half-grin on her face while approaching me with open arms. She always did know when someone needed a hug.

I squeezed Debbie extra tight, hoping this incident wouldn't send her packing. "Well, I certainly apologize to you both for having to deal with that. The nuts must have got wrapped up in a towel when we were cleaning up. We were exhausted and we were mostly focused on having a cold pop."

Dr. Liz nodded. "Completely understandable, if I do say so myself."

"Let's get the laundry closet closed back up and move the candles around a bit to ditch the séance vibe before our friend from the bank arrives." I didn't want him thinking I was some unhinged quack. And I definitely didn't need any snide remarks about this place being unfit to raise a child. "Thanks, ladies, for all your help. Bottles of nice wine are in your future."

We all pitched in and had the place looking somewhat normal just in time for our visitor from town. One thing I learned about overseeing a veterinary business: no two days are ever the same. And that was before I added a curious toddler to the mix!

Later that evening I picked up Lucy from her dad's and walked into the house. I had Lucy in one arm, and I was saddled like a pack mule with tote bags. As I struggled to turn the kitchen light on, Cap ran under my feet, nearly tripping me. I sat Lucy down on the kitchen stool to begin the unloading process. She started making her way around the dining room with her short curly pigtails, sniffing like a hound, and she looked up and said, "It 'tinks, Mom."

"I know, it's a little stinky, honey. I'm sorry. It was just a weird, scented candle. I will open a window." Trying to explain testicles in the washing machine seemed daunting at the moment.

I took one step toward the window and received a page from my emergency answering service. *Goat—F—1 year old—difficulty birthing—heading toward the office now.* Oh great, as if this day hadn't been long enough. I fed Lucy her fancy cuisine of chicken nuggets and yogurt and popped her in the tub for a quick bath. Right as I dried her off and pulled her pajama top over her head, I heard the driveway dinger alert. Our goat in labor had arrived.

"Do you want to help Mommy work on a goat in the garage?" I always asked Lucy what she felt comfortable with when it came to veterinary procedures. She was only a small child, and I didn't want to push her out of her comfort zone too quickly.

"Movie and poptorn, please?" Lucy pleaded, batting her eyes.

"Sure thing, sweetheart, you got it. Mommy will get you settled, then head to the garage. I will check on you in a few minutes."

After I covered her long toes with a blanket on the couch and placed a bowl of freshly popped popcorn on her lap, knowing I'd be picking most of it back out of the couch cushions later, I stepped into the garage on the other side of the wall from Lucy and pulled on my tattered green overalls. A petite young woman stood at the door with a black and white goat in her arms. The little goat let out a bloodcurdling scream as she pushed a small amount of hemorrhagic fluid out of her vagina onto her owner's forearm. I opened the door and instructed the woman to sit the goat on the rubber mat on the floor.

"Hi, Doc. Sorry to bother you after hours, but this goat is a first-timer and the birthing is not going well. I was going to try and help her, but I can't even get three fingers in her vagina. You can see what you think, but I'm thinking C-section." She headed toward the sink to wash her soaked arm.

I placed a long plastic glove on my right hand, lubed my hand, and attempted to check the doe for cervical dilation, to no avail. She was too tight. She was definitely going to need a C-section. I opened the door to the kitchen and hollered into Lucy, "Honey, Mommy has to do a surgery on a pregnant goat. If you need anything you just come to the door. I won't be able to touch the door handle for a bit."

I sedated the young mother-to-be, turned the radio on, and prepped my trusty plastic table for surgery. I carefully laid my knocked-out patient on the table, covered her eyes, clipped her left abdominal region, and injected lidocaine to numb her nerves. Several times, I vigorously scrubbed her abdomen with special surgical soap. I opened my surgery pack, scalpel blade, and suture and placed them on the countertop. Next, I scrubbed my hands with surgical soap and placed sterile gloves on my hands before I placed a sterile drape over the small goat, only revealing an area large enough for me to make an incision. I pitied her; not that long ago, I was draped in a wet sheet, looking like a bloated corpse being pushed into the hospital to deliver my baby girl.

"Nights in White Satin" played on the radio as I delicately pulled the scalpel through the goat's thin skin, parting the liver-colored muscles like Moses parting the Red Sea, until I arrived at her uterus. I torqued the large, swollen organ through my incision for full exposure before I started removing the babies. I shucked the first tiny, wet infant out like an oyster. Just as I was lifting the second baby goat out, I heard the door crack open and saw a small head peering out.

"You OK, Lucy bug? Look at the baby goats." I held up the wet kid proudly for Lucy to see, as if he were mine.

Lucy stood wide-eyed. "Wow, Mom!"

I instructed the owner where to find dry towels to wrap up the babies. Both of her hands were working hard to dry the pair. "Can you hand one of the babies to Lucy in a towel and let her take it into the couch to dry it? I can see there's another baby, and I'm going to need your help with it when I get it out," I told the owner as I removed afterbirth from the uterus with surgical scissors.

"Sure thing. Here you go, Lucy. You dry him and look after him. We'll be in to get him in a few minutes." The kind client gently placed the goat, rolled up like a burrito in a yellow towel, in Lucy's chubby arms. Lucy went back inside and closed the door.

I placed two layers of stitching in the wall of the uterus and made another cut over the goat's other uterine horn to rescue the last baby goat. I had the owner wrap the third baby in a towel and start drying her while I sutured up layer after layer of the patient mother. Finally, I tied the last suture, giving the goat the appearance of a deflated football.

After giving the mother goat antibiotics and pain medication, I sat her back on a towel on the rubber mat and placed two of her babies on another towel in front of her. In a daze, she began to lick her newborns and called out to them in a weak voice. I went in to see how the third baby was faring. When I peeked around the corner into the living room, I spotted the baby goat sitting on the couch while Lucy knelt in front of him, trying to feed him a piece of popcorn. Luckily, the episode of *PAW Patrol* was so interesting Lucy hadn't been able to force any popcorn into the baby's mouth.

"Lucy, honey, it's time for your baby to go back home with his mommy."

"Awww, Mommy, no." Lucy kissed him on his small head, wrapped him back in his blanket, and reluctantly returned him to his mama.

I scavenged around the garage for a medium-sized box to place the babies in. I then carried the mother goat and loaded her securely into the back of the SUV, while the owner slid in the cardboard box with three little heads sticking out and placed them beside their mother. Lucy stood on the patio waving goodbye. I picked her up and kissed her cheek. "Now we have to get you to bed. Thanks for being Mommy's little helper tonight. You did a great job! But remember, baby animals cannot eat popcorn." She laughed while pinching my lips together, which occurred frequently if she didn't like the message they were relaying.

GOING BANANAS

*T*he COVID-19 lockdown had been in place for several weeks. Although Lucy and I were desperately yearning for something exciting to do on a Friday night, assisting the county sheriff's department in serving a search warrant wasn't exactly high on the list. We'd just finished our chicken nugget dinner and were looking forward to a riveting game of Go Fish on the patio before we turned into bed early, when I felt my cell phone vibrating in my back pocket.

"Doc, we're gonna need your help to search this abandoned house. We've been tipped off by the officers in a neighboring county that we might find some interesting creatures inside. Are you available to help?" Chief asked from the other end of the line.

"I reckon. You're lucky I like you. What shall I bring? Anything special?" I pressed stop on the worn-out *PAW Patrol* DVD and beckoned Lucy toward the door. She grudgingly put her tattered mermaid Crocs on the wrong feet as she gathered up the cards to bring along in the truck. Finding childcare during the lockdown had proven to be impossible, so Lucy came with me everywhere. Since a young child couldn't understand the concept of staying in a social unit, we called ourselves a team.

"Probably just some heavy gloves, some patience, and maybe some bananas," Chief chuckled as she hung up abruptly. *Did she say bananas?*

I strapped my sleepy three-year-old into her car seat and kissed her on the forehead. "You look tired, Lucy bug," I said as I tightened the sticky straps.

"I'm not, Momma. Where are we going?" Lucy rubbed her eyes.

"We're going on a little adventure to rescue some animals that need help. You close your eyes and rest, sweet girl. Momma will try to be quick," I said as I grudgingly put the key into the ignition of the vet truck.

"I'm too 'cited to rest. I love rescuing animals, Mom. I want to be an animal rescuer when I grow up." Lucy popped a stale Goldfish cracker in her mouth from the cup holder in her car seat.

Fifteen minutes into our journey, the soft music on the radio coupled with the hum of the truck engine had lulled Lucy to sleep. I was squinting to see the number on the dilapidated sign, struggling to decide if what appeared to be a three could have actually been an eight at one time, when I spotted the police cars through the patch of woods. I prayed that whatever "interesting creatures" we might find inside weren't going to be as neglected as the outside of the two-story house.

I parked the truck in front of the house, carefully positioning it where I could see it from the house, so that I could check on sleeping Lucy periodically. I instructed the young deputy outside to keep watch over my precious cargo in the truck while I went inside to work. He seemed delighted to have a task that didn't involve animals.

"All right, team, the vet is here and Diane from the animal shelter is here, so let's get in there and see what we find. Please be careful—the conditions are treacherous due to the run-down condition of the place. Be sure to search everywhere, inside and outside." Chief put out her cigarette on a crumbling piece of concrete and prepared for entry.

When I shoved the stubborn sliding glass door to enter, I was in a big open room with a high ceiling. It was clear by the poor condition of the wood flooring and lack of furniture that nobody was living here. A strange odor filled the room. It was foul, but not like death or rotting flesh, more like feces. How could there possibly be a type of fecal matter I didn't recognize? Although wearing a KN95 mask had been hard to get used to, I was thankful to be wearing it for this job.

A loud voice hollered from above, "All clear upstairs, Chief."

"All clear in the kitchen," Chief shouted. "Oh, wait a second . . . there's something in the freezer. Would anyone like to play guess what the dead animal is? There's also a frozen pizza if anyone is hungry." Two officers and I played a quick game of "Not It" before filing into the cramped kitchen area like children with our index fingers still on our noses. Chief was holding a frozen plastic bag up to the light.

"Ummm, could it be a monkey?" I offered my professional opinion as I stared at the iced corpse. "I have never seen a monkeysicle before, but I imagine if it were thawed, it would look like a small monkey."

The older, broad-shouldered deputy slid his square glasses down his nose to examine the specimen more closely. "I've seen a lot of sicko stunts in my time in law enforcement, but never have I seen somebody put a monkey in a freezer!"

Chief snickered. "I believe the monkey must have passed away at her property in the neighboring county, and she's storing it here to bury it. Apparently, the county most of her animals reside in has passed an ordinance that forbids the ownership of exotic pets without a special permit that she didn't bother to get. The animal control officers from that county found out she purchased this foreclosed-on piece of property in our county, and they believe she may have brought animals here since we don't have any exotic pet rules."

Chief stuffed the monkey back into the small freezer so the searching could resume. We walked back across the big open room toward an attached garage. Diane pushed the door open with her thin arm and exclaimed, "Oh wow!"

In my business, those words are never good. I decided to sneak a peek out the front door to check on Lucy, in case it was the last time I saw her. She was so relaxed that she was drooling. Meanwhile, my nerves were on edge. I really wanted to bite my fingernails, but I was afraid of what might be on them. I always think of my Mam-Moo threatening to put chicken manure on my nails so I wouldn't bite them. She told my sister and me that we would get worms if we bit our nails. Can you imagine what you'd get from monkey crap?

When I walked into the garage, the first thing I saw was a large wrought iron cage with a small silver and white monkey perched on top, staring back at me. Her black face accentuated by her white unibrow made her appear to be in deep thought. Glancing around the room, I also spotted two animals hunched close to one another that resembled two brown rats with extremely long, furry tails. They appeared to be frightened by our presence. Sitting directly on top of their large wire crate was a brilliant green parrot with nearly every feather missing from its torso. I felt like I was trying to solve a puzzle with missing pieces.

"Are those lemurs, Diane?" Chief asked as she began to quiver from nicotine withdrawal.

"I do believe so," Diane replied. "Can we step out for a quick smoke before we start wrangling these animals? There are a few things I need to get from the van."

I studied these novel species from a distance as the deputies and I waited for Diane and Chief to return. How on God's green earth were we going to trap the loose monkey? I always thought I was gifted at reading an animal's expressions, but this monkey perched on the cage had her poker face on for sure.

Diane and Chief returned with two large crates and a package of grapes. "I'm going to put the grapes in this cage, and we're going to back off to see if the monkey will be hungry enough to come into the cage," Diane explained to the team.

Everyone backed away as Diane placed a handful of grapes into the empty cage, except Deputy Steve, who appeared to be mesmerized by the attentive primate. The pair were locked in an intense gaze, Deputy Steve only about a foot from the cage where the monkey was perched.

I said politely, "Officer, back away from the cage slowly, please." Then, more assertively: "Officer, move away from the monkey cage, now." No response. "Sir, step back now." It was like asking Lucy to turn off *PAW Patrol*. Although I wasn't fluent in monkey, I could tell this one was about to make a move. Right then, she catapulted from the top of the cage and ran across the top of the deputy's blond buzz-cut head to the other side of the room. She made her way into the cage and devoured the grapes.

Diane shut the door with conviction, and I looked over to Deputy Steve, who appeared to be in shock. He reached up to the top of his head and then held up his bloody hand. "It got me!"

"Come out to the vet truck with me. We'll get it cleaned up. Didn't you hear me telling you to back away?" I led him outside to the truck.

Steve sat on my tailgate while I cleaned the superficial cut near the top of his head. "I don't think it needs stitches, but because it's a monkey the sheriff is probably going to demand that you go to the university for further medical attention." Steve rolled his eyes and shook my hand.

"OK, man, best of luck to you. I have to get back in there and figure out how to capture a pair of lemurs without any more casualties," I said. I peered in the window to make sure Lucy was still sleeping. I gave the young deputy a thumbs-up and headed back into the humid garage.

Diane and Chief had positioned the clean, empty cage in front of the filthy cage the lemurs were in. The pair were crouched together near the back of their cage, scared to death. Their fixed topaz eyes made them appear to be in a trance. I attempted to shoo them along with a pen, like moving cattle with a stick, but they didn't respond.

"Let's put some grapes in the new cage and see if they'll move on their own," Diane suggested in her gentle way.

"Yeah, like we're getting men to do something. We'll make them think it's their idea!" Chief snickered and dropped the grapes into the other cage. After several minutes, the curious creatures got brave enough to go into the fresh cage for scrumptious treats. Diane shut the door with a half-grin on her face, and I helped her lift the cage to carry them to the van.

As we passed the vet truck toting the fuzzy captives, I saw Lucy rubbing her eyes, glancing out of her window with a confused look, as her guardian deputy grimaced and took a step backward. Diane and I detoured to the truck so I could open Lucy's door, still holding the cage. Lucy didn't utter a word. She just continued to study the situation while another deputy walked past with a half-naked bird in tow, and two others carried what appeared to be a vervet monkey in a cage.

Lucy lowered her bushy eyebrows, looking concerned.

"Don't worry, honey, we'll get ice cream on the way home. I promise. Look, it's a monkey. You've probably only seen those in your animal books. Mommy will be done very soon."

Diane and I continued toward the van with our newly acquired refugees so they could head to the animal shelter for the night until we devised a plan for their future.

I used the water hose and surgical scrub in the vet box to thoroughly disinfect my hands before hopping in the driver's seat. I was so relieved to be heading out. I looked down at my cell phone and saw a text. *Are you doing something involving a monkey? I just heard on the police scanner an officer was attacked by an at-large monkey.*

Several weeks later, I was placing my groceries on the conveyer belt at the store when Deputy Steve got in line behind me. "How's it going, buddy? Is your head better?" I tried to sneak a peek of his wound.

"Oh yeah, it is. My head is the least of my worries. I had to get rabies prophylaxis, antibiotics, and treatment for herpesvirus since old-world monkeys can potentially carry STDs. I have a sore ass from the rabies shots and a bad attitude from getting bananas and condoms in my work cubby every day! All the weird crap always happens to me." Although it was very hard to discern facial expressions through a mask, I could tell the grocery store clerk was as thoroughly entertained by Deputy Steve's commentary as I was.

"Well, hang in there, man. I feel like a lot of weird crap happens to me as well. Thank you for your service to our community." I pushed my cart full of groceries out the automatic doors.

Loading bag after bag of groceries into the truck, I pondered all the strange and unusual situations I had been in because of my line of work. I knew when I started my career sixteen years ago that no two days were ever going to be the same. The part I never imagined was what my young child would say at school when they asked her what her mom did. From delivering babies to sending them to Jesus, from artificially inseminating cows to rescuing abandoned monkeys, what part of my job would she choose to highlight—and would she get kicked out of school for talking about it?

PRACTICE IN
THE TIME OF COVID

*T*he year 2020 started out with a full staff and a great deal of optimism, and by the middle of March, we were half-staffed in a climate of global uncertainty. As a person who stamps out pestilence for a living, I was deeply concerned about this novel virus that was successfully killing people in every corner of the globe. Veterinarians had been dealing with coronaviruses for years, but this one seemed different. Initially, I wasn't sure how many aspects of my life COVID-19 would affect, but it soon leached out into all parts of my life, just as it did for every person in the world.

A few of my employees who were mothers of young children had to stop working at the veterinary service to homeschool their kids during lockdown. As a mother myself, I realized that teaching children was the most important job parents have. Lucy was just starting preschool that year, and I always managed to sneak a kiss in before I pulled her mask up onto her small face. I prayed every day for her to be protected from the virus, but I also realized that four-year-olds ate boogers for sport and it was probably just a matter of time until we'd get sick.

One spring day, Lucy and I were playing outside when my neighbor pulled into the driveway and asked me to come to euthanize her sixteen-year-old dog. Lucy begged to come along, which was just fine because finding a babysitter in a pandemic is impossible.

I instructed Lucy that she needed to stand quietly while I worked and then we could talk once we got back in the truck.

It was a beautiful sunny day, and Lucy and I knelt with the devastated couple who were petting their beloved family pet for the last time. Lucy greeted them, and I shot her the look to be quiet. I listened with my stethoscope to make sure the dog's heart ceased to beat. I stood up and signaled Lucy that it was time to head back to the truck.

Lucy walked closely behind my heels and tugged at my overalls. "Mom, what happens to the dog now?"

"Well, honey, the dog went up to be with Jesus," I replied as I continued to pack my supplies.

Lucy gazed into the sky, then back at the sobbing people petting their deceased dog. "Mom, bad news, Mom. It didn't work."

"What do you mean, Lucy? Of course it did."

Lucy pointed. "See, the dog didn't go up. He is still over there with his owners!"

Lucy wasn't the only child struggling to understand life and death during the pandemic. At nearly every vet call I went on, there were children searching for answers to life's most difficult questions. The children yearned to know about viruses, treatments for viruses, and how viruses caused death. It became commonplace for me to be science class for children in fifteen counties. It was like they were on a field trip, in a time when field trips were banned. I felt fortunate that I got to teach the subject I loved and was qualified to teach every day, unlike so many parents forced to tutor kids on every subject.

Another time during the pandemic, I was called to a farm to see a sick sheep. After I finished working on the sheep, three elementary-aged girls ran up to me carrying a dead chicken. One blonde, blue-eyed girl with dirt on her cheeks and denim overalls laid the chicken on the tailgate of my vet truck. "Dr. Melinda, can you please tell me why my chicken died? Her name was Dolly, and she was our favorite chicken."

"I suppose I could perform a postmortem exam on Dolly, and we could take a look." I fetched a scalpel from the leather doctor bag, now worn, that Dr. Kate had purchased for me when I started at the practice.

"Would you mind if you were on Zoom with my daughter's class to do the postmortem?" the farmer's wife asked politely. "I'm growing tired of teaching, and so many of my children's friends are at least two generations displaced from farms. It would be good for them to see the exam."

"Sure, that's cool with me." I loved teaching children, and I could tell this group of kids was thirsty for knowledge. The girl in the overalls reminded me of the time on the dairy I necropsied the frozen cow because I needed to know her cause of death. I knew experiential learning was something they were not getting much of in the classroom anymore since it wasn't on standardized tests, and it's exactly the type of learning that sticks with a person through their lifetime.

As I sliced into Dolly's feathers and started peeling back her muscles, the girls got closer and closer. I didn't enforce six-foot distancing, since we were outside and we were masked. I described the organ systems of the chicken and allowed the girls to take turns touching the intestines. We discovered Dolly was egg bound, a condition in which an egg that was stuck inside of her ruptured, causing an infection. Even the kids on Zoom appreciated the cracked egg inside of Dolly's filleted body. I knew the children were excited to get out of school at the beginning of the pandemic, but it was clear to me in my impromptu driveway learning sessions that many of them missed it.

Life was even difficult for those of us who never missed a day of work. For the members of my staff who could come to work, I had to write letters for them to place in their cars stating that we were essential employees so they could get to work without any trouble from law enforcement. When my staff members were out for COVID exposures, my dear friend and neighbor Karen would pop over and help prepare the invoices to go out.

"Karen, I can't even believe you answer the phone when I call. It seems like I'm always needing help," I said as I placed her on a lawn chair by the plastic table in the garage clinic with the stacks of invoices.

Karen pulled her glasses from her shiny silver hair and placed them over her eyes. "Anything for you, my dear. It's actually nice to have an outing of sorts. I need a break from Joe occasionally so we don't kill each other. You're doing me a favor. I will stuff the envelopes if you stamp them."

"Just to show you how much I love you, I'll use those boxes of cow fly tags for my desk so we can maintain our social distance. I will also make us some liquid refreshments." We'd figured out quickly that flexible straws could slide into the side of a mask so that we could enjoy our G&Ts together.

There were so few vehicles on the road that every town looked like a ghost town. I could drive for ten miles sometimes without passing a single car, and on night emergency calls, I rarely ever passed one. Wouldn't you know, this was the one time in history I didn't have to drive home naked from any calls. Selfishly, I found it nice to have fewer vehicles on the road, but it was eerie. For many years, I had taken for granted the ability to duck into a convenience store for a pack of crackers, a drink, and a bathroom stop. At this point, I had peed in so many random patches of woods that I was certain I would appear on a hunter's game camera wiping myself with a leaf because of the toilet paper shortage.

The COVID-19 lockdown period opened my eyes to a lot of things. It was amazing to see how few people in the workforce could nonetheless keep our country running. I distinctly remember hearing a news anchor say, "Stay home and watch Netflix on your couch for the good of your country." This statement was shocking to me. I'm not sure I have ever sat on my couch and watched

Netflix. I understood his point, but the ones of us producing food for the nation were working our fingers to the bone.

I felt fortunate to be able to continue doing my job every single day. Whoever thought that working outside in the fresh air on production animals would allow me to continue to make a living when the entire world had the pause button pushed? I took great pride in being able to work alongside my farmers to continue to help provide the safest and cheapest food supply in the world. This task was becoming more difficult daily.

Most of our production systems are vertically integrated, meaning they are owned by corporations that only operate a handful of large slaughterhouses in the entire country. Once COVID-19 started to affect the workers on the production lines, production started to back up, and grocery store shelves became bare. This was an unusual sight for Americans. In the grand scheme of things, very few of us have seen empty shelves, and even fewer have ever really been hungry. Since the Great Depression, we have become spoiled and accustomed to a readily available food supply 24/7.

When meat began to disappear from the shelves, the small farmers started to send animals to the smaller butcher shops, which filled every slot they had for the next two years in a matter of weeks. My clients who sell animals directly from the farm sold out of all their frozen meat and live animals very quickly.

Some of the country folk were pulling their grandparents' hog-killing supplies out of the barns and attempting to revive traditions they thought they had retired permanently. I fondly remember killing hogs growing up. Our large family banded together to kill them over Thanksgiving so everyone would be off work. It always fell near my birthday, and Grandma Lucile, Lucy's namesake, and aunts always offered to make me a birthday cake with their hands caked in sausage grease. I politely declined because I feared it would taste like a sausage ball. Once my grandma passed away, we stopped killing hogs for several reasons, and in this global crisis, it seemed we may have stopped too soon. At least we still had the knowledge and most of the equipment, unlike most other people.

Several of my clients decided maybe it was a good time to become homesteaders and provide as much of their own food as possible. They feared they had become too dependent on "Big Ag." Dale, who had several children, planted huge gardens, which worked out nicely since he was working from home and had time and plenty of labor. He also purchased chickens to provide both eggs and meat. Dale's wife wanted cows for house milk and steers for beef. They also bought a hog to put in the freezer. This trend became so popular so fast that the suppliers ran out of seeds, canning supplies, chicks, meat processing equipment, and even deep freezers.

By the time I took care of animals all day and half the night, there was no time to grow and produce food for my own family. Nathan, one of my nine-year-old 4-Hers, graciously provided me with eggs, while my friend Heidi kept me well supplied with fresh goat cheese. Since I owned the business, I was all about bartering, and I was happy to provide veterinary service for products that would sustain me and nourish my growing daughter.

One night when Lucy was cracking an egg for dinner she asked, "Mom, the shape of this egg is different. What's wrong with it?"

"Not a thing, honey. Nathan gave us duck eggs instead of chicken eggs today, so we're going to bake some brownies for dessert," I replied with a smile.

"Nathan is cute. He must know that I love brownies. I'm going to write him a note and see if he'll be my boyfriend." Lucy began to scribble her love letter on the paper towel I handed her for her hands.

"You're too young for a boyfriend. Keep cracking those eggs and be sure not to spill. We can't afford to waste food." I leaned over the bowl and planted a kiss smack in the middle of her forehead.

One thing that was particularly frustrating during the pandemic was watching people hoard food and supplies. This atmosphere of greed was toxic, and it was hurtful to the most vulnerable in our society. My pastor friend Sandi and I had learned a lot about the poverty in our community over the past two years. We had been heading up a "Ten Gallon Milk Challenge" that challenged the local churches to provide milk to the food bank. The churches in our county donated over one thousand gallons of milk each summer and over the holidays while the children were on breaks from school.

One day, we were dropping off milk at our county food bank when the director said, "We are struggling to provide food backpacks to the underprivileged children who are stuck at home during this lockdown." He hung his head toward the ground and shook it. "We have an unprecedented number of children in the county who are dependent on this food for survival, and because of the hoarding situation, we have no way to get it for them."

Sandi, who is a North Dakotan, and I looked at each other and knew we'd been called to action. If you tell two farm girls there are hungry children out there, you are going to get a steady supply of food in short order. Sandi and I spread the word that we were collecting donations for the children's backpack program, and many cheerful givers in our church family got on board.

Every Wednesday during the COVID lockdown, we went to Walmart when the trucks made their delivery so we could be sure they had product available. We put on our N95 masks and climbed to the top of the tall shelves to fill grocery carts with copious amounts of kid-friendly foods.

On one occasion while at the self-checkout counter we were approached by a Walmart employee eyeing our overflowing shopping cart. She tapped Sandi's shoulder. "Excuse me, ma'am. You're only allowed to have one of each of those items."

"Sorry for any confusion, ma'am. This food is not for us. We are taking it to the food bank. I'm a pastor and I give you my word," Sandi explained as I continued to unload the packed cart. The woman let us continue.

The food supply certainly wasn't the only supply chain affected by the pandemic. As more and more humans were getting hospitalized with the virus, medical supplies were in short supply. I can tell you firsthand that food service gloves do not hold up well for doing rectal exams on animals. There were times I had more crap on my hand from a hole in the shoddy glove than the animal had in its entire rectum. Luckily, veterinarians are pretty good at improvising, so we figured out how to mix up our own IV fluids, and how to reuse IV sets safely.

I dreaded the mornings when a politician announced yet another possible treatment or cure for COVID. One morning, while drinking my tea, I saw a news story about using dexamethasone to treat COVID. I walked straight into the office to order a case of the steroids, and it was already back ordered. Steroids and dewormers that were critically important to animals' survival were now being stored in people's basements. Fear and paranoia had taken over, and questioning science was the new hobby of many Americans.

I try to find a bright side to every situation. During COVID, the interest rate on federal student loans was 0 percent, which meant those of us paying on those insurmountable loans could actually start making headway on the loan principal. There was finally a light at the end of that damn tunnel. This prompted me to write my congresswoman and ask her why in the year 2020 it takes a plague for a doctor to pay off her student loans. I encouraged her to push for the federal government not only to cap the interest rates on student loans, but to give borrowers a year of 0 percent interest after every five years of good payment. It's shameful that the most developed country in the world has turned education into a for-profit venture. I wondered how many veterinarians' lives could be saved if anyone heeded this message.

Others' experiences with the global pandemic made me realize how lucky I am. I witnessed both frustrated children and stay-at-home workers suffering from Zoom fatigue. I watched an elderly gentleman wearing his colorful World War II veteran hat don his mask and gloves as he prepared to enter the grocery store. I imagined him as a young soldier gearing up for battle, and I pondered how scary it would be at his age to fight an invisible enemy. I prayed every night for the afflicted and for the frontline healthcare workers who were caring for them, putting their own families at risk every day. My heart broke for those suffering the loss of loved ones.

Compared to so many others, I considered myself fortunate. I felt a sense of security knowing that my strong work ethic, my positive outlook, my precious daughter's dependence on me, and my grateful heart could carry me through even the darkest of times.

SIDEWAYS IN A SUBARU

*W*hy *does it feel like a hot piece of rebar has been driven down through my leg?* I awoke thinking I was having a nightmare. When I attempted to stand up from the bed, tears began to fall uncontrollably from my eyes. I hadn't cried in so long that I reckoned the first several tears contained rust. Every step required incredible effort and made me cry to the point of jerking. The clock read 4:00 a.m. What on God's green earth happened to my back and leg while I was sleeping? I didn't remember seeing a pack of ninjas climb through the window, but as tired as I was last night, anything was possible.

I had worked so many fifteen-hour days lately I had stopped counting. My back had been hurting increasingly over the past two months, but that was nothing new in the birthing season. Lying behind those cows and pulling, and occasionally sawing, the oversized calves was pure hell on the muscles and bones that made up the structure of my back.

I had never felt pain this intense in my life. I thought the concussion from taking the pipe to the head or the pancreatitis I developed after a cow kick was the worst until I gave birth, and now this? I decided to try and hobble to the kitchen in search of an expired pain pill left over from the bout of pancreatitis. I leaned on the wall for support and desperately clutched every piece of molding on my way.

After an hour, the pill was offering me no relief at all. My phone alarm rang to remind me to go to the animal shelter to help feed and water a group of seized dogs. I knew Chief would need me because finding volunteers on a Sunday morning in the spring was harder than finding the matches for Lucy's tiny socks. I figured working might take my mind off the pain, as it had done so many times before. I stumbled to open the door of the vet truck and realized I couldn't make the step up the running board to get in. I tried to hold onto the steering wheel and pull myself in, but it was impossible. After fifteen minutes of struggling, the pain was intensifying, and I knew I had to stop trying. I beat my fist on the dusty side of the truck while the tears streamed down my face.

I was upset both emotionally and physically. How was I going to fulfill my roles as a mother and as a veterinarian in this condition? How would my business survive? Dr. Lesley had left over a year ago to start her own practice in a different area. Dr. Sarah only worked for me part-time and had announced that she was moving out of the state at the beginning of summer.

Once the sun came up, I rang Karen and asked her to come over. She came dashing into the bedroom, her shiny silver hair pulled back in a loose ponytail. She was sporting her FARM GIRL shirt and tattered gray pants. "What happened? Are you OK?"

"I'm not sure what has happened, but whatever it is, it's not good."

"Do you want me to haul you into the ER? You look like you need some pain control." Karen rubbed my tense calf muscle to try to console me.

"I appreciate it, Karen, but I don't want to go into the ER. COVID is rampant right now, and I don't want to contract that stuff and bring it back to Lucy." Having a coughing virus right now would be the end of me, I realized, grimacing as I tried to resituate myself in the bed.

"OK, dear, but if you change your mind give me a call. You know I'm here for anything you need." She headed out to get on with her day.

By Sunday afternoon, I rang Lewis and asked him to keep Lucy for a bit longer until I could get myself sorted out. I didn't want Lucy to see me like this.

Early Monday morning, I was finally ready to get some professional help. I held the phone in my hand and gritted my teeth, counting down the minutes to call the doctor's office when they opened. The wise nurse, Kim, advised me to go to the ER so that I'd be able to get the necessary imaging. I called Karen and asked her to give me a ride in her Subaru. I agonized over how I was going to be able to ride in a car. "Can you put those back seats down, Karen? And pop the hatch? I'm afraid I have no other choice but to try to ride lying down in the back."

"Sure thing. I even have a yoga mat I can put down for you. I will drive as slowly as I can." Karen held my feet as I slithered in horizontally while grinding my teeth.

By the time we arrived at the university hospital emergency room and I got unloaded, my heart rate was racing at 225 beats per minute. I got placed in a bed quickly, only to wait for hours for an MRI. Finally, the petite, seemingly experienced doctor entered the room. "Well, dear, it appears you've herniated your L5/S1 disc and it has your sciatic nerve trapped. My husband did that once, and it was awful to watch. Painkillers and weeks of rest fix most people, so we'll send you home with those and a walker. Good luck, and hang in there."

A walker? I was only forty-two years old. My ninety-year-old grandmother didn't even use a walker. And how was I going to keep up with an energetic preschooler on a walker? Would I have to carry the blow dart in the basket in case she got too close to the road?

I called my parents to tell them the news. I was sure my mom, who worried about me even when I was healthy, would not take the news well. And I just knew my dad would think he was a prophet for predicting I'd get injured because I chose a dangerous career.

"Honey, let me pack some clothes and I will head your way. It's gonna take me close to four hours. I will stay as long as you and Lucy need me." Mom's words were the most comforting I had heard in days.

I also called Dr. Lesley to see if she was available to help for a couple of weeks to get the immediate work done. She agreed to help in any way she could. And Dr. Sarah agreed to work some extra days and be on call each day.

For the next three weeks, I lay in the bed only on my right side, using the walker for assistance to get to the bathroom. Even in my unpleasant situation, I had several things for which to be grateful. Heating pads and Percocet were two of them. I was especially thankful I was facing the side of my bedroom with the windows—I was dependent on sunshine for survival. I was most fortunate to have a mother who was a caring and compassionate nurse. She was from the old school, where the emphasis was placed on patient care and comfort as a foundation to promote healing. Mom put a chair outside my window by the azalea bush, with its small white buds forming, so I could safely have visitors. She cooked me nutritious meals and served me in bed. Most important, she took good care of Lucy.

"Lucy, would you like to eat in the bed with Mommy? It will be like having a picnic." Mom walked into the bedroom with a tray of snacks. She always did have a special way of taking a crappy situation and making it better.

Lucy stacked pillows to reach the bed and delicately climbed in. She lay parallel to me as Mom slid the snack tray between us. "Thanks, Grandma. This is cool."

"Lucy, honey, you can eat sitting up if it's easier for you." I pushed back her wispy bangs that were falling into her eyes.

"No, Mommy. I want to be just like you." Her small soft hand patted my flushed cheek. I couldn't believe anyone would want to be just like me. I felt useless to everyone. I was lucky to have a child and a mother who refused to give up on me.

After three weeks in bed and a failed epidural injection in my back, I returned to the surgeon, Dr. Ahmed. He slid his glasses down below his dark eyes as he looked over to me. "Surgery, you need surgery. For six weeks you cannot lift anything, *anything* more than a milk jug. Understand?"

"Yes, sir, I understand. I will do anything to get out of this pain, sir. Will this fix me? Can I continue to work on the large animals?" I tried to process how this would work with my business.

"Yes. It will fix you, but it will be up to you not to undo my good work. You're going to have to work smarter, not harder." As a woman working in a traditionally male field, I'd heard "smarter, not harder" many times before. He scrolled through the surgery dates and handed me a slip of paper with a date and time.

Next, I needed to call my former veterinary student and friend Dr. Jessica, who was Dr. Sarah's other employer. I dreaded calling Dr. Jessica because she'd just had her second C-section two weeks ago and was on restricted activity for six to eight weeks. I knew she was short-staffed as well and already trying to work again. But Dr. Jessica and I were no strangers to adversity. She had been so helpful to me during the earthquake, and I knew we'd figure this out.

Lying awake that night, I remembered my recent conversation with Dr. Margaret, my dear friend who had recently retired from thirty-five years of practice. The next morning, I called her.

"Hi, Dr. Margaret. When you asked if I needed anything, did you really mean *anything?*" I had realized that many friends would offer to do "anything," and a much smaller subset would follow through.

"You bet, dear. What did you have in mind?" Dr. Margaret replied.

"This sounds crazy, but try to follow me. I really need Dr. Sarah here at least four days a week for the next few weeks while I heal up from this surgery. Is there any chance you'd be willing to go work in her place at the small animal clinic a couple of days a week? Dr. Jessica just had a C-section, so they are in dire straits as well."

I hated to even ask for such a big favor. I bit off my last fingernail awaiting her answer.

"Yes. I can do it. I was once in Dr. Jessica's shoes. I had just had my second C-section and was having a hard time recovering, so I hired a relief veterinarian," Margaret explained.

The word "yes" was music to my ears! "Wow, I never knew you had a relief vet. I'm proud of you."

"Well, after just one week, I realized there were major problems in the clinic, so I had to let her go and go back to work myself. A good friend called to check on me and could tell I was struggling. She came and worked in my place for three weeks until I could safely get back up on my feet. I can help you girls out for three or four weeks until you're both ambulatory." Dr. Margaret was the type of Christian who walked the walk.

In the weeks leading up to the surgery, my coworkers placed cinder blocks under the legs of my plastic table to raise the table so it would be easier on my back. Dad brought me a different type of walker, a sportier version, with a seat. I saw simple appointments in the garage to help take the load off Dr. Sarah.

On one of my dad's visits, he saw me casting a young goat's broken leg while bent over the walker. He commented, "This is like the blind leading the blind." Despite the occasional snide remark, Dad was quite helpful. He remembered I had helped him after all three of his back surgeries. After his most recent back surgery, I used a week of my vacation to go home and work in his place. I used all those skills he'd taught me over the years—the ones that made me successful as a veterinarian—to help get his work done.

On the morning of the surgery, as the nurse wheeled me under the blinding lights in the operating room, I overheard one of my clients who worked at the hospital shout, "You take good care of that young lady—we need her back on her feet to take care of our cows." Her comment made me smile and feel at peace. There were so many people rooting for me.

PERCOCET, HIGH-SPEED INTERNET, AND A LITTLE FREE TIME

I opened my eyes and began looking around the room, trying to figure out how I got there. The last thing I remembered was the bright lights in the operating room. "Why do you think Michael Jackson picked propofol?" I struggled to speak with my dry, sore throat.

The recovery room nurse bebopping around the room in her pale blue scrubs replied, "I have no idea, dear. I've wondered about that myself. That crap burns your veins so bad." She pulled out my IV catheter and wrapped a bandage around my arm. "How are you feeling? You ready to stand up?"

"I feel great. My leg isn't hurting anymore!" My facial muscles were relaxed enough to be able to smile for the first time in nearly six weeks. I slowly stood up out of the bed, and she walked me into another room to get dressed and to get discharge instructions.

As I sat down on the bed in that room, a tall, thin nurse entered. "You're awfully young for back surgery. What do you do for a living?"

"I'm a veterinarian, ma'am. I mostly work on large animals, hence the back issue."

"Wow, I bet that's a cool job. Animals are so amazing. My cat, who never really seemed to like people, laid with my husband every day as he battled cancer." She pulled my sock up. "That ornery cat provided comfort to him to his last day."

That was a common theme most anywhere I went. If I said I was a veterinarian, people started to tell stories about their animals. I can't even count the number of times I have heard about puking cats or dogs with diarrhea in the checkout line at the grocery store. I wasn't sure why I was in such a hurry to get back to this, but I was. Veterinary medicine had become my identity. I would be lost without it.

During the recovery period, I felt very lucky to live at work, which hadn't always been the case. A single-story, 1,600-square-foot brick house that contains an office and a veterinary clinic in the attached garage doesn't leave much room for leisure. Any space that wasn't being used to help live animal patients was occupied by Lucy's fleet of stuffed ones. While lying in my bed, I kept my door open, as did my faithful office manager, Cecilia, who worked in the small office in the next room. I kept an office phone, my cell phone, and my computer in the bed with me. I stayed busy most every day answering calls and emails, consulting clients by phone, and conducting job interviews to fill Dr. Sarah's position. Some people may have thought I was curled up in my bed watching Netflix all day, but as a business owner, there was barely ever a time for relaxation.

I was frustrated that I was stuck in a bed when I could have been racing toward the finish line of my student loans. As mentioned before, the federal government had lowered student loan interest to 0 percent during the pandemic, and for the first time in years, I felt like I was making headway. Not only was I not able to make my student loan payment, I had no income at all. I felt like every time I was digging my way out of the hole called debt, someone started throwing dirt back on me.

One day, I called my good friend and mentor Dr. Tom to ask how he'd managed to keep his business afloat after his back surgery several years ago.

"I'm going to give you a very important piece of advice," Dr. Tom said. "Beware of the dangers of Percocet, high-speed internet, and a little free time. One week into my recovery I purchased a new car online and didn't even remember doing it. The day they dropped the new car off, my wife took my computer away and threw the truck keys at me, and consequently, I had a very short recovery."

I was amused by Dr. Tom's story, but I didn't really understand what he meant. I thought the Percocet didn't affect me too much. One day while Dad was visiting, I asked him to take the tax payments I had prepared into the bank.

He returned still holding the documents. "Honey, the bank teller says these tax payments are all screwed up. I apologized and told her you were on heavy-duty pain meds. She laughed and said she had her driveway paved while on painkillers, so she understands. She's sending it back with me so you can try again." Dad chuckled as he reported the news. Even when being supportive of me, he had to rub my nose in it if I messed up. Once, while Dad was teaching me how to pull a calf, I mistakenly placed the obstetrical chains on the same foot of the calf—deep in the womb of the cow. When I began to pull, one foot emerged with two chains, and my dad pointed and laughed as I hung my head in shame. He definitely prepared me for the tough critics I'd face in veterinary school.

I didn't like being on the pain medication, but I couldn't do without it yet. Being from the Appalachian region of southwest Virginia at the height of the opioid epidemic, I had seen the drugs damage a lot of young people's lives. Unfortunately, I had lost friends who succumbed to overdose, one a father who left behind a wife and two young daughters. I didn't want anything to dim my bright future. I'd worked hard to get where I was, I'd spent twenty-one years in school and nearly $100,000 on my education, and I wasn't about to let some little white pills destroy everything.

One evening during Lucy's bath time, Mom accidentally left the door open. From my bed, I could hear my sweet four-year-old splashing and giggling. This little girl deserved the happiest childhood I could provide for her, and Percocet would have no role in that. I decided at that moment I would only take one pill before bedtime to help me rest through the night for a couple more weeks, and by doing so, I'd wean myself off the opioids altogether.

Despite having to use a handicapped toilet seat and a sock puller, I had a lot to be thankful for. I was surrounded by fresh flowers nearly every day of my recovery period. One beautiful day, Mom yelled down the hall, "Do you think there's any possibility the lady that does your prayer list at church may have said you died?"

"I certainly hope not. Why?" I rubbed my forehead.

"This is the fourth bunch of flowers you've gotten today. I'm going to put them in a vase here on the windowsill in front of your chair." Mom sneezed as she trimmed the stems.

Nearly every day a neighbor, a friend, or a colleague would bring or send a delicious meal for us. The people who were extra thoughtful always included a bag of chicken nuggets to appease Lucy. The phone calls, cards, and visits lifted my spirits daily. I spent one entire day writing thank-you notes.

It was a strange feeling for me to be in low gear. Normally I would have spent the past two months in constant motion, unable to keep up with the mountains of work. This year, I got to see spring emerge gradually while I lay still instead of seeing it through a windshield at sixty miles per hour. During a normal spring, I would have driven an average of a thousand miles each week. Every year, it seemed like the grass turned green and the flowers bloomed all in a matter of days. I knew going forward I would need to take some extra time to watch nature unfold.

My physical limitations meant that my sweet Lucy had to mature ahead of her time. She had to learn how to climb into the bed by herself and how to hug gently. She became a stellar egg cracker and dressed herself proudly each day; her underwear was only occasionally on the outside of her pants. Her light brown hair got longer by the week, and every time she ran past my bedroom window, she seemed taller.

Lucy was my biggest cheerleader, and she was all about positive reinforcement. "Great job, Mom. You walked out to the patio. Want to see how far I can throw the ball for Cappy?" she'd shout from the yard as she cocked back the ball chucker. I got to see my baby girl growing up in slow motion just like I got to watch the azalea bush outside my bedroom window go from barren and green to covered in bright white flowers over several weeks. Both were physical representations of my healing process.

A DRAFT HORSE
AMONG SADDLEBREDS

*F*inally, after six weeks of good behavior, I was cleared to start physical therapy. This would be my ticket to getting back to work. As I walked around the corner from the lobby, I gazed at the huge, open room filled with a row of padded tables, mirrors on every wall, and weights and tension bands of every color and description. I wondered which torture device I'd get to use first and how soon I could get started. I was like a puppy who'd been penned up for three months and released into a roomful of toys. I sat down on the exam table, and a tall, athletic woman with strawberry-blonde hair walked into the room and started her evaluation.

"My name is Anne—myself and Stephen will be your therapists for the next two to three months. What type of work do you do?" she asked.

"Great to meet you, Anne. My sister's name is Ann too. I'm a veterinarian, and there are a lot of animals and farmers depending on me, so I'm prepared to work hard for you every session." I struggled to push my left foot against Anne's strong hand.

"It appears you have a lot of weakness in this left leg, but we're going to help you get where you need to be. What goals do you have for yourself?" Anne asked.

"I need to be able to chase my four-year-old, run from crazy cows, and ride in a truck for extended periods." I could feel my face light up when I fantasized about chasing Lucy through the yard.

In the months that followed, I did two thirty-minute sessions of exercises every day at home, before and after work, with the help of Coach Lucy. "Mom, that was only eight, not ten, and you didn't squeeze your butt cheeks very good." Lucy critiqued my form as she lay beside me on the hard floor.

I turned my head to look into Lucy's big eyes. "Do Anne and Stephen pay you in lollipops to fuss at Mommy?" We both giggled before repeating the last exercise with more gluteal conviction.

Twice a week, I'd drive forty minutes to Charlottesville for physical therapy. The traffic was always fast-paced, as were the people. Every time I went to therapy, I remembered why I loved living in the country. I remember watching the city women lying on the table with a heating pad, getting a calf massage while they scrolled through their social media feeds. Meanwhile, I moved large wooden boxes around the large, open therapy room with a harness around my waist. Mallory, a young blonde PT student, was attached to the other end of the harness, sadistically trying to pull me backward. Occasionally, the other patients would look over curiously, probably secretly hoping they wouldn't have to be harnessed—or maybe that they would? I looked like a Clydesdale in a stable full of saddlebreds. Even though it didn't seem fair, it didn't upset me. I was used to life not being fair, after years of watching my small animal veterinary colleagues work in climate-controlled offices for far more money than I made. Initially, I had an equal opportunity to work in a cushy office in an urban location, but that wasn't for me. My therapists were training me for the type of work I needed to do to be successful in my life and to achieve my goals.

"Great idea with the harness, Stephen. Wouldn't it be cool if there were live animals involved in her therapy?" Anne commented, casually strolling past us.

"You want live animals? Just say the word," I offered. "They would probably crap on your carpet if we brought them in here, but I have done some sketchy stuff in parking lots. I once euthanized a goat with a broken leg at Giant and nobody even noticed. I can arrange for a client to bring an animal to the parking area next time." I was delighted to be graduating to live animal wrangling.

When Thursday afternoon rolled around, I checked at the front desk. The young receptionist shouted through the open door, "Anne, your four o'clock is here, and she claims to have a goat in the parking lot." Several patients in the waiting room laughed, while one looked confused.

Anne peeked around the corner and smiled. "You really did it, didn't you? Let me get Stephen and Mallory and we'll be right out. I'm excited!"

Sitting in the parking space was an older-model green pickup truck with Farm Use tags and a camper top. A goat peered out of the open camper top, with his owner, Pat, bracing his strong horn to keep him from jumping out. My team of therapists admired the goat, with the long, white, crimped locks of mohair covering his body.

"What's wrong with him? He looks perfect," Mallory exclaimed.

Pat said, "He's got a swelling under his jaw. I think it's an abscess, but I wanted Dr. Melinda to look at it to make sure." She popped the tailgate and pushed the eager goat patient backward.

"How are you going to handle that goat to safely examine him?" Anne asked, encouraging me to think before I acted.

"Well, I'm going to get Pat to pull him to the edge of the tailgate so I can check the swelling. If it needs to be lanced, I will sedate him with some Valium. The Rolling Stones didn't call it 'Mother's Little Helper' for nothin'." Stephen snickered as I drew up a dose of sedative and stuck it in my shirt pocket.

"Smart girl," Anne said. "You need to let those clients do the restraining and use those sedatives liberally for a while until you're able to handle the animals safely. Now I'm heading back in before I see anything too gross. Come in once you're done, and we'll do the rest of your therapy." She made a beeline for the door as I pushed the sharp razor into the swelling. She barely got away before thick, yellow, purulent discharge rolled out of the abscess like lava from a volcano. Pat helped our drunken patient get back to his feet. She was relieved that it was just an abscess.

On our way back into the building, Mallory asked, "Dr. Melinda, is the goat going to be OK?"

"You bet. He'll be right as rain once he wakes up. It's just like popping a gigantic pimple. Lancing abscesses is one of the most gratifying tasks we perform as veterinarians." She breathed a sigh of relief.

Slowly but surely, I was regaining my ability to do what I loved, and I was delighted. I remembered anxiously signing the pre-surgical forms for the back operation, praying I wouldn't have any serious complications. As a surgeon myself, I knew one small slip with the scalpel could have paralyzed me. Having always been a person who likes to have my affairs in order, I submitted a collection of veterinary stories to a publisher the morning of my surgery. I knew I might need a way to support my child and myself if things didn't go well, but both went better than I could have ever expected.

MOTHERHOOD'S THE BEST HOOD

"**M**om, why is Julie here with her cat?" Lucy asked, shrugging her shoulders. Her eyelashes were so long that when she looked up, they nearly touched her eyebrows. She was three years old then, and she always wanted to be right in the middle of the action.

"Well, Lucy, she's bringing a cat for Mommy to work on," I replied.

Lucy didn't always know exactly what was going on, but she always seemed to ask the right questions to figure it out. "But, Mom, you don't usually work with cats. What are you going to do to it?"

"Mommy is going to make the cat go night-night . . ." I tried to explain the need for euthanasia to her in the most practical way I knew how: "Honey, the cat is old, nearly twenty years old. He won't eat anymore, and he has health issues. It's time."

"Then what happens to the cat?" Lucy tugged on the leg of my green overalls.

I carefully drew up the fatal solution into the syringe and paused, surprised by her question. "I suppose the cat will go see Jesus."

"What on earth would Jesus want with an old dead cat?" Lucy exclaimed. As I looked down at my geriatric, emaciated patient with matted fur and bad breath, I had no answer.

I knew from the time Lucy was a baby that her childhood was going to be unconventional. She'd lived in two different households for over two years now and was being co-parented by a veterinarian and a dairy farmer. She'd already seen a lot of things other children hadn't, but now she could talk and think. In some ways, I was envious of her childhood. She was growing up on a dairy in a time where women were employed on dairies, women were prominent experts in dairy science, and women veterinarians serviced dairies. Lucy clearly had a much different situation than I did. I'd always encouraged her to ask questions, and no question was ever out of bounds. I was fully expecting her to get kicked out of preschool at some point for her choice of show-and-tell.

One warm afternoon, Dr. Sarah, Karen, Pastor Sandi, and I stood around chatting in the garage clinic, watching Lucy digging out a ball to throw for Cap. Lucy didn't realize she was surrounded by four women with doctorate degrees, all of whom loved and supported her. For Lucy, it was just a fun afternoon with friends.

One summer day when Lucy was three, I strapped her in her car seat to go on a call. "What are we going to do, Mom?" Lucy asked, chewing up an old red M&M she'd found hiding in her car seat.

I always tried the matter-of-fact approach first. "We're going to breed a cow."

"What does that mean?" Lucy's thick eyebrows raised as she continued to mine for M&M's.

"Well, honey, we're going to put something in the cow that will hopefully turn into a baby." I fastened my seat belt and put the vet truck in reverse.

"Where do you put it?" Lucy asked. A thin stream of chocolate ran down the corner of her mouth.

"You'll see when we get there." I turned the volume up on the radio to buy myself time to think of a better explanation.

Lucy chose to watch from the truck window. With my gloved right arm tucked into the cow's rectum to stabilize her cervix, I used my left hand to slide the long, thin silver rod methodically into the big Angus cow's vagina. I deposited the dose of semen in her uterus and pulled off my long plastic sleeve.

When I got back in the truck and fired up the engine, the phone rang. My dad's voice came loudly through the truck's speaker. "Hi, Lucy, what are you and Mommy up to today?"

"Grandad! Mommy shot a baby up a cow's butt!" Lucy seemed delighted with herself, like she'd answered her own question. Dad was laughing hysterically.

I wasn't sure if seeing my work on animals was inspiring Lucy or dissuading her from veterinary medicine, but at her age, she didn't have any choice but to come along. For better or for worse, that was the life she was born into. Lucy had gotten a Doc McStuffins veterinary kit for Christmas when she was just two years old, followed by several more veterinary kits on subsequent special occasions. The more procedures she saw me perform on animals, the more excited she was to get home and play animal doctor. She possibly had more equipment in her kits than I did in the garage clinic.

It could be exhausting to be out working on animals all day long, then come home and see the lineup of stuffed animals Lucy had waiting for me in our bedroom "hospital": a pink rabbit with a crooked ear, a teddy bear with a laceration from Cap, the blue dog from last week needing his cast changed. I always tried to act excited to play animal doctor, even on the days when I didn't feel like looking at or talking about one more animal. I didn't want her to see what burnout looked like. Sometimes I regretted encouraging her to put on her little white coat and do a complete and thorough physical exam on every single patient. Occasionally, if it was my turn to be the doctor after a long day, I was guilty of skipping ahead.

"Mom, you didn't listen to my teddy's heart first. You just started sewing up his cut. I want a new doctor." Lucy snatched up her fuzzy brown bear with the stuffing hanging out and marched away. The good news was she wasn't planning on paying the bill anyway and she didn't know how to give me a one-star review on Google.

Having a child renewed the fire I once had for my career. It had been quite a while now since I was young and eager. My body was physically wearing down, and dealing with the attitudes of people in a changing society was exhausting. I had spent most of my career educating producers, clients, students, and children, but during the pandemic, there was very little education going on. Lucy's enthusiasm and desire to learn came at just the right time for me. She made me remember how important it is to learn something new every day.

RESURRECTION
OF THE LAMB

"What time are we leaving tomorrow, Mom? I can't wait to see those cute lambs," Lucy asked with her eyes closed.

"Lucy . . . You're supposed to be asleep already; it's nearly ten o'clock. I told you we'd leave when Mommy finishes her vet calls. Now get some rest so you'll be ready for the long trip tomorrow." I lifted her soft bangs and kissed her forehead.

"I'm gonna try counting sheep in my head. It will be good practice for Grandad and Grandma's," Lucy mumbled as she began to doze off.

Easter was rapidly approaching. Lucy and I were headed to visit my parents in southwest Virginia for a quick weekend getaway. Our Good Friday drive down Interstate 81 was pleasant, with redbud trees and daffodils blooming along the roadside and the trees blanketing the mountains in front of us displaying their spring foliage. Lucy quivered with excitement at the thought of playing with her grandad's baby lambs, but listening to "Ol' Red" on the radio kept her calm as we closed in on our destination.

Upon our arrival at my parents' small beige house on top of the hill surrounded by sheep, we were greeted by my mom waving and smiling on the back porch. Although this was not my childhood home, it was on inherited land, and you couldn't throw a rock without hitting a family member. I always looked forward to sitting on the porch shooting the breeze with all my uncles and aunts. Mom bolted toward the truck and pulled open the back door.

"It's my Lucy bug!" Mom wrapped her arms around her five-year-old baby doll as if she were going to squeeze her in half.

"Grandma, I missed you so much. Can we see the baby lambs?" Lucy pried herself from her grandma's tight grip to run to the board fence surrounding the yard.

Just as Lucy climbed onto the first board, my dad pulled into the driveway in his bright blue Ranger. "Lucy! Want to go see the lambs?" Dad ran toward Lucy with open arms.

Lucy hopped off the fence into her grandad's arms and planted a big wet kiss on his cheek. "You're right, Grandad. I want to see those adorable baby lambs." Grandad and Lucy headed to the sheep field to scope out his latest arrivals while I unloaded the truck. Within fifteen minutes of our arrival, I got a text from Dad: *We have a sick lamb.*

I nearly hadn't brought my vet truck on the trip just so I could actually have a day off, but I feel helpless without it. I hated the feeling of helplessness so much that it drove me to become a veterinarian. I hopped in my truck and headed down the hill to the sheep pen, ready with a stethoscope draped around my neck and a thermometer in my pocket.

Lucy grabbed my hand and dragged me into the field. She pointed at the lamb in question. "Me and Grandad have a patient for you. He don't look good at all."

Curled up against the dilapidated fence was a small white lamb with his head on the ground and his ears down. "Dr. Lucy already told me it's probably got some kind of -itis." Dad glanced over to see my reaction to Lucy's diagnosis. His half grin could not disguise his look of pride.

I crept toward the lamb, trying not to startle him. I crawled on my hands and knees, then grabbed him. Once I had the lamb securely in my grasp, I placed him between my thighs to examine him. I could hear Dad whispering to Lucy, "Well, that's not a good sign if your mom can catch him." I squinted my eyes, smiled, and kept all the curse words I wanted to say in my head for the sake of the impressionable child watching.

The lamb's heart rate and respiratory rates were markedly elevated, as was his temperature. It was 106.5, which is nearly four degrees above normal. I lifted the lamb into my arms and announced to Dad and Lucy, "The lamb has pneumonia. We need to take him to the back of the truck and give him some medications and fluids."

I placed the weak lamb on my tailgate workstation and injected him with a strong respiratory antibiotic, fever reducer, and a shot to boost his immune system. Then I spiked the bag of fluids with a dose of B vitamins, turning it a brilliant yellow color. I placed Lucy on the tailgate, standing behind the lamb, and gave her the bag of fluids. "Lucy, you're going to help Mommy by being the IV pole. Can you squeeze the bag?"

"Sure, Mom. What are fluids and why are they yellow? Are we giving the baby Mountain Dew?" Lucy sat down quickly but continued to squeeze the bag.

"Fluids are like Gatorade for the lamb. He's dehydrated because he hasn't felt too much like nursing milk from his mommy. The fluids will help him feel better faster." I was delighted that Lucy felt comfortable asking any question that came to her mind, even in the presence of her grandad.

When the bag began to get close to the end, Dad asked, "Do you have anything you could mark him with, so I will know which one we treated?"

I grabbed a shamrock-colored livestock paint stick from the top drawer of the vet box and made a cross on the lamb's forehead. It looked like he'd attended an Ash Wednesday service during Holy Week. I figured that, in his condition, he'd need all the religion he could get. As I made the T part of the cross, the lamb started to squirm and jerked his head.

Lucy said, "Way to go, Mom, that looks like a cactus." I rolled my eyes. I turned off the fluids and unhooked the needle from the lamb's tough skin. I carried the lamb back to the gate and set him on his feet so he could attempt to find his mother. He staggered back off into the flock.

When Lucy and I snuggled up together to say our bedtime prayers, we were sure to include the wee lamb. I woke from my slumber when I heard the heavy rain pounding the roof. All I could think of was the poor ill lamb stuck outside in the dark, cold rain. I knew the odds were stacked against him, but taking him away from his mother would be too stressful. Sometimes all you can do is realize you've done your level best and let Mother Nature handle the situation.

Early the next morning, I felt a soft hand patting my cheek. "Get up, Mom. We need to see if the Easter Bunny came, and then we need to hurry out there and check on our patient!" Lucy could barely contain her excitement.

I watched through the kitchen window as the sun rose slowly over the majestic mountaintops, with a thin layer of fog steaming atop the green pastures from the overnight rain. Occasionally, I could see the silhouette of a sheep's head pop up above the haze.

I poured a cup of tea while Lucy rummaged through her giant Easter basket. "This basket is great, Mom. I must have been good. I can't wait to pick out all the chocolate, but first, we need to go find the lamb." Lucy pulled her pink rubber boots onto her bare feet over the legs of her pajamas, and I followed suit.

Walking out the back door, I contemplated how to share with Lucy the wisdom imparted to me by one of my veterinary school professors: "When you're dealing with sheep, never forget the four S's. Sick Sheep Seldom Survive." I always thought that was a rude generalization until I started practicing veterinary medicine eighteen years ago—then I realized he was onto something.

Lucy stepped off the porch and looked up. "Look, Mom, no buzzards. That's a good sign!"

"Who taught you that?" I was beginning to think somebody had already explained the four S's to her.

"Grandad. He said that's how you know if there's a dead one." Lucy struggled to climb over the board fence. I smirked when I remembered Dad telling me the exact same thing when I was her age. Walking through the sheep pasture that Easter morning, I couldn't help but feel guilty that we weren't in church. After all, most Christians believe Easter is the holiest day of the year, and here I was braless in a field dodging sheep poop in Crocs with my kid in tow. The sad reality was that if a lot of people hadn't been celebrating a major holiday, I likely couldn't have gotten out of town.

"Lucy, we'll need to look through the sheep carefully to find our lamb because it rained last night, and his paint probably washed off. So, we'll need to try and find the lamb that looks like he doesn't feel well." I glanced ahead at the seventy sheep, mostly white, standing in front of us, and I wasn't even sure I could follow my own instructions.

Lucy started walking through the flock confidently. "Well, that one's not sick—it just peed and pooped. And that little one over there is a girl 'cause it pees from the butt end, so that's not him. And that one's ears are perky, so it's not him either." I was impressed with her astute assessment of the flock.

I peered over the next knoll to start checking another group, and my eye caught a glimmer of green. In the distance, standing beside a big white ewe, was a wet lamb with one ear up and one ear down, sporting smeared green paint on his head.

"Looky there, Mom! Looks like ol' Cactus Head is gonna pull through." Lucy's face lit up as she reported her findings.

Witnessing her excitement over a lamb's recovery from what seemed like a lethal condition made me ponder the sheer surprise and amazement Mary Magdalene must have felt when she discovered Jesus's empty tomb. Those of us who work in the agricultural sector aren't always able to make it to church on Sunday because of the nature of our work, but sometimes, church comes to us in a unique way.

"You better take a picture of him for Grandad. You know he's not going to believe us," Lucy said as she grabbed my hand.

"Good idea. Now let's get back in there and check out that Easter basket and make some breakfast."

When I see the bright smile on Lucy's face after saving a baby lamb or playing with a new litter of border collie puppies, it takes me right back to my childhood on the dairy farm. Lying on the hillside surrounded by the rolling green hills with cattle and sheep grazing, I, too, started out as a little freckle-faced girl who enjoyed mothering orphan lambs and giggling while a mob of pups deluged me with their warm puppy breath on my face.

As Lucy and I walked hand in hand back up the hill toward the house, I couldn't help but count my blessings. Last year at this time, I was unable to walk and my future was uncertain, but this year, I was back out in the field doing what I love with the people I love.

ACKNOWLEDGMENTS

*F*irst and foremost, I'd like to thank my family. Thank you, Mom and Dad, for setting the bar high and for cheering for me as I struggled to get over it. A special thanks to my sweet Lucy for making me laugh every single day and providing me with endless amounts of material.

Thanks to my loyal clients. Without you all, I'd have a boring life. If I wrote about you in this book, please don't be offended by anything I said; it all comes from a loving place. I'm eternally grateful to all of you who produce our food and clothing.

Thanks to my patients, even though you can't read, for teaching me so much about many aspects of life. I'm not going to lie—some of y'all have really been a pain in my butt.

Many thanks to a special friend and former neighbor, Cathy Collins, for riding me like a rented mule until I wrote this book and for doing some early editing.

A huge thanks to my book coach and kindred spirit, Candace Coakley, for helping me find my voice and for encouraging me to "show, not tell." Candy, even if this book were never published, I would never regret learning everything you taught me and the friendship we have developed.

I'm also thankful for my friend and neighbor Karen Hulebak, who not only helped with the early editing but made me sit down and write the first page of this book and encouraged me every step of the way.

Thanks to the dearly departed Judith Truesdail, who helped with the early editing. I miss you and wish you could have been here to see the finished product.

A huge shout-out to my beta readers: Abigail Raeke, Jess Fefferman, Gus Gatti, and Judith Havasy. Thank you all for your next-level input.

Thanks to everyone at She Writes Press, not only for your publishing expertise but for taking a chance on me. Brooke Warner and her team—Shannon Green, Lauren Wise, Samantha Strom, Addison Gallegos, and cover designer Julie Metz—are a talented group of ladies.

Many thanks to my copy editor, Jackie Parkison, for your diligence.

And last, but definitely not least, thanks to my interns, Gracie Warda and Shruthi Krishnan, who have taught me more about websites and social media than I ever wanted to know.

ABOUT THE AUTHOR

Photo credit: Jacob Capozella

*M*elinda McCall, DVM, owns a large animal mobile veterinary service in central Virginia. She and her all-female staff specialize in beef and dairy cattle herds, swine, small ruminant animals, and camelids. Dr. Melinda earned a BS in Biology from Queens University and a Doctor of Veterinary Medicine from Virginia-Maryland College of Veterinary Medicine. A woman in a male-dominated field, she has mastered the ability to do the work she loves while educating and inspiring others through her expertise, passion, and grit. Dr. Melinda is passionate about agricultural education and loves giving back to her community. She resides in Louisa, Virginia, with her daughter, Lucy, and their beloved border collie, Cap.